C000101697

TALKING TO MY SELVES

TALKING TO MY SELVES

A Journey into Awareness

Betty Hughes

The Path

Distributed by Gardners Books, 1 Whittle Drive, Eastbourne, East
Sussex, BN23 6QH
Tel: +44(0)1323 521555 | Fax: +44(0)1323 521666

www.primallaugh.com

British Library Cataloguing in Publication Data
A catalogue record for this book is available from the British Library.

ISBN 978-0-9563386-0-0

Typeset by Amolibros, Milverton, Somerset
www.amolibros.com
This book production has been managed by Amolibros
Printed and bound by T J International Ltd, Padstow, Cornwall, UK

CONTENTS

DEDICATION

I dedicate this book to any fellow traveller who is struggling to make sense of life's journey.

LIST OF ILLUSTRATIONS

Facing page 16   **Section One**

Charming black and white 'snaps' which bring alive the history of those times: early years to late forties when the therapeutic journey commences.

Facing page 144   **Section Two**

Sandplay – the exciting discovery that the deepest secrets of ones inner world can be expressed in a medium more meaningful than words by using miniatures and other intriguing objects to create life stories in a box of sand. This section contains deeply revealing sequences of story-telling including those created by the author.

Facing page 176   **Section Three**

Kodak Instamatic to Sony Digital – adventures with a camera, capturing the world in colour, including action-packed wildlife photography in East Africa. This section also includes very early ventures into using pictures as an alternative to words.

Artwork in acrylic, collage and even primitive sketches scribbled at dead of night: a progression of creativity that opens up a new dimension to the therapeutic journey. Described by Valerie Sinason, who has written a foreword to this book, as 'powerful artwork to communicate in the spaces where words might have been too hurtful'.

The Endpapers

I am fascinated by trees and the endpapers represent a creative project described in Chapter Sixteen.

Copyright queries for quoted text

Healing in Depth. Culver Barker. Hodder and Stoughton. 1972.
Frank Lake – the man and his work. John Peters. Darton, Longman and Todd. 1989.
Sandplay. Dora M Kalff. Sigo Press 1980:

Note. Despite attempts to track down the copyright holder for quotations from the above titles I have been unsuccessful. Any information regarding this would be most welcome.

Betty Hughes

ACKNOWLEDGEMENTS

I have been struggling with this manuscript for about twenty-five years. The repetitive patterning of my attempts to complete the task has followed the repetitive patterns of my growth path. The project has been thrown aside as worthless many times yet retrospectively I can see that this was because there was always a further stage of my journey to be lived. This has meant that numerous drafts of the MS have been painfully edited by my loyal helpers and reams of pages have found their way into the bin.

For this reason I wish to thank **every single person** who has been concerned with the project for their endless patience, affirmation and encouragement. Many have maintained their belief in the venture in spite of the dark days when the story disappeared – disappeared as if forever.

First of all I would like to thank Lloyda who struggled for many weary hours on a manual typewriter, editing and typing the very first drafts of my narrative and giving me vital feedback along the way. I am deeply grateful to Nikki who first gave me courage to venture into creative writing and photography, and who has given so much time and patience to editing the various versions of this manuscript. Evidence of her unique skill and creativity can be seen throughout the book. My thanks to Denise and Harvey who have waded into unknown territory (my story is not always easy reading) and have helped not only with grammar but also by making sure that they, and therefore subsequent readers, were able to understand what I have written. Thank you, Bridge, for your encouragement even though you have not been able to put as much into the project as you would have wished. Yolanda, your appraisal was an inspiration and you have aided and supported me practically in so many ways.

In the text I have expressed my enormous gratitude to various people who have aided me on my therapeutic, creative and spiritual journey: Dr Peter Lomas, Dr Frank Lake, Dr William Swartley, Dr William Emerson, Richard Mowbray and Juliana Brown; Bishop John Perry, Tim Laurence and the Hoffman Institute, Dr Jim O'Donoghue and the Bridge Pastoral Foundation, Dr Paul Allan and, of course, Dr Sarah Kenny who played such a crucial part in my journey.

Others, many of them busy people deeply engaged in their own pursuits, have helped this project reach completion by giving me generous support over many years: not just listening to me talking aloud, giving feedback, helpful suggestions and encouragement but openhearted perception and understanding of my human frailty and vulnerability. Thank you Jan, Anna, Tim, Clare, Lisa, and many others, including my clients from whom I have learned so much.

Last of all, my thanks to Valerie Sinason, founder of The Clinic for Dissociative Studies for reading the manuscript and writing the foreword and to Sir Richard and Xenia Bowlby, well known in the field of research into Attachment Theory for reading the final manuscript and writing a plaudit for the cover. These three gave my doubting selves a final burst of courage to venture into print. My thanks to Tony Hill of Sarsen Press, Winchester for preparing the illustrations and, last of all my deep appreciation to Jane Tatam of Amolibros for all the work involved in launching my book on to the shelves.

PREFACE

by Yolanda Ironside

Betty Hughes has written a unique, extraordinary and important book. It is the story of her life, how it unfolded and how she undertook a long, tortuous and profound journey using psychiatry and psychotherapies to find a place in herself and the world: that she becomes able to 'be'. It is *a journey into life and awareness*.

It is a story showing the devastating effects that early childhood trauma has on the development of the person, the experience of life and the consequences these can have on one's ability to reach full potential.

The gift of the book is Betty's ability to record and express her journey deep into the myriad depths of her psyche to a point where she is barely hanging on to life by a 'gossamer thread'. We become aware of the pain, the confusion, and the fragility. She makes the unconscious visible. Betty then follows this through with a powerful articulation of the multifaceted understanding, knowing and healing she has achieved.

This is neither a quick journey nor an easy one. It is one that could only come from a long life and a very brave person's journey through it. And this is the importance and the unique quality of this book. There are few who will ever undertake such a journey or be able to write such a book. It is a gift to anyone on the quest for recovery. It is a story of courage and hope and attainment. The personal work and the self-exploration through expressive art, which she shares with the reader, adds further rarity to this book; I will treasure it for life.

For psychiatrists and psychotherapists it is the gift of deep knowledge of the experience: the journey deep into a person's psyche, the effects on mind, body and spirit. Something far beyond the textbook – which indeed should be prominently highlighted for those going to work with the troubled soul.

For anyone in therapy it tells a brave courageous and heartening story. I myself am still struggling to be in life – to get a life. I read Betty's book in two sittings. I have laughed and I have cried. I have felt this woman's deep warmth and compassion. I did not move for hours and hours. Her journey, her understanding, her knowing, her deep, deep knowing – such a gift. It is a book which has made me feel not so alone in my darkness.

My gratitude to Betty is beyond words. She has given me hope – hope that maybe I too will find a way to reach a state of peace and a pleasure and joy in life.

Thank you, Betty, for the RICHNESS of your voice.

FOREWORD

by Valerie Sinason

"Grow old along with me! The best is yet to be", wrote Robert Browning. Betty Hughes at ninety is living proof of this. After years of confusion and pain as well as courage and creative resilience she has finally understood herself-or rather herselves – and now she, with the co-operation of her others (alters/personalities) has written a book on the process. It is never too late to grow, to change or to gain a correct diagnosis and this book might inspire others to come forward.

In making most of the positive experiences in her life and her strong visual memory, the reader is allowed to enter the world of a very different historical moment.

From the vantage point of ninety, these memoirs provide an elegant reflection on times past. The language is clear and gracious and easy to read.

The book provides a window into a range of therapies that have helped Betty along the years and they offer the reader the important insight that a life journey requires different companions at different times. There is eloquent expression of overwhelming frustration, rage and hopelessness at her plight but she has been able to appreciate the good intentions of all those who have tried their best to offer help, whatever the historical limitations. Indeed, Betty has been able to welcome the progress in treatment and research on post-traumatic stress disorder, dissociation and attachment theory in the last decade and sees it as providing further backing for her account.

The book spares the reader the unbearable toll of trauma that causes DID. There is no gratuitous dwelling on pain and the multiple causes for fragmentation. There is only a small verbal window into the reasons for her predicament. This leaves the powerful artwork to communicate in the spaces where words might have been too hurtful.

And of course, there is something in the creative space between the words and the artwork that allows the reader time to reflect.

The story is not over. Betty and Co are vibrantly alive and present. Here's to the start of 'the best' new decade for Betty and to all survivors who dare to go forth on their hazardous long journeys.

Dr Valerie Sinason PhD MACP M Inst Psychoanal
Director, Clinic for Dissociative Studies

PART ONE

IN THE BEGINNING

CHAPTER ONE

BROADMEAD FARM

– the journey begins

Down the decades, the winding trail of my life journey is marked with 'milestones' that are uniquely intriguing and I find it fascinating to look back to the beginning where it all started.

I was born on a farm at West Knoyle, a hamlet near Mere on the Wiltshire/Dorset border. My father came from a well-known farming family and his father, my grandfather, was a tough, hardworking disciplinarian who sired eight children in much the same mould. The five daughters were tall and well-built and had forceful personalities: three married and two followed successful careers. The sons automatically took up farming, except my father who broke with tradition and went into business in London.

After my grandfather's death, it was my father's brother, my Uncle Will, who ruled the family home and maintained the old traditions such as collecting the family together in his beautiful old farmhouse at Christmas. We did not join in when I was very young but I remember the awesomeness of a family dinner in my teens. I was surprised when the ladies withdrew to the drawing room at the end of the meal and left the men to enjoy their port. In my ignorance I thought this only happened in books.

Uncle Will was a familiar figure in the neighbourhood, sitting his horse with ramrod straight back as he rode round his estate on his daily inspection. He was once thrown from his mount and broke his neck, but completely recovered – amazingly, to ride again. The Hughes's were hard taskmasters; authoritarian, insensitive, and stubborn, but there was also a tough, tenacious, 'leathery' quality about them and I like the idea of having some of this in my genes.

My mother came from quite different stock and had French ancestors. I also like the idea of having French blood in my veins. She was a vibrantly pretty woman, with soft, clear skin and beautiful eyes. She and my father met in London and must have made a handsome pair. He was over six foot tall, broad-shouldered and good-looking in a rugged, robust kind of way. She was deeply religious and, in order to win her affections, my father had to be converted to her narrow, restrictive beliefs. He also had to 'sign the pledge' – promising not to touch alcohol for the rest of his life. The only time I remember my father resorting to alcohol was immediately after my mother's death. I became worried because I could hear him laughing and singing during the night. I told my sister Helen and she tackled him about it. He stopped and as far as I am aware did not touch alcohol again. Helen was very courageous.

The first years of their marriage seem to have been quite happy. My father preached locally accompanied by my mother who had a clear soprano voice and sang solos. They had a wide circle of friends and my eldest sister Mary remembers a warm, cosy atmosphere in the home. *She* was allowed to sit on her father's knee by the fireside! But ill-health forced him out of London and back to the land: his roots were in the soil so the move to a small dairy farm was a challenge which he took up with vigour and enthusiasm. Like his brothers he soon became a farming workaholic.

My mother was used to a modern house in suburbia. She had never, to the best of my knowledge, lived in the country; certainly not in a tiny hamlet with no near neighbours. The picturesque old farmhouse with its rambling rooms and staircases, draughty passages and cold stone floors must have filled her with dismay. When they

4

first arrived there was no running water, no indoor sanitation, no electricity: baths had to be taken in a tub in front of the huge black coal range. We enjoyed snuggling round the cosy warmth of this stove during cold winters and at bedtime were loath to light our candles and climb the steep stairs to bed. Next day it was exciting to discover that the frost had made feathery designs on our bedroom windows. But how mother must have struggled to get that fire going on cold, dark mornings when father was already out milking the cows.

I have a clear picture of her as I write. She already had three children – my brother Pat the eldest, then about six; Mary, around four, Helen about one year old and myself on the way. I wonder how she felt when she became aware of my presence. Did she wish I wasn't there? I *do* wonder. Life must have been increasingly stressful for her as her pregnancy progressed. Both my parents wanted a boy and had two names ready – George Ernest. But I was a girl; a good girl from the start. My mother didn't want me to be born on the Sabbath so, I am told, I duly arrived late on Saturday night. I was christened Betty Ernestine.

I understand that I was fed strictly by the clock and I have no doubt that, however much I may have roared and screamed, this regime would have held firm. Undoubtedly this was intended for my good. With equal regularity my pram would have been placed out in the garden, come wind, rain or shine. My cries may not have brought my mother, or my father to my side but there must have been comfort in the sights and sounds of the garden and the farmyard. I was an April baby so pale pink petals would have been floating to the ground from the apple tree. I would have been near to the heavy clip-clop of the cart-horses in the yard and the cows shuffling impatiently near the gate waiting to be fed. I would have heard voices – voices carrying the possibility of somebody's face coming into my line of vision around the hood of my pram. Of course, it would have been the old-fashioned type of high-built pram which mothers were proud to use in those days.

The happiest memories of my childhood are associated with being outside in the fresh air. To be out of doors was to feel alive, to be free, to be in tune with growing things, to savour a harmony of colours, sounds and fragrances. There was a sense of order and congruity, a built-in pattern of events, a precise inner programming which could be observed and wondered at. This early identification with the trustworthiness of Mother Earth has nourished, influenced and encouraged me throughout my long life – right up to this present moment.

It has been my deepest, affirming truth during the darkest of doom laden days of my life. It has motivated, stimulated and inspired me to keep going in my search for meaning, purpose and cohesion. When repetitive patterning has seemed to deny rational explanation for my deep feelings of guilt and shame, this truth has upheld me. Even at times when I have lost the plot – when I have disappeared out of sight into the darkest pit – mysteriously it has had the power to hold me in its trustworthy arms.

Some people give names to this mysterious power that lies behind the universe – many different names, depending upon the culture. I still find that labels, in this or any other context are not very useful. They tend to be restrictive and narrow one's vision. If God is God and he created us then he must be beyond our capacity to know or comprehend him. I think I felt this even as a child.

But, back to my story. Quite early on I seemed to find out that animals were far less complicated than humans. Although they could be unpredictable in their behaviour, the signals they gave were easier to read than the unfathomable secret codes used by grown-ups. We had pets – many pets. Mother had a grey parrot who mimicked everybody, including the farm workers. He was called Sammy – although once to our great surprise he laid an egg – and in good weather he was put out in the garden. He used to say 'Whoa' or 'Gee up' to the cart-horses standing in the yard and one of the men complained in broad Wiltshire tones, "That there bird do make a fool o' I." Every spring there were motherless lambs to bottle-feed and cuddle, and oh, the grief when we had to carry these tenderly in our arms and reluctantly release them to rejoin their companions in the meadow.

I well remember Tootsey, a lame hen and my very own baby duckling called Khaki Bill who followed me faithfully wherever I went. He was so soft – so very, very special and I loved him dearly. He was most distressed when some obstacle was too high for him to clamber over and he would often stand flapping his little wings plaintively at the bottom of the stairs waiting for me to come and fetch him. At this time we each had our own small plot of land which we tilled with great pride. One day I left Khaki Bill with my sister Helen when I had to go off to school. When I returned home I found that she had put her small garden fork through him. I never forgave her. Was this deliberate or was it an accident? I shall never know. *How intriguing it is to look back and wonder about some of the imponderables of childhood.*

I have mentioned 'Sammy' Mummy's parrot, 'Tootsey' the lame hen, and 'Khaki Bill' my very own baby duckling but the horses were my favourites, especially the ponies – Star and Sprig. They were so immediate in their response and nuzzled up to my face affectionately. They loved to be touched and stroked – their coats were so soft and silky. I could talk to them and they seemed to understand – everything – my innermost secrets. I felt that they loved me. I felt attached to them in a way which I never achieved with humans. Recently I was in a small growth group in which the facilitators had placed a collection of cuddly toys on the mantelpiece. Right at the beginning I spied a small pony and very deliberately stepped out of the neat circle and grabbed it! I held it throughout all the sessions, touching it tenderly – stroking it fondly. As the life of the group unfolded it became obvious that as a little girl I had been extremely tactile and my pony had supplied a vital lack in a very sterile life.

Father at this time was just managing to make a meagre living from the farm yet somehow we always managed to have ponies.

I learnt to ride almost as soon as I could walk. Mother used to take my sister Helen and I by pony and trap to do the weekly shopping in Mere or Gillingham. Sometimes one of us was allowed to follow on horseback. On the way out we had to urge the ponies along with a stick but, on the way back, they would trot briskly with no encouragement at all and even break into a canter on the homeward stretch. But, woe betide us if we let one of them stumble and graze its knees. If this happened we were deeply upset about the pony but this very real concern was swept away by our fear of facing Father's wrath. I say 'we' but it could just have been me because Helen always had her own unique method of dealing with emotions – she adopted a fearless stance. We both rode everywhere on our ponies but I was never as brave as she was, especially when it came to jumping over streams and tree trunks.

Although we were living out in the country and were allowed to roam freely, observing animals mating or giving birth was strictly prohibited. This taboo created in me an element of profound, secret curiosity around this mysterious area of everyday life on the farm. Sometimes I hid furtively behind a tree or a bale of hay and watched with guilty fascination. Occasionally I happened to be in a secret hiding place when our massive bull was taken from its stall. I thought that the large metal ring through his nose must be very uncomfortable as Jack, the head cowman, led him on a long rod to a bizarre rendezvous with a cow.

I was also enthralled by the weird activities in the rabbit hutch which stood in a corner of the garden and was completely baffled at the speed at which the tame mice seemed to double in numbers overnight. Nevertheless, we welcomed all new arrivals and made a great fuss of them – especially the calves. When we went to feed them they raised wet shiny noses and licked our fingers with long, pink, sandpapery tongues.

Father claimed that pigs were the cleanest of all the animals on the farm and this seemed a bit odd. After all, they were the ones who seemed to delight in sloshing about in squelchy mud. They even put their filthy feet into the trough. Sometimes a pig would be killed and there was great excitement and a highly distinctive smell when the carcase was put on a bonfire to singe off the hair. Mouth-watering aromas wafted from the kitchen (which now had an oil stove as well as the old coal range) as tasty titbits of pork and chitterlings were cooked for family dinner.

Huge hams were cured. They were hung in the scullery before being hidden away in a deep wooden bin full of sawdust. We used to hide in this bin when we played Hide and Seek or Sardines. There was a strange musky smell as we crouched among the hams. If I were alone I was always afraid that if nobody found me I might not be able to lift the heavy sloping lid from inside. Yet it was such a good place to hide so I always jumped in and pulled the lid down before I remembered that fear always jumped in after me! This bin often featured in therapy sessions later on. It was the scene of dramas enacted with children who came to play with us. Were these dramas based upon actual memories or were they figments of a vivid imagination? *This is a question which has become a persistent theme throughout my therapeutic journey in all its phases.*

Indoors had a different feel in comparison to outdoors and I have carried this feeling with me throughout my life: a sense of freedom out in the open air swallowed up by a weighty sense of foreboding on crossing a threshold. Retrospectively I can see that my mother became progressively more obsessive in the practice of her religion as my father slowly strayed from the fold in his total preoccupation with the demands of the farm. She would attach herself to any church, chapel or gospel hall which she thought was 'sound' and which preached the pure gospel of salvation through the blood of Jesus shed upon the Cross. This could be Plymouth Brethren, Baptist, Evangelical Church of England or any group which was staunchly fundamentalist in its literal interpretation of the Bible, which ruthlessly denied any indulgence in the 'lusts of the flesh' or other worldly pleasures and proclaimed the inflexible alternatives of heaven or hell. The only way to be 'saved' was 'to be born again', to be cleansed from sin by being 'washed in the blood of the Lamb'. Over a long period of time I have slowly managed to disentangle myself from the aftermath of the continuum of religious verbosity that I was subjected to. It became interwoven into the very fabric of body, mind and spirit. The degree to which it was intertwined in the recesses of my guilt-ridden spirit still amazes me.

It was my mother's constant prayer and admonition that her children should remain 'pure' and without blemish and this profound desire was focussed upon me with explicit intensity. I was her last-born child – her last opportunity. Weighty, unresolved conflicts about her own sensuality and sexuality, her own efforts to obey the Pauline instruction about not letting sin reign in our mortal bodies in case we obeyed the lusts thereof, affected my mother's response to me at the breast and affected her attitude to all bodily functions and pleasures. It created an atmosphere of severe restriction and repression which completely stifled spontaneity: an oppression and enslavement which were to condition my future life and result in deep-seated problems with sex, eating and basic communication skills.

We were taught not only that God was head of our house but that every single word in the Bible was true in a literal sense. Long chapters of both Old and New Testaments were read to us daily and we sat and fidgeted through endless talks, exhortations and prayers. We sang hymns and jolly choruses about love, joy, peace and happiness but the words were like presents permanently hanging on a Christmas tree and never handed out to be opened and enjoyed. In a mysterious way I managed to file away in secret compartments my bewilderment about these puzzling inconsistencies and it was intensely interesting, decades later, when trap doors, deep inside, opened and those repressed selves gave voice with great glee.

My clearest memory of my mother is of a sad, burdened woman, always praying loudly to her Lord as she knelt at her bedside, or talking to us about Him and telling us how wonderful He was. I used to try desperately hard to smooth the furrows from her brow and always felt that somehow her sorrow was my fault. I recall her sad, gentle face when she sang solos in the chapel at East Knoyle. I would be standing up on the hard wooden seat so that I could get a better view of what was happening. I can still hear the lilting tune of a familiar hymn being played on the ancient harmonium and my mother's clear soprano voice singing:

"There were ninety and nine that safely lay
In the shelter of the fold.
And one was out on the hills away,
Far off from the gates of gold;
Away on the mountains wild and bare,
Away from the tender Shepherd's care.

And all through the mountains, thunder-riven.
And up from the rocky steep,
There rose a cry to the gates of heaven,
'Rejoice! I have found my sheep!
And the angels echoed around the throne
'Rejoice', for the Lord brings back His own."

Lyrics: Elizabeth Cecilia Clephane 1830 – 1869
Music: Ira David Sankey 1840 – 1908

Even then I didn't picture myself as snugly safe and cosy in the shelter of the fold, nor did I feel sure that, if I were to stray up the rocky steep and become lost in the thunder-riven mountains, a tender Shepherd would come and find me and carry me home rejoicing. If I strayed and got lost it was more likely to be *my* fault. My dear mother's religion overwhelmed our house and was a profound source of anxiety, bewilderment and confusion robbing me of any sense of inner security.

Clearly my mother was married to her Lord. Yet, His precious book, the Bible, every word of which was true, was full of horrifying drama. Someone was turned into a pillar of salt, someone else lost his strength when his long hair was cut; an important baby was hidden in a basket in the bulrushes. The walls of Jericho fell at the drop of a hat, Jonah was a moaner who was swallowed by a whale but was vomited up again. And that is not even to mention all the plagues and pestilences, the thunder, lightening and balls of fire and the whole world going up in a God Almighty explosion. Then there was the fact that at any moment mother's Lord was expected to come again. He would descend from heaven with a mighty shout and the righteous ones would join Him in the sky. I always wondered, "Would they have clothes on?"

Yet, I also had a father, a hero kind of person, who worked from pre dawn to dusk on the farm, made meal times a misery by having a cane ready to hand or snoozed in his special armchair and mustn't be disturbed. I was terrified by his loud voice. Not quite up to Uncle Will's standard – *he* prided himself upon being heard from one end of his extensive farm to the other – but Father bellowing at his workmen or at the cows was enough to scare you from being within range at the wrong moment. One of the most perplexing decisions I had to make was how to read the signs. I was like a little shadow following him around, peeping round corners, springing up if I thought I could help yet never knowing whether being seen would be one of those treasured moments of recognition or another tragic, painful disaster.

My sister Mary recalled holding a chicken with trembling hands while father killed it for our dinner. This is a good example of the desperate need 'we girls' had to find any chink of a possibility of being useful – such was our craving to be noticed by father, to be important to him, to feature in his life. I think 'we girls' also tried to make up for the fact that Pat, the only son, wasn't a macho 'Hughes' male and therefore must have been a great disappointment to his dad.

The farm workers were our close friends and 'Bertie' was our favourite. We loved all the rituals of their daily tasks: grooming the cart horses and trying to lift their massive feet to get the mud off, cleaning the harness and making the brass bits sparkle, getting the cows in, though this was a bit scary when they suddenly turned on you with big eyes and pincer sharp horns. Mucking out the pigs made you dirty even though Father said they were the cleanest animals and collecting eggs from the nest could be quite tricky because when you lifted the lid of the nesting box a hen might suddenly pop up and squawk at you. But the newly laid eggs were warm and so delicately fragile. You carried them very carefully to the kitchen knowing that they would appear on the breakfast table to be eaten scrumptiously with 'soldiers'. In the summer we often took picnics up to the fields where the men were working and helped to turn the grass or stack the corn and as a special treat we were hauled up on top of the wagon as we all headed for home at the end of the day.

CHAPTER TWO

MY SIBLINGS

– I was the youngest of four

My siblings and I each chose our path very early. I was good but messy. I loved splattering my food around and getting it all over my face – imitating the favoured pigs I guess. Keeping the most tasty bits till last – such as the thick icing on top of a cup cake – guzzling them lusciously at the very end was a delight but Mother disapproved of this – it was a sign of greedy lustfulness, one of the Pauline sins. Pulling on my father's massive black 'wellies' and wallowing in the squelchy mud near the farm gate or in the pongy dung heap was a favourite pastime. When I pass near to a farmyard I still enjoy the ripe fragrance of manure and I still love putting on my bright red wellies to slosh along muddy paths or squish through autumn leaves.

Helen, eighteen months older than me, was naughty, didn't care about anybody and always made quite sure that she got what she wanted. Once when she was about four she was punished by being locked in her upstairs bedroom. She stuck it out for a while, calling and banging on the door but finally she dragged a chair to the window, scrambled onto the sill and jumped out. My father, struggling with farm accounts in his office below looked up to see her fall past his window. But she got up, ran in, chirpily saying, "I called you and you didn't come so I jumped." Another time, she was given a new jumper for Christmas; she wanted to wear it

14

immediately but was told that she had to wait until after her afternoon rest. Maybe she didn't quite trust them but she was so determined to make sure of enjoying her wonderful present that she purloined a pair of scissors and, when mother went to wake her, she was flabbergasted to see the whole bed covered in bits of wool. A triumphant voice greeted her saying, "Look! I have cut up my old jumper so now I can wear my new woolly."

Helen and I argued and fought a lot, chasing each other round and round the big chesterfield in the sitting room. She teased and taunted me until I was bursting with fury but when I lashed out she called plaintively, "Mummy, Betty has hit me." We often went together to a large farmhouse to play with a family of boys, all older than I was. I hated going because there were so many dark passages with murky corners, winding staircases leading to eerie attics and it was easy to open the wrong door and find startled grown-ups inside. There was a pond with ducks and sometimes tiny yellowy balls of fluff would appear like magic and these minute ducklings would paddle their little legs with remarkable speed, pecking at insects in a very grown-up way as they scuttled to keep up with Mum and Dad. But I couldn't really enjoy the pond because I never knew when geese would unexpectedly appear out of nowhere with outstretched necks and ear-splitting squawks or Helen and the boys might shut me inside the large enclosed garden and then taunt and jeer at me from the other side of the high wall. I was a perfect victim and can still feel intimidated by any group of young boys who gang up together in a threatening stance. On the way home I even allowed Helen to terrify me by saying that when we passed Jim Carey's cottage, massive black dogs would spring out at us. I hated going to the Coleses but when the next visit came around I couldn't tell my mother that I didn't want to go. *Many decades were to pass before I realised that Helen was jealous of the little brat who had pinched her place on her mother's knee and stolen her place in her father's heart.*

Helen was also extremely interested in her body and sometimes, when we sat among the bales of hay in the loft, she would have a good look at our genitals and poke around. This made me feel *so* guilty. She played with boys and even let them touch her intimately. Later, when she and I were at boarding school together, I was guiltily fascinated when she got into bed with another girl and I knew that something was going on under the bedclothes. They were touching each other in 'rude' places and whispering about what was nice but even nicer when done with a boy. I was horrified. What *would* Mother say if she knew?

It is interesting that Helen's 'modus operandi' served her well in certain respects. By not following the guilt route, she didn't have the hang-ups that the rest of us were saddled with and was able to have much more fun and freedom in her life. She really enjoyed her teens and twenties, wasn't remotely troubled about hurting Mother, yet once confessed to me that she was terrified of death. After an eventful life, which included moving to join her son in Australia, she became an alcoholic and sadly ended her days vegetating in a nursing home much to the distress of her son and his family and friends.

In the early days I didn't really get to know my older sister Mary, who had spent her early childhood years in the smoother running environment of the London era. She must have been about six when the family moved to Broadmead. I have vague memories of there being older girls in the Coles family who went by pony and trap to a small private school near Mere. I think they must have been one of the more successful farming families in the area, whereas we were quite poor. They certainly had much more money than we had and both adults and children seemed to adopt an air of superiority. Mary accompanied the Coles girls to school and apparently became *their* victim. I understand that they bullied her relentlessly but, like me, I doubt whether she ever told anyone.

Mary took a different stance from Helen. She did everything she possibly could to help, support and please her mother. She turned over backwards to be Mother's perfect eldest daughter, being kind, thoughtful, caring – always trying to please – always avoiding

1 (above) We loved Broadmead. The farmhouse was a gracious, ivy-clad home surrounded by outbuildings and yards where the horses were groomed and the cows were milked.

2 (right) I like to think that this was my parents' wedding portrait. What an elegant pose – so traditional of that period.

3   In some secret corner I was always sure that I was very special to my daddy and here he is – standing behind my mother – looking directly at me!

4   Haymaking was such fun. We spent hours out in the fields tossing the sweet-scented grass into neat rows; when it was sufficiently dry it was collected by the wagon. Father stamped with impatience if it rained! Then more tossing onto the elevator to form a neat haystack that was thatched to weather the winter storms.

5 *This massive bull filled me with a mixture of awe and curiosity. I knew that he fulfilled some essential, mysterious, yet bizarre function among the cows but being interested was strictly forbidden. Needless to say, whenever I had a chance, I watched his antics from a secret hideaway.*

6 *This is 'Star' the old pony which I rode to school one day when she needed to go to the blacksmith. We weren't allowed to wear trousers and our bare legs always got pinched by the stirrup straps.*

7 *(above right) Pets were my daily companions. I like the plaits and the black woollen stockings, although I probably hated them then.*

8 *(left) A pensive picture of me. I seem to be both protecting myself and comforting myself with the cosy body of my much loved cat.*

9 The house at White Place Farm was very unusual with its wide porch, cascade of Virginia creeper and beautifully landscaped front garden which was Father's pride and joy.

10 This picture still surprises me! The escape to Minehead. My first experience, not only of the beauty of Exmoor, but of receiving attention from the male sex! I am the girl with the centre parting and the handsome lad stroking the horse's head was my daily companion. Helen is tucked away, almost out of sight.

11. *Lee Abbey has lost none of its charm. The wooded estate, with extensive views over Lee Bay, must occupy one of the most beautiful sites on Exmoor.*

12 *This is a classic picture of 'Pop', my father, standing in front of the house watching for new guests to chat to. He was quite benevolent during the latter years of his life and was much loved by Lee Abbey visitors.*

13 (left) How old am I in this picture? I am intrigued by the look in my eyes. Does this young girl have any idea of the journey that lies ahead?

14 (below) Roger de Pemberton, the first Warden of Lee Abbey, is seen here, in characteristic pose with his wife Peggy. He was the pioneer who first conceived the vision of a centre of evangelism sited on this enchanting estate. The venture thrives sixty-four years on.

15 (below) While I was working in the Community, the Dowager Queen Wilhelmina of the Netherlands attended sessions and planted a tree which is now flourishing. I remember having breakfast with her one morning!

16 (left) Definitely 'the hostess with the mostess'.

17 (below) I seem to know how to choose spectacular views! The Hotel Mattenhof in Interlaken, Switzerland – the hotel which I managed – was another impressive building overlooking the famous Jungfrau range of mountains in the Bernese Oberland.

18 (below) 1st August, Swiss National Day, saw all the staff in festive Swiss costumes and our chef excelled himself with a spectacular spread.

19 (left) There is something quite unforgettable about learning to ski. Moments of gliding gracefully down the piste followed by an ungainly tangle of skis and sticks, a flurry of snow and a big bruise on the rear end.

20 (below) The Travel Consultant retires and receives a handsome bouquet from a grateful client.

upsetting her in any way and feeling guilty if inadvertently she did something which was out of line. It was deeply painful for her to do anything to hurt her mother who controlled with such determination yet seemed so fragile. *There was a strange twist to the relationship between mother and elder daughter. In later years Mary sometimes talked to me about this. She could never come to terms with what she felt was a flagrant injustice. She had turned over backwards to be Mother's good elder daughter, yet was branded by Mother as a 'martyr', whereas Helen didn't give a damn about anything or anyone and got away with murder! What does that tell us about my mother?*

Later Mary was uprooted from this simple rural setting and was sent to a well known girl's public school in Malvern. Poor Mary. The exorbitant school fees were kindly paid by my father's two successful, career orientated sisters, Aunties Dulcie and Mary who, I suspect, did not let her forget the fact that she was beholden to them and should be grateful. Aunt Dulcie was a senior mistress at this school and Mary was placed in her 'house' – 'houses' being part of the public school system. This meant that Mary not only felt beholden to her aunts, and was constantly under scrutiny but, worst of all, she was saddled with the heavy burden of never doing as well academically as was hoped and expected. Later Aunt Mary paid for my sister to go to a secretarial college in London but I don't think any consideration was given to whether this was a career that really suited Mary; I don't think it entered anybody's head to consult her in the matter. Aunt Mary engineered a job for her in the Civil Service but I don't remember her enjoying this. I cannot recall exactly when Mary married a chemical engineer whose work took him up north where her two children were born, a boy first and then a girl. She seemed to disappear out of my life for a long periods and I only had glimpses of the children when they were small. All I have is a few pictures.

Another strange twist is that right up to the time of her death, my sister Mary had a strange eerie feeling about Bertie, one of our farm workers. At one crisis period in her life she spent a long period in psychotherapy. She told me that when reliving her childhood there was always a point at which she came up against a brick wall. It seemed to be associated with Bertie and a certain place on the farm. Interesting.

I have very few memories of my brother Pat at this time. He was at boarding school in nearby Shaftesbury and was a quiet presence in the background at the farm, but only during the holidays. It's bizarre – I have no sense whatever of having related to him when I was child yet I *do* recall that Helen used to bait him, and Mary was her victim as well. She was skilled at driving them both mad and had a knack of winding them up and then gloating over their responses.

I recall that on leaving school Pat started a career in business in London just as his father had done. He lived 'in digs' and I remember having a weird picture in my head of what 'digs' might look like!

Later Pat, like his father before him, felt the call of the land and decided to take up farming. Mistakenly, in my view, he went as a pupil to Uncle Will's farm near Swindon. Here he was surrounded by all the Hughes clan – all well-known and respected farmers who were influential in local affairs. Uncle Will was the prototype of macho Hughes males. He could be a threatening bully. Similar to my father, nobody could do jobs as quickly or as efficiently as he could, and for Pat, who was gentle and sensitive, working with Uncle Will must have been a nightmare. He did not fit in – he was much too docile, thin-skinned and tender-hearted. The setting is the Second World War and Pat was living under his uncle's watchful eye in the farmhouse. So, when he fell in love with one of the Land Girls who was working on the same farm disaster struck. Needless to say, she wasn't good enough for a Hughes male.

Pat loathed this atmosphere of intimidation and disapproval. Finally he plucked up sufficient courage to leave his uncle's farm, marry his girl and set himself up on the farming ladder. He became a very loving father to two beautiful daughters. *My feelings are of deep sadness as I write about Pat. I don't think he ever enjoyed the satisfaction of becoming his true self. He had been his mother's favourite but must have sensed at some level that he was a bitter disappointment to his father. Living under the tutelage of his uncle must have reinforced those early imprints with disastrous repercussions.*

When I embarked upon my therapeutic journey Pat was living with his family on a small farm in Somerset. At this time I was intensely interested in my childhood, as one is when delving into one's secret underworld. I would sometimes try to engage Pat in discussions about those early days on the farm when he was a schoolboy and I was very young. After all, he could remember so much more than I could. But he would never be drawn. He would clam up immediately and right to the very end, when he died of Parkinson's disease, his mother was still standing like a holy goddess high up on her pedestal.

But back to Broadmead Farm. Although Pat and Mary are such shadowy figures in my package of childhood memories, they must have been around during the school holidays. Looking back, I see myself in a totally different world. Even Mary, who, during the last few years of her life, was often happy to reminisce, freely admitted that she carried no picture in her mind of what it must have been like for me. I presume this is because there was no direct communication in our family. We lived very separate lives, each relating to our parents by our chosen route – a route determined by the unique, individual way in which we had adapted to our parents and the environment which they had created.

But to return to the story. One day on which magically we became a real family was Christmas Day, with its familiar rituals and an air of excitement. It all started when you crept down to the bottom of the bed at crack of dawn knowing that Father Christmas would have filled your stocking. You felt its shape first of all: an orange in the toe, some pink sugar mice, one of those 'blowyouty' things which squeaked and sprang into life when you blew it, a painting book and lots of other surprises. I was furious when Helen told me that it was mother in her red dressing gown who put the stockings there and not Father Christmas.

We had to wait for our big presents till after the magnificent Christmas dinner – dinner, not lunch – complete with crackers and mince pies. Then we all sat round the huge log fire and opened our gifts one at a time with lots of oohs and ahs. Even Father was present – not just present but in a jovial mood; this was most unusual because he seemed to work all the time and when finally he came indoors he was tired and irritable. Best of all, there was no fuss about the mess of paper and string, strewn all over the floor.

The atmosphere was so special on this festive day. A spirit of plenty replaced the usual meagre 'just enough to go round' routine. There were sweets, wobbly jelly and Christmas cake, silvery three-penny pieces in the luscious fruity pudding, and no one said, "No, you can't have any more." We seemed to be a happy family and even religion was quite jolly – a baby lying in a manger, being warmly welcomed by shepherds and lambs and honoured by kings in exotic robes bearing presents. So entirely different from the Lord who usually ruled our house and demanded instant perfection and obedience.

This picture of my father on Christmas day reminds me of the fringe position he normally took up in the family hierarchy. He ruled the roost outside with Mother and her Lord ruling inside. Father always backed her up – told us to do what she said, told us not to worry her, told us to do nothing to upset her. But if we *did* upset her, by doing something *very* bad, we were informed that we would be spanked by Father when he came in from work. I can still remember the agony of living through the day waiting for his footsteps on the stone floor of the scullery. I knew that when he came in, Mother would tell him what I had done and I would have to pull my knickers down and have my bare bottom beaten. I think it was the humiliation as much as the pain – now I would probably label it as shame. I still cannot remember what sin I had committed to merit such punishment.

Guilt, shame – shame again – and a kind of awkwardness were never far away. There was always a curious feeling around bodies and touching each other. Mother always used a different flannel for washing her private parts as if they, in themselves, were dirty and impure. She was extremely meticulous about our bowels and gave us pills every week as well as brimstone and treacle in the spring and syrup of figs in the autumn. In addition, she used to lay us across her knee on our tummies and de-worm us. This was an intimate experience which held a strange tinge of excitement, yet also there was a trace of revulsion when her fingers picked these white, wriggling worms out of your bottom and showed them to you with satisfaction: almost as if she was purifying you and ridding you of something evil which was distasteful to *her*.

Father was a bit like a coiled spring. A grating irritation often got past his guard and came through in his voice. An intense rage, just under the surface, was kept tightly leashed while in the house but was vented with venom outside at the animals and the farm workers. *I have a flicker of recollection of being held gently in his arms as a tiny baby and of a special look of pride and joy in his eyes: but, later on, like other things, I began to wonder whether this was a real experience, woven into the fabric of my being, or whether it was a sign of the depth of my need for my father's love and attention. Regretfully, I have found that many years of psychotherapy and personal growth can sometimes make things more rather than less complex and convoluted. Recently, a child self was quite jubilant when I came across an old photograph which affirms my original perception! He is looking at me intently – I was his pride and joy!*

Certainly when I became a toddler father was unable to be gentle or tender. He poked with a sharply pointed finger, pinched a soft cheek with talons that felt like pincers or tickled with a ferocity which built up a crescendo of excitement which Mother disapproved of. He was totally unable to be what the Bible said Jesus was like with little children – tender, gentle and compassionate. As an adult I have often observed the loud, jolly, cumbersome way in which he related to small children – even his own grandchildren. He obviously loved them dearly but he was ham-fisted and had no idea how to touch them gently. When one of my nieces was reading this manuscript she immediately recalled how frightened she had been as a small child by his loud voice and his heavy-handedness. *This affirms the deeply entrenched conflict which I have unearthed about my father. I had a deep longing to be held closely and tenderly by him but this yearning lived side-by-side with nervous anxiety and terror.*

Early experiences of primary school are hazy except for three incidents which stand out significantly. After a short period at West Knoyle village school Helen and I started to travel by bus to Mere. One day the driver stopped to watch a gypsy dancing round his brightly painted caravan which stood in a clearing in the woods. The gipsy was cavorting around holding his penis in both hands, playing to the gallery and enjoying the children's laughter. The bus driver, Helen and the rest of the children chortled with delight and watched for a long time. I was shocked. My immediate reaction was, "I mustn't look. I shouldn't look. What would Mother think? She would be horrified and disgusted." Years later, Helen and I recalled this incident, which we both remembered vividly. I was fascinated by her response. She said, "I recall thinking what a silly little thing 'it' was to make such a fuss about." How extraordinary! I remembered a penis the size of a police truncheon and thought how wonderful it would be to have one of those! *A very reasonable response from a little girl who believed that she would have been much more acceptable had she been a boy and had male advantages and appendages. Needless to say this event also featured prominently in therapy sessions.*

The second incident took place during a singing lesson at school. I was about six. The mistress was seated at the piano and the little boys and girls took it in turns to come out to the front of the class with a ruler and conduct the singing. My turn came and I stepped forward with great pride and took my place. But alas, after a few minutes I wanted to spend a penny. It was urgent. We were not permitted to leave the room without putting a hand up and asking 'to be excused'. For a few minutes I alternated between using both hands to conduct the class and raising my right arm with a pleading look towards the teacher at the piano. There was such urgency and panic. What a predicament! She didn't catch on, nature took over, the inevitable happened and a puddle started to spread over the floor. I was overcome with shame and humiliation – *such* humiliation and *such* shame.

The next incident has a weird sense of connection to the above but I don't really know why. Perhaps it happened on the same day. Occasionally we were allowed to ride one of the ponies to school and leave it at the blacksmith's to be shod, then collect it when lessons were over. My luck was to take Star, an old friend who was very slow and had to be the encouraged along with a whip. Although I left early and took the same route as the bus, I arrived at school extremely late. For some reason there was a lot of fuss and hullabaloo about this and I never quite knew what it was all about. I can picture the head teacher talking to my mother in front of our coal range in the farmhouse kitchen and there is something about the village policeman but it is all extremely hazy.

Spring, summer, autumn and winter came and went – spring was always my very special time of year. The cows were released into the meadow after months of being confined to the barns. They would scamper up the hill beside Puckwell Wood, kicking up their back legs and waving their tails with glee at being let out again. I always hoped that this was going to be one of the days when I would be allowed to take my little stick and help my daddy. If this happened I grasped the opportunity to peep into my own very special wood to see if the first celandine, the first primrose and the first bluebell had arrived. This was such an exciting ritual.

But back in 1929 farmers were having a difficult time and when I was nine my father was forced to sell up and take a farm manager's job. I can recall the sad, heavy feeling at the farm sale. All the implements used for haymaking and harvesting were laid out in a field. Strangers wandered round the buildings looking at the animals, *our* animals. There would be no more picnics in the hayfield, no more riding home on top of the wagon, no more collecting the warm, brown eggs from the nest, no more anything at Broadmead Farm. I was desolated when we moved to a farm at Cookham in Berkshire.

I often go back to Broadmead Farm. It is quite difficult for me to drive down the A303, in either direction, without taking the short diversion and passing through West Knoyle.

The very first time was just after I had started psychotherapy. It was a delight to find that the scenes so closely matched the pictures in the old family albums. I felt compelled to knock on the door, explain that I had been born in this beautiful farmhouse and ask if I could look around. The new owners didn't seem to mind at all. The furnishings were all updated but the basic structure had changed very little. Wandering into the front lounge brought a vivid picture of my father, sitting in his armchair, hidden behind his Daily Express. *Next, I strolled into the school-room where Helen and I had lessons with our governess and Helen had dared me to strike my first match.*

In pensive mood I stood in the living room which had been dominated by the black coal range and the large table around which meals had been such purgatory because 'children should be seen and not heard'. A sudden picture of mother flashed into my mind. She was unpacking the shopping and I was an excited child wondering whether there was going to be something nice to eat – maybe a cup-cake with icing on top.

Climbing the steep stairs to bedroom level, I looked out of the window, with its wide window sill, from which Helen had jumped. Just imagine Father busy in his study below, suddenly looking up and not being able to believe his own eyes when her small body dropped from nowhere and hit the hard ground. This was a large room and in our day had a double bed with shiny brass knobs – Helen had slept here when she had rheumatic fever and was visited by nice Dr Farmfield. It led into a tiny dark 'cupboardy' room where spiders lurked. This was where Pat got into trouble because he cut Mary's hair off. When I first heard this story I was very surprised because Pat seemed to be such a good boy.

Later on, my sister Mary, her daughter Nikki and I made a pilgrimage to Puckwell Wood every spring for a number of years. We would stop at the top of the drive which led to Broadmead Farm and look out for any alterations to the house or farmyard. Then on to Colses Farm to reminisce about those awful children who had made our lives such a misery before strolling through Puckwell Wood to look for primroses and bluebells. After Mary died Nikki and I continued the tradition whenever we could manage it.

Chapter Three

WHITE PLACE FARM

– *a significant move*

We moved into a beautiful house just a couple of fields away from one of the most famous reaches on the River Thames. My father was managing the dairy farm on the estate of Lord and Lady Astor who lived at Clivedon, a stately home high up among the trees on the other side of the river. Yes, this was the famous Nancy Astor with the razor sharp tongue who was the first female Member of Parliament. Yes again, this was the mansion where the world-famous 'Clivedon set' had cavorted.

We children were interested in the farm but everything was different. It was no longer *our* farm, the cows were no longer *our* cows, we didn't belong in the same way and we didn't have ponies. But these weren't the only changes.

The early parts of my life at Broadmead are still alive and vivid. Although some of the elements were deeply confusing, up to a certain juncture there was a strange way in which I was able to trust my own perception in regard to the contradictions that were expressed so blatantly in my world; as if I looked out from a secret spy hole through which I was able to observe the subtleties, yet hold on to my own truth. But as I re-live the move to Cookham a grey dreariness takes over.

In the new house there were two very large bedrooms at each end of a long passage and three small single rooms in between. I found myself sharing Mother's large double bed, while Pat, Mary and Helen had the singles and Father was alone in the equally huge bed with brass knobs at the far end of the corridor. Mother and I slept very close together like two spoons and when she turned, I turned. By this time, I was already unhealthily attached to her and sharing the vast marital bed increased this sense of intimacy. I felt quite detached and had little involvement with my father from then on: he was the breadwinner and was called in to administer punishment when we had been particularly badly behaved. He frowned over my school reports when he read, "Betty *can* do good work" – a phrase that irritated him most of all. It was strange, as if an emotional link with him had been broken for ever. The small child who had followed her daddy around like a shadow wasn't present any more.

But as my deep emotional attachment to my father disappeared, my fear of the Almighty grew in intensity: the wrath of God was like a sword of Damocles, every moment of every day and every night, for ever and ever, hanging above my head. It could fall at any moment. If every single word of the Bible were true in a literal sense, there were *so* many potential pitfalls. The body was a temple of the Holy Spirit, not a home in which one lived, to be revelled in and enjoyed. Sex was something to be endured strictly for the procreation of children and any form of lust, greed or bodily pleasure was a temptation of the devil. This teaching bound me in an inflexible strait-jacket as I made the transition into my teens. I came to hate my body with a deep abhorrence because, the more it began to develop female characteristics, the more it became the seat of inextinguishable flames of sinfulness. People have found my breasts a place of great comfort and cosiness, yet I detested the first signs of their bulging curves and, when my periods started, I knew I had to tell my mother. I lay beside her trembling in every limb and eventually she asked me what was the matter and I was able to confess. It felt like the last straw – the final shame. I can still remember the moment of telling her and can recall the awfulness of the feelings that accompanied that revelation.

Helen and Mary started to go out with boys, and this caused my mother deep pain and grief. At first they were probably just flirting and petting, but in my mother's eyes they were succumbing to the devil and were on the road to hell – doomed for ever. Her anxiety was tangible and she made me her confidante – continually offloading her distress. She spent longer and longer kneeling at her bedside, pouring out her heart to the Almighty – praying out loud and weeping. I could hear the dreary lament of her moaning and wailing as I sat in the sitting room below and I felt heavily burdened by her sorrow. As I emerged into my teens I knew that *I* couldn't add to her worries. One day we were cleaning Helen's bedroom and Mother opened a letter which was lying on the table. She was deeply shocked by the references to intimate sexual contact and she turned to me and said, "If you follow in your sister's footsteps it will break my heart." I can see now that my mother was a sad, frail woman who was totally unaware of her obsessions. She used me as a cushion of support in her fight to serve and please her Lord and Master. At the time, I knew that I couldn't add to her burden of grief, nor could I allow her to collapse because I was deeply dependent upon her emotionally. It did not occur to me that I had rights of my own: the right to exist as a separate individual, the right to develop as a sexual woman, the right to explore and have fun with other teenagers. I seemed to have no choice. I *couldn't* hurt her. If I succumbed to the wiles of the devil it *would* break her heart and she would die – that was my explicit perception at the time.

*A friend editing this passage remarked that I must have been aware that my mother's heart wouldn't really have broken if I had followed in my sisters' footsteps. I am not sure about this. I can picture the exact moment when Mother spoke these words. A profound feeling of fear overwhelmed me – as if her heart **might** break, and it would have been **my** fault: as if my spirit was being crushed by a leaden weight of doom. Maybe I was **already** carrying a load of guilt and this threat added to* *the dreary greyness – the ever present weight of the world on my shoulders.*

So I remained a good, dutiful, obedient daughter, living a zombie-like existence, escaping whenever I could. In good weather I would climb to the very top of a tall fir tree and spend hours there, gently swaying in the breeze with a book and some apples for company. I would go for long walks or cycle rides and allow my mind to drift into dreams and fantasies. In winter I took my book and my apples into the airing cupboard and hid in the warm cosiness of this secret hideout.

I had friends at school but they always had to be vetted by my mother. I remember one girl who was great fun, but she wasn't permitted to come to tea because her parents were divorced. Later, Helen and I were sent to a boarding school carefully chosen by my mother to match her narrow Christian views. In addition to a restrictive religious regime, food was strictly rationed and we were always hungry. For breakfast we were given three half slices of bread with a scrape of butter and four slices for tea. Worse still, one pound of preserves and one pound of sweets had to last for the whole term. We used to go for long walks in crocodile and all heads would turn to the right when we passed the local baker's shop, and we revelled in the tantalising aroma of the warm, crusty bread as it wafted across the pavement.

Every night, before going to bed, we stood in a long queue outside the Head's study and went in one by one to say goodnight and to receive any reprimand that might be awaiting us. Two sisters, the Misses Fenn, ran the school and when we opened the door they would always be sitting like bookends, one each side of the fireplace. One evening, Helen and I and another girl stood trembling as we awaited our turn because we had decided to go in together and complain that we were hungry. I can still remember the shocked expression on the faces of the sisters at our audacity. After an intimidating pause, Miss Fenn, the elder, turned to me and said, "Well Betty, I suppose it is just possible that *you* might be hungry because you are so big…" a remark calculated to boost one's teenage morale indeed! Anyway, much to the envy of everybody else, after that they gave us doubly thick slices of bread both for breakfast and tea – huge delicious hunks piled like a castle on a large dish, just for us three. But this gesture of plenty didn't last. As term progressed the slices gradually grew thinner and there came a day when we were once again treated like the rest.

I was terribly homesick at boarding school and can still remember how painful it was being away from my mother. Learning was a struggle. I can recall the dreadful feeling. It was as if my head was clogged up and I was unable to absorb information. The only thing that motivated me was gym classes. However, I remember one occasion when we all had to recite a poem and I was surprised that I stood out as one of the best performers. Finally, regardless of important forthcoming examinations that might affect my future career prospects, I was glad when they let me leave and I spent the following year helping my mother run the home.

A highlight of this period was a holiday we three girls spent at Minehead in North Devon. I have never been able to fathom why my mother allowed us to go, because we were joining a house-party consisting mostly of young men. Mary and Helen must have made up some tale to deceive my mother. It was my very first experience of being let off the lead and as I was the youngest at about sixteen I came in for a lot of teasing and spoiling. I was surprised that they liked me because I always saw myself as an uninteresting, insipid person. I felt inept and naïve but again it was a surprise when I paired off with a handsome young man and we sat on the settee holding hands in the evenings. Three other young men were also interested in me and kept in touch afterwards. One sent long, poetic letters, but my mother had sussed out by then what was going on and when he called to see me one afternoon she sent him packing. Looking back, I find it so painful to picture myself: a young teenager, so completely out of touch with her emotions at such a crucial stage in her development. It is almost inconceivable that not only did

I allow my mother to send him away without protesting, but I wasn't even aware that I minded.

After a year at home I was sent to a domestic science college in London because I was good at cooking. I did well there and was popular enough to be elected as representative of my set in the Students' Union. This surprised me because I saw myself as bland, colourless, sexless, and without any unique characteristics. This element of surprise was going to be an on-going experience as I was gradually forced to recognise that there was more to me than I thought. Yet, this was imposed from outside and did nothing to modify or counteract the feelings of intense inferiority which I carried as a life sentence.

My mother died while I was at college and this *did* touch me. She developed cancer and was taken to hospital for an emergency operation from which she did not recover. My father, Helen and I were at her bedside when she passed away but I don't think she knew we were there. Pat and Mary came home for the funeral. I recall walking like a zombie behind the coffin but afterwards I was distraught and felt that life could never be the same again. The bottom had dropped out of my world.

I was to find that the imprint of my mother's influence was deeply entrenched and it was many years before I recognised this. The acknowledgement, when it dawned, led to a long, hard struggle to release myself from the straitjacket which had restricted my development and robbed me of any sense of self.

CHAPTER FOUR

TEENS TO FORTIES

– wandering in a wasteland

When my mother died I felt both anguish and relief. I experienced a deep sense of loss and emptiness – a dreadful, doom-laden sensation that nothing could ever be the same again. Yet, at the same time there was a glimmer of light. I began to realise that at long last I was free to spread my wings. I started to venture out in small ways that would have caused my mother great pain. For example, I joined a broadly-based Christian fellowship which in her eyes would have been 'unsound' and 'of the Devil'.

When I first wrote this paragraph I started with the words, "Once again I was surprised to find that I was popular and recognised by my peers as cut out for leadership and responsibility", so perhaps it is necessary to acknowledge once and for all the degree to which my true character and personality had been subjugated by the time my mother died. Throughout my life it has never ceased to surprise me when people see qualities that I am unaware of. At eighteen years old, I had no knowledge of myself; simple data and awareness of my true personality – my vitality, my colourfulness, my exuberant energy – were not available to me. I was totally 'greyed out' in my own eyes and in my own estimation, but fortunately, the quite extraordinary, lifelong experience of 'unpacking myself' started as I ventured out into life as a separate individual after my mother's death.

My first real boyfriend appeared on the scene. We went around together for several years and enjoyed each other's company, walking, discussing, playing tennis, lazing in a boat on the river; sometimes in a group, sometimes just the two of us. We grew fond of each other, yet the relationship was very innocent, nothing more sinful than petting and cuddling. I was quite content to meander romantically for hours, to lie snugly together in a punt on the sunlit River Thames in summer, or cosily tuck up together in the farm hayloft in the winter. But, as we grew closer and older and the possibility of more intimate sexual contact seemed likely, I started to become aware of deep-seated conflict and a burden of guilt. A bewildering jumble of chaotic feelings took me over. It was like opening up a man-hole leading God knew where.

In addition to a profound sense of shame, I also felt pathetic and inferior, even defective in some way. I compared myself unfavourably with my sister Helen who apparently had no such taboos or inhibitions and happily flitted like a butterfly from one attractive male to another.

The Second World War had started by the time I ended the relationship. I was working at the Domestic Science College where I had trained which had been evacuated to Bournemouth. The break was extremely painful and left me with a deep sense of loss. He was posted overseas with the Army and I worried about him continuously but the indoctrination about sex and sin embedded in my roots went so deep that even pining for him seemed wicked. What happened to him? He survived the war and I met up with him once. He was studying at a Bible College in London and was already engaged to be married. Sadly, the last I heard was that he had developed MS.

It could be said that, at no point in history, had young women been presented with such a unique opportunity to socialise with such a concentration of eligible, personable young men in their prime. If I could go back and pick up the trail again, I think this might be a fun point to choose. The town was full of handsome

RAF and Army officers from the UK and abroad, and organisations recruited every available young woman to help entertain them and give them a good time. All my work colleagues were having exciting dates and every morning I had to listen enviously to on-going sagas of encounters with fascinating men.

Instead, I set out on a more deliberate search for a radical Christian experience: I felt this would release me from the burden of guilt which held me prisoner and bring me the happiness and peace I yearned for. I went to evangelistic meetings and responded to emotional appeals to surrender my life to Christ. I confessed my sins and, although an inner sense of being forgiven didn't follow, I was assured that it was a matter of faith and not feeling. So I persevered. I came into contact with the Oxford Group, one of the movements afloat at that time, but their 'absolute' standards regarding honesty and openness filled me with terror and panic, although I didn't know why I felt so intrinsically bad and sinful – just like an apple rotten to the core. I joined another less threatening Christian Fellowship, which met in somebody's house, and I was able to make a new circle of friends: there were always interesting men around but no close relationships developed.

Later in the War I found myself working in a London hospital during the phase of the doodle-bugs and buzz bombs. Catering for the whole hospital was my responsibility and I enjoyed the rank of Sister. This was deeply resented by the nursing hierarchy because I was a trained caterer and had not risen step by step through the strict, disciplined ranks of nursing. There was a firm pecking order. Everybody was placed in order of seniority in the dining-room. At the high table Matron sat at the head, the most junior Sister at the foot and I came last. In the normal course of events if somebody left everybody moved up a place. The day came when one of the sisters moved to another hospital and I knew that they all expected me to remain in my lowly seat. Courageously, I decided to move up and leave the new Sister the humbler seat and this brought me withering looks of disapproval. I was starting to assert myself – at long last.

There was a feud between two groups of Sisters and they had not spoken to each other for many years. However the vendetta was always dropped on Christmas Day and once, when bombs were falling nearby, one sister offered her rival refuge under her red-lined cloak as they crossed the yard! I ran the dangerous course of fraternising with both groups and from time to time found myself 'sent to Coventry' by both sides.

It was a tradition on Christmas Eve, when the hospital was brightly decorated with holly and gift-laden trees, for all the staff to don their cloaks red-side outwards and, carrying lighted candles, trail round the wards singing carols. Once, for some strange reason, Matron mistakenly thought that I had a good voice and as we started out on our pilgrimage, she turned to me and said, "Miss Hughes, perhaps you would give us the note." I have never been able to sing in tune and felt paralysed. There was a deathly hush until I nudged a friendly Sister next to me and she came to my rescue.

If the air-raid siren sounded during the night we all shuffled our way down into the basement and slept on bunk beds. This was a great leveller of ranks: from Matron downwards, we lay side by side, tucked up in sleeping bags, waiting restively in case we heard the engine of an approaching missile. That was the most petrifying moment of all: the deadly second – the deathly silence between the mechanism cutting out and the bomb landing and exploding – which you might or you might not be alive to hear. You didn't know and that was terrifying. When a missile landed in our area, the basement of our hospital became a hive of activity as casualties poured in from every direction. I made myself available to lend a hand in any way that was useful in the well organised chaos which followed.

By this time my father had undergone a number of operations and finally he was forced by ill health to leave his farm manager's job at Cookham; arthritis had increased, walking was difficult and he had to use a stick. So I left the hospital and moved to a boys' school in Surrey where we were allocated a cottage in the school grounds. My father was fond of me and proud of me too, but our relationship was a strange one because I had no emotional feelings around him at all. I felt a sense of duty to look after him but otherwise my relationship with him was a blank, a space – my heart was cold and empty. *It was an unforgettable experience – both deeply moving and exhilarating to discover many decades later, that as a small child I had loved my father deeply and had been very close to him.*

At about this time I enjoyed my first holiday house-party run by Roger de Pemberton at Lee Abbey in North Devon, and I became interested in the exciting project that was about to be launched there. This large country mansion, set in one of the beauty spots of England on the edge of Exmoor, was being purchased as an act of faith, and destined to become a famous centre of evangelism within the Church of England. It was to be run by a Community of men and women who would work together and share a common life. I was excited and challenged by the idea of joining this venture and felt called by God to be one of the early pioneers.

When I told my father about joining the Lee Abbey Community he agreed rather reluctantly to come with me, although later he was often heard to say that it was the best thing that had ever happened to him because it led to a renewal of his Christian faith. We moved to a house on the estate in 1946, just after the end of the war, and he gradually became interested and involved in the venture.

When I joined the Community, full of zest and enthusiasm, I was responsible for the food, and in those early days we had to cook for some two hundred people on an ancient coal range reminiscent of our farmhouse kitchen. Cockroaches crept out from the shadows at night and rustled back into hiding when we went down to stoke the fires at crack of dawn.

I became a member of the Inner Team who organised the day-to-day running of the centre, as well as being a member of the Management Committee who were responsible for wider issues. I also took part in the pastoral work, playing a prominent role and becoming well liked and respected. A fellow Community member describes me:

"I remember Betty as a decisive, strong personality, who ruled her department firmly but kindly. Highly efficient in her work and a perfectionist who expected high standards from others. She was completely discreet and never joined in any gossip; she was liked by most of her colleagues, held in awe by some. Socially she was excellent with house-party guests, due in part at least to her attractive appearance and her ability and her willingness to listen. She had a pronounced gift for seeing the nub of a problem or situation and for disregarding irrelevancies. She was a wise, sensitive, intelligent and imaginative counsellor."

Another colleague sent me his observations:

"My main impressions are of you as a very cheerful, ebullient and at times all-too-hearty person. You came across as a workaholic who was a perfectionist, extremely capable at your job, and someone who set the highest standards for yourself, and also demanded them of others. I remember how you stayed up all night icing our wedding cake (which was really magnificent), but was also very irritated on another occasion when my wife humbly asked for an extra rasher of bacon for a meal on our day off – and you refused in no uncertain manner!

"I suppose my chief recollection is of you as a woman of great vitality, fun and humour, well able to communicate the Christian faith by word and action. No doubt there was a down side, but it was well hidden, and looking back, I wonder what your relationship with your father was really like."

I can see myself clearly in this description of an all-too-hearty perfectionist who kept the 'down side' well hidden. And I recognise the creative artist who would gladly stay up all night to ice a wedding cake, yet, on another occasion, would snap somebody's head off in frustration if she was interrupted when under pressure. Pressure was a typical, on-going state of affairs in the kitchen in those days of minimal equipment and it was a miracle, which incorporated relentless hard work and culinary skill, that allowed reasonably presented meals to reach the dining-room tables during this period.

This is how I was seen by my peers, but looking back I perceive myself as an unhappy person striving for something I couldn't attain. As in childhood, the Christian gospel seemed to have everything on offer and all you had to do was accept in simple faith and all the treasures would be yours: lay down all your burdens and you would be filled with love, joy, peace, freedom, a sense of forgiveness and untold spiritual riches. But it didn't work out that way for me.

For the first few years I seemed to flourish. The sense of belonging, of being accepted, of having a significant role, of being involved in an exciting adventure seemed to free me up, but as time went on, when Geoffrey Rogers replaced Roger de Pemberton as Warden, the rules upon which the life of the Community were based became more clearly defined and discipline was tightened up.

A humorous anecdote illustrates the basic flavour of this era. Two of the liveliest young sparks decided that they just **had** to go to a dance in Lynton even though it meant walking two miles through the Valley of the Rocks in the dark. They dolled themselves up in their most glamorous long-skirted gear, tucked their skirts up at the waist with a belt, set a guard at the foot of the wide staircase leading down to the front door, and started to creep furtively down the stairs. Did they make it? No! Jack Winslow appeared and sent them back to their rooms.

On the serious side there was much more emphasis upon openness and the Community promises included the question: "Are you prepared to live in fellowship, being open to be known for what you are, accepting one another in Christ, and saying of others nothing that could not be said to them personally if love and wisdom required it?"

Although I didn't understand it at the time, this rule about openness was like a noose around my neck – it made me feel threatened and filled me with a feeling of doom, a dread of being found out, a heavy sense of shame. We were all expected to start the day with a time of prayer and meditation but for me it was effort enough to face the day at all, much less to sit with an open Bible in front of me or to kneel by my bed with a weight of profound guilt as a companion. A friend always woke me with a cup of tea in the morning and once, during Lent I felt called to be the one who got up first and took tea to her. She was always fully awake, patiently waiting. Seeing my dead pan face with its false smile peer round her door – shaking hands carrying a cup rattling on its saucer – was her penance for forty days.

Life in the Community involved attending meetings of many kinds and I listened, as in childhood, to high-powered, emotional exhortations about the need for forgiveness and cleansing, to low-key persuasive declarations of the love of Jesus, and to clever intellectual expositions of the eternal truth about God and His Universe. I discussed my problems, bared my soul, confessed every sin I could identify – and some more I hatched up – time and time again. I sat face to face in studies, prayed in chapel, paced the well-worn path to Jennifred's Leap with holy people steeped in the ways of God and experienced in helping people to overcome problems in their Christian lives. Many of these were later to become well-known in the upper echelons of the Church of England. On each occasion I would expect to feel different: "This will be the time something will really happen," I thought. "I will feel myself accepted and forgiven, I will feel close to Jesus and will know that He loves me." When nothing changed I had to remind myself that it was a matter of faith and not feelings, and I would battle on again with a sunny smile. But my burden of guilt and shame was growing heavier all the time. I felt that it must be *my* fault that I couldn't feel forgiven and accepted – there must be something fundamentally wrong with *me;* there was no other answer.

After some years at Lee Abbey I was given sabbatical leave and went abroad to work in a Swiss hotel for some months and then spent a while in London. During this time, perhaps because I felt myself to be so bad and so guilty anyway, I thought I might as well give myself a reason for feeling this way. So, I had a number of adventures, including a hilarious 'naughty weekend' with a male friend in Paris. It was interesting to discover that I didn't have any problems with sex when my emotions were not involved, but that is not to say that I didn't feel guilty. I did, and when I returned to the Community I had to confess my sins to Geoffrey Rogers. At least this time I knew what I had done and why.

Looking back, it is obvious that I was still trying to come to terms with my mother and her Lord, but I had no clue about this at the time. Simple information about the psychological impact of experiences in childhood and the effects that such indelible imprints can have on a child's early development and sense of well-being was just not available in those days. Such knowledge was certainly not accessible to us in our daily strivings to be good Community members so, like others who were struggling with similar issues, my happy Christian smile hid an acutely troubled, profoundly unhappy woman.

My only safe haven, as in childhood, was to wander out into the countryside either on foot or on Acorn, the Lee Abbey pony, and I developed a deep love of Exmoor which remains to this day. Some essential core of me sensed that a secret clue to life itself was embedded in this experience of being near to the earth, especially when I had a pony for company. Yet, it was an escape route which also held a certain haunting sadness for me. The sheer beauty of the surroundings contrasted with the profound heaviness of my spirit; everything around was vibrant, exciting and alive and I felt cold, benumbed and dead inside.

I have been concentrating on the down side of my time at Lee Abbey, yet foundation blocks were laid during those years that I value deeply; some of these may have their roots in the very difficulties that I experienced. I am thinking of my ability to listen with quiet attention, my deep conviction that everyone is unique and valuable and has the right to be seen and heard, that each one of us experiences truth in our own individual way and that even when situations don't, on the surface, appear to add up or make sense, we are not in a position to judge: that cursory judgements can denigrate and, above all, that each and every person matters.

Lee Abbey has flourished; it has expanded, moved with the times and is now recognised within the religious hierarchy of this country and beyond as a powerful, innovative centre of spiritual growth and development. Because I tend to undervalue the positive contributions I have made during my long life, I think it is appropriate for me to put on record that I made a significant contribution to the launching of this venture. I made my mark as a valued member of the team whose opinion carried weight; people sought me out, confided in me, trusted my judgement, were nourished by my warmth and my ability to understand and 'see beyond' what they were trying to tell me. I was a good speaker and often graced the platform at major events and even took part in a Radio Four broadcast.

A number of valuable friendships from this era endure to this day and I don't want to give the impression that Lee Abbey was a negative experience for everybody, because in fact the reverse is true. For many, during those early years and right up to the present time when Lee Abbey has celebrated its sixtieth Jubilee, a period spent as a member of the Community or as a guest is remembered with great thankfulness as a time of joy, growth and spiritual renewal and development. For example, an ex member of the Community writes:

"I originally came to Lee Abbey when I was twenty-two to a Student's House-party. I thought I could sidestep the religious aspect of the place, and an aunt had guaranteed that there would be plenty of Oxbridge undergraduates there. What struck me most was that there were 'normal' young people who seemed to take the teachings of the Bible seriously and attended all the talks enthusiastically. The evening epilogue opened up a whole new world to me – one that made Christianity seem relevant to living life with a deeper dimension than anything I had considered or even experienced.

"What happened was that I was pulled up in my tracks and over the next two years I went through emotional conflict. The impact that the message of 'giving our life to Christ' had had on me, together with the memory of the quality of the lives I had seen there, seemed to have pricked the rather superficial balloon of my egocentric existence. My parents seemed at a loss to understand my situation, so I was drawn back to Lee Abbey. If this Life works for some, then why not for me? So I applied for a position in the Community and quit my London job.

"I can look back now and still say that the eighteen months that I worked on the Community were some of the happiest of my life. The basis of modelling one's life on that of Jesus was the beam of light that my upbringing had not given me. Here was something deeply meaningful, and living with others who were committed to a common goal was the bonus. For me Lee Abbey was a pointer of the Way at a time when I was walking in an unrecognised desert. It was a starter for a life of self-discovery and self-responsibility and the foundation of the inner depths of stillness that have never left me, however much the surface may be disturbed."

I was very interested in my niece Nikki's reaction when I asked her to read this chapter. She used to visit Lee Abbey as a child, to see me and to see Pop who was, of course, her grandfather. Her reply was spontaneous and enthusiastic and she writes:

"Lee Abbey was a haven for me. I roamed my favourite aunt's domain of the kitchen where all the machines had biblical names: ovens Matthew, Mark, Luke and John, the sink and the auto potato peeler – something in my brain right now says 'Moses! – where I was allowed to labour over the spuddie 'eyes'. There was never a feeling of being in the way, only a sense of security and belonging in the Community, all of whom were immensely kind to me.

"Ancient photographs show my brother and me joining in house-party frolics and fancy dress evenings in the fifties. I could see the scenes in my middle eye long before I dug the pictures out of the archives: me on a pantomime elephant, with my face blacked and looking about to fall between the two-man team that swayed me in state across the lawn: with my brother Mike, two sub-team siblings dressed as Darby and Joan – a disguise I remember which took Betty patient hours to achieve. Her own outfit for the same occasion still puzzles me – a frumpy suit, glasses and a school-marmish expression very alien from the warmly affectionate character I have always known."

After ten years I decided to leave Lee Abbey, although reaching this decision involved me in much soul searching. Was I doing the right thing? Was I being guided by God? Doubts like this became an obsession when an important decision like this had to be made. But I left, and in my new life I tried to maintain my Christian witness and practice, but clearly this path was not working for me so gradually I let it go. To my great surprise I found life much easier when I stopped trying. Yet, I still seemed to have a compulsive need to repeat a deeply entrenched pattern, to live under pressure of some kind and to strive for the unattainable. My new work became my next field of endeavour.

I applied for a job in a travel company which operated hotels and organised house-parties in Europe and, after a successful interview, I was appointed House-party Hostess at a large hotel on the shores of Lake Como in Italy. Following my years in the Lee Abbey Community, it was second nature for me to welcome guests warmly, make them feel at home and create a comfortable, friendly atmosphere in the hotel. Arranging entertainment every evening was no real problem, but socialising became really onerous when I had to prop up the bar with the last stragglers till the early hours of the morning. I yearned for my bed, and the smile on my face became gradually more rigidly fixed as I stifled my yawns. Although, as at Lee Abbey, there were plenty of eligible men around I didn't make any close liaisons: trying to relate intimately was an effort, it was always a struggle, there was no joy or sense of fulfilment in it.

Later I was promoted to managing a large hotel in Switzerland which employed a staff of about sixty men and women of mixed nationalities. The establishment was also run as a house-party and, in addition to my managerial duties, I was hostess to some one hundred and twenty guests, and once again was responsible for arranging entertainment each evening. My remit included engaging and handling staff, and endeavouring to maintain high standards of service, overseeing the buildings, greenhouses and extensive gardens, responsibility for expenditure, accountancy and the expectation of running the hotel at a profit; general organisation and administration, trouble shooting, and keeping guests contentedly amused and likely to give positive feed-back on their return home. It is interesting to note, that prior to my appointment, the position had always been held jointly by a married couple as manager and hostess. No doubt I felt flattered at being considered capable of doing the job single handed.

It was a life of perpetual tension and stress, as if, at some deep level, I was driven to be in a position where I was stretched beyond my capacity to deliver – a situation where the possibility of failure, humiliation, or disaster lurked round every corner. It was a life that fitted my unconscious need to feel inadequate, to have little time to think, to be permanently extended and to end each day exhausted and depressed. I had given up on trying to please God because the quest seemed to be a non-runner, but work had become just as onerous a taskmaster. Retrospectively, it is easy to see the imprinted pattern which I was continuing to act out. My refuge was to escape to the spectacular beauty of the Bernese Oberland – an area which I still love to explore in my favourite mountain boots every springtime when the gentians are at their most beautiful.

This Swiss hotel was only open during the summer months so my winters were spent in Austrian ski resorts looking after the needs of in-coming tourists – far less arduous and an opportunity to enjoy a lighter side of myself. I still have friends from that era. It was the time when I was left a small legacy by my Uncle Will and I learnt to drive and passed my test on the snow-bound roads of Mayrhofen in Austria. I bought my first car, my beloved Karman Ghia and, when the season closed, I enjoyed many holidays meandering around mountain villages and city sights of neighbouring countries.

After my departure my father continued to live at Lee Abbey where he had become a much loved member of the Community. Once I had to go home for a few days because he was in hospital. It was strange. I remember a colleague remarking how I stressed

I was during his illness – how extremely thin I had become. He even said that he thought that I was near to having a breakdown. My feelings about my father were safely locked away, yet, it was obvious to an onlooker that under the surface his failing health was taking its toll on me. He became ill again while I was working in Austria, and I flew back to the UK and watched like a zombie at his bedside. He seemed to have been waiting for me to arrive and he died very peacefully a few days later. He is buried in the little graveyard in the Valley of Rocks near Lynton where I have also purchased a plot and plan to be buried.

At this period in my story I was not making noticeable headway with relationships, although my pattern seemed to be to make one very close friend in each decade of my life. So I feel myself to be wealthy in this area. People liked, respected and valued me. When I was in the role of leader or organiser I could cope quite well socially, but I was very slow to make close friends, especially with men. If I did open up, I discovered an unfathomable inner chaos deep within me. Why, I used to ask myself? I wasn't all that different from others who seemed to fall in love, settle down, have children and make family life work in a fairly satisfying way. I was deeply puzzled by this and eventually my curiosity led me to read more widely and to seek help outside religious circles where I had been led to believe the only source of true peace and happiness were to be found. To my great surprise, books on psychology began to make sense and opened my eyes to the fact that my restricted childhood had contributed to making me the person I had become; the conditioning I had received from my mother had affected my way of 'being' in the world. So, well into my forties, while still working in Europe, but spending some months each year in London, I went into therapy with Philip. He had been recommended to me as an experienced psychotherapist. I had been told that he was a practising Christian and this encouraged me because I thought that he would be able to understand the degree to which my religious upbringing had influenced and, in many respect, given shape to my development.

PART TWO

INTO THE UNKNOWN

Chapter Five

PHILIP – THE START OF A JOURNEY

– the mystery of therapy

When I started seeing Philip I felt anxious and apprehensive. I knew little about psychotherapy and the world of the unconscious, and I felt that I was embarking on a hazardous enterprise. I didn't know what to expect. Fears about opening up my inner world – fears which had dogged my footsteps for so long – all rose up to haunt me. What hideous monsters might be lurking in my underworld?

Philip seemed to be a gentle, kind, understanding person and this helped me to gain confidence. I lay on the couch in his consulting room in the traditional manner. He sat out of sight beside my right shoulder. We talked about my childhood and in particular about my mother and the way in which her obsessive personality and her restrictive religious beliefs had dominated my whole life. It became apparent that, although she had been dead for some years and I had freed myself from her rigid opinions, she was still controlling me from within. She often appeared in my dreams and the scenario was usually the same – my inner world was subjugated by her internalised presence and this was paralysing my everyday life.

I found myself recapturing tiny vignettes from childhood and we would examine these carefully. For example, a memory of me as a small child sitting on my father's lap and playing with his face, always accompanied by the fear that my mother might come in and spoil the fun. This led to other incidents and the deep sense of anxiety I always felt about choosing the right moment to approach my father. I saw a small child sitting pensively – pondering and studying the signs. Was he asleep? Was he in a good mood? Was his attention fully on his newspaper or was he pretending? If I interpreted the signs correctly we might have some frolicking fun but if I got it wrong I would feel squashed, flattened, demolished. It always seemed such a risky decision to make. Sometimes the fun would be riotous, with him holding me very tightly and tickling me. There was a certain fiery, turbulent, blustery heavy-handedness in the tickling and I would struggle and kick and thrash about, trying to get away. Sometimes he would tickle me very low on my tummy and I became almost hysterical with excitement.

I gradually built up a memory bank of interactions with my father. He was tetchy and irascible and, when he was under pressure, which seemed to be most of the time, there was this ominous 'he's going to explode, wait for it, it may come my way' atmosphere in the air. I had a deep fear of his anger; it hovered threateningly, it was oppressive. I hated it – and I dreaded his stentorian voice. Whether he was angry at me, or at somebody else, or even at one of the animals, the sound itself was menacing and I used to find myself searching for what I might have done wrong – I must have done something bad, it must be *my* fault. *Even as I write this all my muscles scrunch up in fearful anticipation and my body language tells its ancient tale.*

As I lay on the couch in Philip's study, I recalled those early days so fraught with angst. I pictured this small child looking around nervously with a puzzled expression, constantly troubled and perplexed, trying to read the expressions on people's faces, desperate to pick up clues. It was a picture which reawakened all the feelings associated with an ever-present perception that something was wrong, wrong, wrong: the child didn't know what it was, but it always seemed to be her fault. *It is interesting to observe that later on, when I created a collage of this scene, there are two little people with troubled faces – a little girl and a little boy.*

The embarrassing incident at school which I mentioned in Chapter Two, when I urinated on the floor in front of the whole class, was painfully called to mind, together with something about being cleaned up and people looking at my knickers. I recalled the headmistress coming to the farm and talking to my mother in front of our coal range, although this seems to be a strange thing to have happened. It was quite a journey to our lonely farmstead, so she must have considered the matter to be of some importance. There was a sense of discomfort – the headmistress and my mother seemed to be talking about me, there was a vague picture of a country policeman being there.

I reconnected to the vivid picture of the gypsy dancing at the roadside, and heard again the laughter of my sister Helen and the other schoolchildren, sitting at the back of the bus. I experienced the intensity of the feelings deep inside myself. It felt wicked to be fascinated and curious as I watched this bizarre figure revelling in the attention he was receiving as he danced in front of us with his penis exposed. I also remembered the profound sense of guilt I experienced at even wanting to look! These incidents and many others presented themselves at random and were always accompanied by a picture of my mother and her heavy exhortations to be good, pure and holy. I could see her sad face as Helen and I sat through long Bible readings and I could feel the rough texture of the green armchair with its black zigzag pattern, as I knelt and fidgeted through endless prayers. *This profound indoctrination was ever present and, even as I write, I can still feel the deep-seated sense of doom which it cast upon me. It crushed my spirit.*

My sister Helen, who was a year and a half older than me, also came in for much recall as I pondered the events of our childhood. As a baby I had usurped her place on my mother's lap, and, while working with Philip, it dawned on me that she was probably very jealous. I had stolen her place at my mother's knee and also her place in my father's arms and, with the benefit of hindsight, I think her jealousy was expressed in many subtle ways. While exploring with Philip, I remembered that she often worked me up into a frenzy of rage – she knew just how to do this – and when I chased her round the sofa and started to hit her she would call out, "Mummy, Mummy, Mummy, Betty has hurt me," so I would be the one to get into trouble. I have already mentioned that she was able to wind Pat and Mary up in similar fashion.

And there was the day she killed my little duck 'Khaki Bill'. I still wonder whether unconsciously she meant to do it?

An incident in the street outside my office one day many years later was to jog my memory. A toddler was standing beside a pram watching his mother through a shop window making her purchases. I saw the toddler, when the mother's attention was firmly fixed at the counter, lean over the side of the pram and give the baby a vicious pinch. The infant's roar of protest brought the mother hurrying from the shop, by which time the toddler was looking completely innocent and apparently concerned about the baby! This incident brought up a whole package of feelings about being threatened and attacked when I was very small lying in my pram. It made me wonder when Helen's bullying started.

Psychotherapy is a fascinating experience. The process of focussing on the inner world and at the same time connecting to the outer world, allows an unfolding of significant information to take place. In some ways it is like doing a jigsaw puzzle. A few pieces fit together here, and a few more pieces fit together there; then, with a sense of excitement, several of the clusters are discovered to belong together. A larger panorama opens up. As the sessions proceed there is a growing sense of design and structure, of shape and meaning, of emerging patterns, of an orderly journey. Sometimes you find yourself remarking, "Oh, that makes sense", or "So that's where that feeling comes from!", or "Oh, so-and-so makes me feel just like that, I'd like to hit her/him". Or even "I could kill him/her". Sometimes there is a shadowy awareness of approaching unexplored territory; fear and uneasiness develop – a premonition of pain and terror, and yet, at the same time a tinge of expectation and excitement about the discoveries that may be waiting to emerge.

In the first chapter I mentioned the family of boys who lived at a nearby farm. They featured quite frequently in my explorations with Philip, mostly because I hated their constant teasing; but they also ganged up with Helen to torment and bully me. In therapy, I was able to recognise that I became their victim. A number of my recollections centred around the huge sawdust bin where the smoked hams were stored. I recalled choosing this bin for Hide and Seek – it seemed *such* a good place in which to conceal myself, even though I was scared as I jumped inside. Once with Philip, I relived a ghastly panic. I was trapped inside the bin and couldn't get out because the lid was too heavy for me to lift up. I don't know how long I was there before being discovered, but it seemed like a lifetime of intense terror. *I still get an uncomfortable feeling in the pit of my stomach as I write about it.*

Another recollection popped out of the bag. The boys were there and we were playing Sardines. I hunted around and eventually found them in the sawdust bin. Acting on impulse, I jumped in too. The experience I relived was a jumble of complexity – I was never sure exactly what happened: it felt totally confusing – a package of emotions which emerged in sessions a number of times, and I was never able to differentiate between truth and fantasy, what actually happened and what might have been figment of a vivid imagination.

When Philip talked at length in sessions, I often became angry and this rage seemed to connect to my mother's prayers and exhortations that had droned on so incessantly. I felt that even when I was developing in her womb and when she held me to her breast, she had prayed aloud, offering me up to her Lord and exhorting Him to keep me pure and unblemished. It had penetrated deep inside me like an actual invasion of my guts as well as my embryonic brain. An authentic experience of indoctrination. I reconnected to a feeling of profound resentment about this concern for my soul, when all I wanted was to be close to her body. I longed to be allowed to relish her warm cosiness. She was thinking of her own needs – she wasn't thinking of me. It was only much later that I was able to see her within the context of her own upbringing and could then understand that she was the product of her own formative experiences. My dear mother – how tortured she must have been.

In therapy I became aware of the deep repugnance I felt about my body. A sense of it not really belonging to me, of living outside of it, of being an observer. The fact that men friends liked and admired me seemed to make no difference: I loathed my body with an intense revulsion. Philip and I talked about this often in our sessions: about my relationship with men, about sexual matters in general.

One night, between sessions, I had an extraordinary experience. It was intensely vivid and traumatic. I felt myself to be a small child and a large man was on top of me. I was being abused sexually. I felt deep shock, a sense of outrage, violation, terror and excruciating pain, followed by sinister threats about what would happen if I told anybody.

I told Philip about it at my next session and we discussed whether it was a dream, a fantasy or whether I had relived something that had actually happened. As we talked, the scene returned to consciousness with more detail and I quote from the notes which he took verbatim as I relived the experience:

> "I can move the top part of me but not the bottom part. I am being hurt. It's the gypsy. There's a very peculiar look on his face – an odd look – cruel. Go away. Go away. Go away. He's hurting me. I mustn't remember. The lower part of my body is fixed but at one time I think he put his penis in my mouth. Get it away. Get it away. He's trying to get it into my mouth. He's so strong. So strong. His face…his legs…I mustn't remember. It's not nice, not nice. I'm going to be sick (nearly chokes and vomits). He's hurting me –

the lower part of my body. He shouldn't be biting me there. He's hurting me. I could scream. He's like a wild beast. I'll scratch him. Get away. Get away. I feel as if I am going to pass out. I mustn't remember. He seems to be biting me. He seems to explore me with his mouth and tongue. My genitals. Then he hurts me, bites me, gets all steamed up.

'He seems to have a fire and heats a poker in it. He won't touch me with it, will he? Did he touch me? He says that if ever I tell anybody he will find me and put this poker into me. He kills a chicken by wringing its neck. Says he will do this to me if I tell anybody.

'Puts things into me again – terrible pain...pain...pain. Forces my mouth open and puts his penis in – makes me cough and choke. I can't take any more. I feel in a coma. He must have done all that to somebody else, it's nothing to do with me. It's dead and buried. Gone for ever. I must cut off that part of me (my genitals?) – must never remember. Nothing to do with me. The only thing left is a horrible grey cloud. Whatever happened was *my* fault. Everything's *my* fault.

'How do I get away? I let him put my clothes on and tidy my hair. I'm in a daze. Only half there. Shocked. He put me on my pony. I go to the blacksmith's. Then school. I'm late but quite matter of fact about it. The pony was slow and I lost my way. At the end of the day I picked up the pony and went straight home. I didn't go round by the gypsy's caravan.

"From then on – part of me goes on – the rest stays behind. Everything is terribly grey – everything grey – just grey."

Philip gave me time to relax and recover from the shock of what I had experienced before we talked about it. Then I recalled the day I was allowed to ride the pony to school. Star needed to go to the blacksmith's to be shod. I remembered losing my way and being late for class. But the rest of the drama I hadn't remembered until this moment and we quietly pondered it together over many sessions.

Were we considering a memory of a ghastly experience that had actually happened? If so, what impact would such a criminal, abusive offence have upon a child – especially a child with my religious background? Alternatively, could what I had experienced so vividly be a conglomerate of a vivid imagination? Could it simply be a combination of repressed material linking the dancing gypsy, the boys in the sawdust bin, my secret observance of animal behaviour, Oedipal fantasies, and my mother's inhibitions and prohibitions concerning sex and any expression of physical intimacy?

But…after this cathartic experience, a curious and, to me, astonishing thing happened. As I drove to work in my sporty Kharman Ghia, the greyness suddenly lifted and the until-then ever present feeling of self-loathing floated away. I experienced myself in a new way. I seemed to be living in my body and looking out through my own eyes. The sky was a more intense blue, the trees had fascinating shapes and were more vividly green, the sun caressed my skin and made me feel vibrantly alive. I sang as I drove and I wanted to skip and to dance.

There was a change at work. I was much more at ease socially and communication and interaction with people no longer drained my inner resources. I felt attractive and there was a sparkle in my eyes. The sense of doom and gloom which had oppressed my spirit for most of my life had dissipated and, instead of a foreboding of disaster, I woke up each morning with a feeling of zest and excitement about the new day and what it might bring.

I was highly attractive to men at this time and had a brief, amusing, exciting affair with a handsome, Don Juan type holiday-maker. A pattern had changed. I took the opportunity of starting another relationship during this period and, although the person concerned didn't really attract me, the experience increased my confidence.

This magical existence – this feeling of being really alive instead of half-dead – lasted for about three months. A glorious summer of freedom among the lakes and mountains of Lucerne. Then, suddenly, without warning, within a couple of hours, the heavy oppression returned like a thick grey cloud drifting across the sun. No particular event pinpointed the cause of this abrupt reversal – it just happened and I was back into deadness, the familiar greyness...just greyness...greyness...deadness.

CHAPTER SIX

IT ALL GOES WRONG

– disaster strikes

When I told Philip what had happened he thought we should look again at the gypsy material which had preceded my spell of living in the sunshine. Fact or fantasy? This is a question which was going to haunt me for endless ages to come – haunt me like the arrow of a computer 'mouse' flicking its devious trail through the twisted paths of my brain. I told myself that it didn't matter one way or the other – whether it was true or not true; whether it had happened or whether it was a drama created by my imagination. Either way I was exploring an area which was taboo in my childhood, and Mother's strict ban on sex and any enjoyment of the body was sufficient in itself to cause erotic fantasies resulting in feelings of guilt and self-loathing.

And yet, the experience of being abused by the gypsy had been so vivid in its intensity. Reliving the shock, the terror and the physical agony, plus the threats and exhortations not to tell anyone – had a resonance of authenticity. Did it happen or didn't it? Rationality didn't lay the question to rest – it dogged my footsteps and added to the burden of living once again under the heavy grey cloud and not knowing how to get back into the sun.

My sessions with Philip continued and about this time I started to read books by Freud, Guntrip, Fairburn, Winnicott, Klein and Balint. My attention was riveted by a paragraph in a book by Dr

Peter Lomas in which he refers to Winnicott as "perhaps the most creative thinker in the field of psychotherapy – whether inside or outside the psychoanalytical movement – since Freud". I quote:

> "Perhaps the most valuable of Winnicott's contributions to psychotherapy is his conception of a 'true self' which can remain intact, though hidden, during infancy, awaiting the possibility that in later years circumstances may permit it to emerge. During this period of concealment it is protected by a 'false self' which makes an apparently successful adaptation to society. The task of the therapist, in this event, is to engender sufficient trust in the patient for him to abandon his 'false self' and then hold him during the subsequent period of confusion while the 'true self' is developing."
>
> (*True and False Experience.* Peter Lomas
> First published by Allen Lane – a division of Penguin
> Books Ltd. 1973)

My attention was riveted by this concept. I recognised the 'false self' with which I had adapted to the outside world: it was a self that had incorporated many of my valuable characteristics and it had served me well in spite of the deep negative patterns which controlled my behaviour and left me depressed. I was uptight, unhappy and often irritable but I still managed to make the most of what was available to me. I did a semblance of coping, provided few emotional issues were involved. The deeply entrenched pattern was to be over-stretched, fraught, and 'driven' in a way which soaked up my energy and masked my deepest secrets. Underneath was a vulnerable, needy, fragmented, severely damaged person and deeper still a secret self who was vibrant and full of colourful energy. I lived on the edge of this knowledge – this deeply hidden infrastructure, and it was a relief to read that, as a result of my personal history, it was a rational position to be in.

While exploring with Philip I had suddenly touched into this extremely profound level; I had actually, in the here and now, experienced an amazing three months when my life changed dramatically. For the first time I knew what it was to be fully alive – to be living wholly in the present. I had actually experienced this but it had come and it had gone – and I didn't know how to get it back. This was *so* tantalising, one might even say torturing, tormenting – the essence of life here, in my grasp, at my disposal and then, the essence of life here no longer, but with no explanation. I could only assume that I needed to dig deeper.

So, my relationship with Philip started to change and I regressed into a small child tiptoeing out of a secret hiding place. I began to trust him, to reach out towards him; I felt warm towards him. It was quite new for me to feel like this. He would place his hand on my arm as I lay on the couch and this felt very safe and comfortable. I was reacting to him quite simply as a little child relates to a parent, and I found myself creeping out of my underground haven of isolation. I felt myself wanting to make contact with Philip and be held by him. This emerging self felt real and alive, it had energy, a life force and a spirit of expectancy. It felt like the essence of myself – a small person version of the self I had experienced in those magical three months.

Philip had already told me quite a lot about his life and I knew that he was going through the painful process of separating from his wife. I sensed his loneliness and his un-met needs. It reminded me of the uncomfortable feeling between my parents – they didn't fit together, they weren't close and compatible; the atmosphere between them was tense and uneasy and I longed for them to be happy – especially my father. This is where Philip, the detached, expert therapist should have observed what was happening. This was unprofessional behaviour. It was malpractice. At this crucial point my own needs gradually became submerged in an awareness of *his* needs. I slotted in to the well worn pattern of looking after mother and father.

The feelings of revulsion about my body had returned with the 'greyness' and Philip tried to help me distinguish between feelings from the past, resulting from my upbringing, and the truth about my body in the present. I think it was an attempt to show me that *he* found my body attractive that prompted him to open my blouse one day during a session and place his hand gently on my breasts. I felt disturbed and uncomfortable about this gesture but did nothing to express my uneasiness. I allowed him to continue to touch me in this way during the sessions that followed. I felt exceedingly confused because, in spite of my disquiet, it was also comforting to have his hand there and I felt very special, singled out and *so* important. I cannot overemphasise the significance of this staging post in our therapeutic relationship. *I was no longer just a client – I was someone who really mattered to Philip in a personal way in the here and now.*

It is curious to look back and observe what was going on with me at this time. Did I seduce him? I know that I didn't find him sexually attractive so I wasn't grappling with *that* problem. I was an adult experiencing myself as a regressed child but was I sufficiently aware to recognise that he was attracted to **me**? If he was, then this would have been puzzling because I felt myself to be so worthless, so tainted, so undesirable. But that was not all. The intricate tangle of my relationship with my parents, which had ended up with me taking my father's place in the marital bed, had left me profoundly disturbed about my sexuality. I think I was aware that what was happening was wrong, yet I felt helpless to do anything other than go along with it.

The day finally came when Philip lay beside me on the couch, unzipped his trousers and took out his penis. I think he said something like, "Perhaps this will help," which was a perplexing remark. I didn't register shock or surprise – I just felt frozen, paralysed, until the end of the session. At some level there must have been an impulse to push him away but…it was deeply buried – way out of reach. I just felt numb, blanked out, totally non-reactive.

I could as well have been a spectator of the scene – way up on the ceiling, certainly not a main participant. When I emerged from the consulting room at the end of the session, I was surprised to see Philip's secretary still working in her office next door. My eyes locked with hers. I felt intensely guilty and was sure that she must know what had happened. Her eyes were like the eyes of my mother and her God. This powerfully increased the heaviness of my burden of shame.

After this Philip and I started to meet socially, although he was rightly uneasy about the professional ethics of the situation. Our meetings had a clandestine element which fitted into my secret inner world. But working with him in a therapeutic way became impossibly confusing, so after a while I stopped my sessions. It is curious to look back at the relationship which developed between us. I was coming from a very childlike place and loved holding his hand as we walked the hills and I cherished snuggling close to him on the sofa in front of the fire. It was an exciting adventure to go on holiday together, exploring new places; all the things which I would have adored sharing with my father.

I was very aware of Philip's sexual needs and desperately wanted to give him pleasure but this degree of intimacy aroused a discordance of confused feelings in me: deeply profound longings for affection and specialness, affirmation and understanding, warmth and closeness vying with revulsion and violation, rage and destructiveness, bewilderment and vulnerability.

The destructive relationship continued for several years because I seemed unable to end it but the situation between us deteriorated as I found it increasingly difficult to bridge the gulf between the little girl who had found a father and the so-called adult woman who was trying to relate to her boyfriend.

It is hard to do justice to the chaos which exploded in my inner world at this time. Confusion was tangible in every aspect of my being – mayhem, entrapment, chaos and utter disorientation. I would pace up and down my room in a level of distress which was awe-inspiring and overwhelming. The package of emotions became too convoluted for me to handle in a kind, polite, adult way. The complexity of feelings included an element of ruthless rage and resentment that I didn't understand and this spilled over on to Philip with a force that I was unable to prevent. For Philip too, the liaison turned out to be a disappointing, intensely painful experience. As things soured between us I appeared to be a second edition of his wife – spiteful, vindictive and rejecting.

When we finally parted I was infinitely more confused than when I had embarked on the therapy trail. I was left with this child self, isolated, out on a limb, cut off, yet still holding Philip in my heart, fantasising, missing his company, missing walking with him, holding his hand, observing birds, trees and flowers, exploring new places. I once said to him, "You found me when I wasn't anywhere." This may sound mysterious but that is exactly how I felt – as if I had been lost and then found. Found, as in rediscovered – rediscovered in the therapeutic relationship which was developing with him before he allowed me to 'act out' the scenario of a little girl wanting to make her daddy happy. Found only to be abused? Is it too dramatic to say that this child felt that she had been found only to be physically abused?

CHAPTER SEVEN

ANOTHER ATTEMPT – WITH JAMES

– hopes rise and fall

This is the fifth redraft of my manuscript and I am struck afresh by the quality of the therapeutic journey which had slowly unfolded with Philip in the first chapters of our endeavour. It seems to me that my early history was unpacked piece by piece. A glimpse of the picture on the jigsaw box began to emerge out of the mists of time. Many of the essential imprints and conditioning elements that had deeply affected me in childhood were revealed, parcels of authentic feelings had been expressed and put into context. Why did it all go wrong? What part did I play in what transpired? Did I seduce Philip? What was my responsibility in relation to what developed between us? I have asked myself these questions countless times through the years but in this account I can only pick up the pieces at the point at which I found myself at the time. I have no problem remembering.

I was back in England managing a travel agency: once again losing myself in a job which satisfied my need to work under pressure and left me with energy enough at the end of the day only to sleep and then start the cycle again next day. There was plenty of scope to strive for perfection, and to repeat familiar patterns of behaviour. Stacks of paper appeared on my desk with exact precision every morning, masses, which, however hard I worked, were consistently topped up the following day. At that time it was difficult to find skilled, well trained personnel, so we were frequently short-staffed; this meant that we had to deal with constant demands and interruptions. Often, when there were already enough tasks listed on your pad to keep you occupied for the whole day, a special client could come in, or phone, who required your complete attention. Not only that, but when the client left you probably had another extensive research job to be tackled – and then the phone would ring yet again.

Oh yes! The job equalled the Hotel Mattenhof in diversity and intensity. It was just the kind of atmosphere in which tangles in relationships flourished: a situation in which to get utterly stressed out, to feel frustrated and defeated, not to mention ending up feeling depressed. Days off and holidays were my only solace and were a rich source of excitement and adventure. They represented the 'just enough' quota of interesting, motivating things in my life – the miserly ration on which I managed to exist.

The only part of the travel agency job that I found rewarding – in addition to dressing the shop window for which I once won a prize of a week in Austria – was the challenge of trying to determine, by a process of careful deduction, just the type of location and even the precise style of hotel that would suit each customer. I was good at this when I was allowed both the time and the opportunity. I remember one day a local tradesman walked in, placed an open brochure in front of me, with a hotel clearly marked in red ink. He slapped down a pile of smelly, fishy banknotes and said, "I'm in a rush – book me in here – first available date – I'll be back in ten minutes." That was the gist of it and I obeyed instructions. The interesting thing is that I knew this location well and had enjoyed staying at this particular hotel. By coincidence, a few days earlier, after very careful ground work, I had suggested it to a very discriminating lady and she had made a booking. They both came in to report after the holiday – fortunately not at the same time; the lady said it was paradise and 'Mr Fish' said it was purgatory – but he hadn't asked for my advice!

I found it extremely useful when I had seen places for myself and had sampled the hotels and locations at first-hand, so I took every opportunity that presented itself to travel around. As a manageress, some interesting 'freebies' came my way such as travelling first class to Australia. This proved to be a hectic week, being lavishly hosted while flying and motoring between Perth, Adelaide, Alice Springs, Melbourne and Sydney. Before returning home I was able to add on a weekend visit to see my sister Helen who had settled down in a neat bungalow not far from Adelaide. It was situated a bit too near to the vineyards of Maclaren Vale for the good of her health, but she enjoyed some delightful years there. Her son Simon had built himself a house nearby and Helen played a major role in the early life of two of her grandchildren. She always got on well with youngsters and revelled in having them to stay; her house was constantly alive with all kinds of hectic activities. Dressed in a bikini, in the height of the Australian summer, she always cooked full Christmas dinner – with all the trimmings – for the extended family. She even bought a pony, which she kept in a paddock at the bottom of the garden, and she was able to relive an enjoyable part of her own childhood by teaching them to ride. This was the last time I saw Helen. She died in a nursing home in January 2003.

I also luxuriated in the inaugural cruise of an elegant vessel *The Cunard Princess*, flying out to San Juan via Miami. We watched Neil Armstrong, in traditional manner, break a bottle of champers over the brow of the ship and then we sailed away and dropped in for a few hours to explore a couple of Caribbean islands. Shipboard life was a dressy affair and it was interesting to note how distinguished the English contingent looked; gents immaculate in black, allowing the ladies to flaunt their multi-coloured finery, whereas the American men seemed to vie with each other for vibrant tailor-mades and often seemed to outshine their partners.

I flew to Sri Lanka for the opening of the new Intercontinental Hotel by the first lady President, Sirimavo Bandaranaike. I found that the combination of humidity and car fumes spoilt my wanderings around the city of Colombo and I was not tempted by the tempting offers to buy precious stones. Had I ventured into bargaining and doing some deals, I would probably have made a good profit on my return to the UK.

Any group of local agencies throughout the world, combining to entertain a bunch of travel consultants and journalists know that they will only get a good press if they are generous with the amount of alcohol on tap. Once I had a deeply humiliating experience. Glasses were being constantly replenished and I had not observed just how lavishly they had been laced with gin. Unfortunately, I became ill instead of merry, so now on these occasions, I always creep away as soon as I can manage to do so without offending the hosts.

In Colombo, most of the party stayed up all night at the Bar and I think I was the only person awake enough to enjoy an unforgettable trip by train up to Kandy with a night spent at the Hunas Falls Hotel. On the way back we visited several of the well-known places of interest for which Sri Lanka is so famous.

A week touring Israel brought to life many of the Biblical names which were so familiar to me in childhood and I found that our tour guide often seemed to be watching me with interest and curiosity. Quite obviously I didn't fit neatly into any of the precise categories with which he was familiar. I am not at all surprised by this because I was constantly operating on two levels; I was the mature travel agent, asking sensible questions, eager to explore all the sights, not missing a thing, but I was also a child for whom Bible stories had been fairy tales. Hearing all these names again, visiting these places and finding that they really existed, was incredibly exciting; this child could almost imagine that at any moment we might bump into Abraham or Isaac, get lost in the wilderness, the walls of Jericho might fall down or we might see someone escaping by being lowered to the ground in a laundry hamper. Equally, New Testament place names evoked all kinds of possibilities; a baby might be lying in a Moses basket in the bulrushes, a modern Lazarus might be brought back to life, water might be turned into wine or Jesus might turn up walking on the Sea of Galilee. My memories of the trip are still astonishingly vivid. I bought two candles in Bethlehem, kept them for years waiting for the right occasion to light them. I lit one of them during Bill's group; I wonder what happened to the other one.

The trip which outclassed all the others was a visit to Kenya and my very first safari experience, but this is an event which had far-reaching repercussions and has an important place in a future chapter.

For my own holidays I enjoyed visiting famous cities of unique originality and charm, and I loved meandering in my car around the highways, byways and hamlets of France and Italy. In particular, I enjoyed small pensions where Monsieur was the chef and Madame was the bustling hostess. You could be certain of an excellent meal and, in the morning, delicious coffee and croissants for breakfast. Italy, with its unrivalled art treasures and the diversity of its countryside and coastline, never failed to be of interest and the original Yugoslavia, mainland Greece, together with the Greek Islands were great favourites.

I lived and worked in both Austria and Switzerland but they never lost their magic; I returned to the Bernese Oberland and visited my friend Maria in Bonigen and the Brunner family hotel in Wengen every June for many years. I never tire of exploring our English countryside and there are still many places that I want to see before my last visit to Lynton where I have purchased my plot in the graveyard in the Valley of Rocks.

I cannot recall how long it was before I decided to give psychotherapy another chance. It was James this time who had been recommended to me by a friend. I was in a quandary from the beginning. A mistaken sense of loyalty forbade me sharing with him the account of what had transpired with Philip. I don't blame James for the tangle that developed between us: after all, I had denied him the essential clue which would have thrown light upon my state of mind at that particular time.

In my everyday life I was used to being irritable, snappy, prickly, touchy, sulky – call it what you will – in fact anything but overtly angry. With James, I began to experience – to allow myself to experience – intense anger, vehement fury, even violence. I boiled over with rage. After a session, I would storm out of his house, slam the door of my car, churn up the gravel as I reversed down his drive and then shout at him all the way home! I even considered crashing my car. When I reached home I felt an urge to fling my radio against the wall, bash my television to smithereens, trash my refrigerator, wreck my flat and destroy all the treasures that were so valuable to me. I also wanted to tear my own flesh to shreds and often bit my clenched fist till I drew blood. Years later, when I participated in growth groups, I learnt safer ways of expressing murderous rage, such as bashing cushions with fists or tennis racquet, tearing up old telephone directories or battering a huge log of rotten wood to pulp. But at this stage it was a bewildering experience for me to be in touch with my wrath and to express it openly.

At the time I didn't understand why all these feelings came bursting out like steam from a pressure cooker and what added to my ferocity was that I was paying good, hard-earned money for the doubtful privilege of giving vent to my frenzy in this unfocussed way. Retrospectively, I know that I could have given priority to my own needs rather than shielding Philip. But this perspective was not available to me at the time and I found myself in a very lonely, isolated place, raging against the confines of my prison, a bit like a lioness angrily pacing the limits of her cage while protecting her cub and resenting the enforced restrictions.

The rage brought me in touch again with the very vulnerable child self and, although perhaps I do James an injustice, I had the impression that he was confused by the extremes that I presented. I felt that he was unable to contain the chaotic turbulence of my negative feelings *and* the fragility of my most vulnerable self; that he was unable to 'hold' what he could not understand unless it could be expressed in words.

Words! Words! In certain circumstances I experienced words as a threat – as if they were an expression of a power behind the throne that left me feeling powerless, inferior, inadequate and without an appropriate response. This is understandable. In my childhood 'The Word of God' had reigned supreme; it was a tangible force, because in Mother's eyes every word in the Bible was true in a very literal sense and there was no way of avoiding this menacing threat – no safe place where you could be out of danger. Further details regarding what this particular child made of her Bible-ridden environment will be revealed later on, but for the moment, to put it quite simply, Mother followed these precepts to the letter and Father, even though he wasn't actively identified with her beliefs at that time, backed her and his response always followed the same line: "Do what your mother says", "Don't hurt your mother", "Children should be seen but not heard".

Clearly I was brought up in a way which denied me an opportunity to grow up naturally, to become rooted and grounded in myself, to be established in the core of my being, to communicate, to develop the right to have opinions and to express them. In many ways I was extremely immature and I felt both threatened and at a disadvantage in the world of words.

James seemed to have considerable power, as if the phenomena of 'transference' were an 'X' factor on his side, a weapon which always enabled him to translate what was happening into something else and that 'something else' always seemed to put me in the wrong. He said that it could be resistance on my part, a defence mechanism, avoidance, denial, a subsidiary gain or some kind of acting out. Obviously, in his position it was important for him to observe and weigh up these considerations but I felt that, as a person, I was lost sight of in the process, that his psychological 'doctrines' took priority, just as my mother's religious ones had done.

I well remember the extremes of the heart-searching that I

endured at this time. I had high hopes of this, my second therapeutic endeavour; dependency was involved and I found it incredibly hard to consider, once again, leaving the therapeutic relationship in mid-stream. I tossed the pros and cons backwards and forwards. I was aware that I might be left with a deep sense of disappointment or failure. My thoughts, my fears and my feelings were intensely complex and confused over a period of several weeks. Could I trust my own perception? James was the expert, so did I need to trust him and work through the issues which were coming up between us? On the other hand, I hadn't protected myself when I worked with Philip, so was I taking care of myself by leaving or should I stick it out? This was a see-saw of doubt that tore me apart in its intensity.

While I was struggling with these issues I slept badly and one disturbed night I had an vivid dream. I was in James's consulting room, which in reality was pleasant and comfortable but in the dream I was having the session with him in a small, bare chamber with plain white-washed walls. The only piece of furniture was a rickety little couch – rather like an infants' cot but without any safety rails round it to keep the baby safe. It was ill-constructed – it tilted and didn't stand squarely on the floor. In the dream, I turned to James with feelings of deep anguish and desolation and said, "Is this where the baby has to go?" I felt extremely vulnerable, anxious and insecure. Finally I stopped seeing James and I think the next few weeks were the nearest I came to a complete breakdown.

Would it have been a positive experience of personal growth to have worked my way through this impasse? I shall never know but I have a sense that I was too vulnerable at that time to cope with deep transference issues; I just needed to be 'held' while I re-established the ground of my being.

I was also finding it hard to function in my working life, I felt painfully exposed, vulnerable and fragile, as if the very fabric of my being might fall apart – as if I was a minuscule speck suspended on a gossamer thread. One morning, I was following my usual routine of walking in the park at the beginning of the day and I saw a minute, pink fledgling lying on the ground – it had fallen out of its nest and was almost dead. I looked down at it and said out loud, "That's exactly what I feel like."

This is a period of my life when I thought very seriously about suicide as a way out. It wasn't new to contemplate ending my life: this solution had been around for a long time and I always kept some tablets in my bedside cabinet. Yet, whenever I gave really serious consideration to this way out, two thoughts would halt me in my tracks. The first was that I couldn't die because I hadn't really lived yet, except for that wonderful period of about three months. The second was somewhat more menacing – I might be sent back to do the job again!

But it transpired that at this crucial point, I read again the book previously referred to: *True and False Experience*, written by Dr Peter Lomas. I was impressed by his intuition, by the sensitive way in which he wrote. There were many indications that he would understand my plight. When I contacted him he was about to go on holiday but after some delay I started to have sessions with him.

CHAPTER EIGHT

PICKING UP THE PIECES WITH PETER

– *another journey*

In psychotherapy, as in everyday relationships, it usually takes time
to establish trust between therapist and client. I felt I already knew
a lot about Peter from reading his book and when we finally met
I felt at once that I could trust him. It was the deep intuitive sense
that children have – they know who feels trustworthy and who
doesn't. So I was able to lower my defences and allow myself to
be small and vulnerable which was exactly how I was feeling in my
innermost self. I did nothing to cover it up – I acted as I felt.

It was not so easy for Peter who knew only what I had told him
about myself, but even in that brief telling it was obvious that I
was in great distress and he recognised this immediately. Much later,
in his book *The Case for a Personal Psychotherapy*, using the
pseudonym 'Margaret' he wrote:

> "For the first months Margaret behaved in a very regressed
> way during sessions. Much of the time she curled up on
> the couch, sometimes in apparent anguish, sometimes
> crying like a baby or speaking like a very small child. I felt
> rather unsure of the way to respond to her but at certain
> times I reacted to her in a manner that was more like a
> parent to a tiny child than as one adult to another. The

result of this was that, in her own words, she 'was beginning to come alive'."

(*The Case for a Personal Psychotherapy.* Peter Lomas. Oxford University Press. 1981.)

And that is exactly how it was. I felt split off from the main stream of my life, existing in a lonely, isolated place – a very secret place. Although some of the feelings were deeply painful and my hold on life felt extremely precarious, there was also a mysterious, almost exciting sense of re-connecting to reality, of finding my 'core' self again. The difference was tangible, a remarkable sense of being truly present as opposed to experiencing life from a distance. I remember talking a lot about finding what I called 'a place' – almost as if I didn't actually belong anywhere. The feeling was quite basic – as if I was talking from a part of myself that was floating in space and needed to implant somewhere. It was exactly the same feeling that I had described to Philip when I said, "You found me when I wasn't anywhere." I felt minuscule, detached, disembodied.

From an observer's perspective I was aware that my need to please my mother plus her injunction that I must 'be dead to the body' could have made me feel uneasy about my physicality, yet I felt that there were deeper causes for my estrangement from my true self.

When I had been seeing Peter regularly for about two months he went on holiday for three days. I was extremely dependent on him at this stage and was desperately anxious about him going away – it felt as if my foothold on life was moving out of reach. I used to carry a little doll around at this time – clearly a very special 'object' for me. I considered asking whether I could leave this symbol in one of the drawers of his consulting room. Whether this idea would have reassured me that *he* would come back or that *I* would come back I am not sure. Later I wished that I had had the courage to ask him because, on his journey to the West Country, an approaching vehicle ran out of control and in the ensuing collision

Peter could have died. He was seriously injured, had to be cut from the wreckage and was taken to hospital.

I heard the news by telephone from his daughter and my immediate reaction was one of shock. I felt cold and started to shiver, my legs felt unsteady and liable to collapse under me and these feelings lasted for some days. It was that same 'near breakdown' space that I had experienced before. From then on I was constantly worried about Peter. Although he took the trouble to write to me from his hospital bed, which moved me deeply, and I received news from other sources, I was still full of anxiety. My connection to him felt like a gossamer thread which was too delicate and fragile to survive a prolonged period of separation.

It is well-known that young children have particularly limited tolerance to the anxiety caused by the absence of mother or some other special person upon whom they are dependent. There is an excellent film called *John* which is part of a research project featuring the experiences of a small child who was separated from his mother for nine months when he was in hospital. When the child and his mother were reunited he was not the sunny little soul from before the separation but a hurt, angry child who didn't trust life any more.

The anguish of that child was echoed in my feelings when Peter was ill. Weeks were passing without sessions and I feared that time was running out. I contacted a colleague of Peter's called Nick who had offered assistance and I shall always be grateful for his kindness and support.

An obvious question was whether the break in sessions was reminding me of other separations during my childhood. I recalled anxiety when my father went into hospital to have his appendix out and my childlike fantasies about his operation. I also remembered a state of appalling panic which I once experienced when I became separated from my mother in a department store, but reliving these incidents didn't seem to ease my anxiety about Peter. Before the accident I had been creeping out of my secret hiding place but now I was finding that the 'no man's land' of separation was more than I could tolerate.

It still interests me as I look back, that even though in my adult self I was aware and understood what was going on, yet I was completely unable to halt the process. I knew that Peter would not let me down; he was getting better, he was keeping in touch and my sessions would resume – I had no doubt about this at all. Yet, this knowledge did not reach the subterranean enclaves of the troubled child who reacted quite independently. It felt as if some type of safety device had been preset: preset way back in time to respond in a precise, unequivocal, protective way to any situation that overstretched an explicitly limited tolerance level. It seemed that no cognitive reasoning in the present was capable of overriding this system.

When sessions were resumed things were terribly difficult between us. On an adult level I was really pleased to see Peter again: we discussed his accident and he told me what it had felt like being trapped in his car on a country road. While waiting for the fire brigade to come and cut him out he did not know whether he was going to live or die. He talked about the serious effects of his injuries and of the shock, his concern about his patients, his concern about me, the long convalescence and the fact that he was still experiencing the side-effects of the accident. I really cared about him, so it was devastating and also extremely confusing when I turned on him and switched to being a furiously angry child who had been abandoned.

In the first edition of this manuscript I went into all the details of how things went dreadfully wrong but somehow that does not feel necessary this time round. Peter's accident wasn't his fault and my reactions were not my fault – the circumstances themselves were thoroughly unfortunate. In any case, experience has led me to the conclusion that it is an exceedingly daunting undertaking to attempt to unravel heavy, complex transference feelings *at the same time* as regressing and attempting to bridge the gap and build a bridge between true and false self positions. I believe that this transitional stage is extremely delicate and requires the strong support of our adult self and a trusted other person who knows the territory. It is sufficient to say that I left Peter for a while, had some sessions with his colleague Nick and then returned to Peter for a period of several years. This helped me to ground myself and provided me with a more stable base from which to venture into deeper explorations.

The second period of sessions helped me to accept that, although I had been deeply affected by my childhood, this did not give me licence to allow my emotions to gush out indiscriminately. I needed to take responsibility for my way of being in the world and I wasn't at liberty to 'dump' my emotional baggage at random. I found this a hard task to take on board because, quite often, I didn't understand what was going on within me. I felt so divided, so split; parts of me felt beyond the reach of cognitive decision making. However, I made a start at this time and often feel grateful to Peter for encouraging me to take up this challenge.

After a lengthy struggle I did manage to tell Peter the full truth concerning my relationship with Philip but mysteriously the telling left me feeling even more guilty. It also raised the same uncomfortable questions. Was I responsible for what happened? I had certainly wanted to be 'special' to Philip, so had I manipulated him into *making* me 'special'? In effect had I seduced him?

The scene with the gypsy was laid out again and discussed at length. This incident always had particular significance because it had led to the spectacular, though temporary, lifting of my depression and other symptoms. Yet I seemed unable to reach any clear decision regarding its authenticity. A fantasy? A memory? A false memory? Retrospectively, I find it interesting that although I was still suffering from depression, still keeping a reserve of tablets in my bedside cupboard, hated my body, had sexual inhibitions, somatic flashbacks, and a degree of dental phobia, yet I continued to sit on the fence in relation to this issue.

One thing that was really helpful in my interactions was that Peter always gave me a direct answer to my questions. As a child, one of my unfathomable and perplexing preoccupations was trying to read my parents' minds from the expressions on their faces – specially from the look in their eyes. I did this with Peter too and it was fascinating to find out that the truth often bore little resemblance to what I had feared or what I had conjectured from the look on his face. As an example, once, as I entered his consulting room, I sensed that something was troubling him and I asked him if he was all right. He replied that he had just seen from his bank statement that his balance was lower than he had expected. Not a pleasant discovery, but nothing particularly drastic and as I had paid my fees certainly nothing to do with me. Yet I was worrying and wondering whether his disturbed expression was my fault.

Another time I had exactly the same feeling that something was disturbing him and when I questioned him he told me that his sister had just died very suddenly. The scale of my anxiety was the same on both occasions and some therapists' avoidance of such questions *might* have been useful but could also have compounded my problem. Peter's openness and honesty helped me to identify an area of deep worry and concern that I endured as a child. I had been troubled and deeply burdened by the worry lines on my parents' faces and had tried to interpret them without success. I had taken careful warning from my father's tone of voice and had feared that my mother's sadness would overwhelm her, but I had no open, honesty gauge to help me assess the true significance of what was happening in front of my eyes. Anxiety became a heavy burden to carry when I was a child and usually ended up with a sense that *I* must have done something – it must be *my* fault. This lesson has been of great benefit to me because now I seldom – I hope never – assume that what I am interpreting from somebody's expression is the truth!

Towards the end of my time with Peter I felt a need to interact with a larger range of people and to express myself in new ways, so I decided to try some of the group work which was becoming available at that time. I was extremely nervous and scared. I was also embarrassed, because I thought that I would be much older than other members of the group which almost always proved to be the case. It felt risky and daring to launch out in this way and it was comforting having Peter's interest and encouragement in this venture.

The time finally came when I felt established and grounded enough to manage without the support of regular sessions but I have always maintained a link with Peter over the years. I still choose his Christmas card with care and am pleased when his card, always with a few items of news, drops through my letter-box. I shall enjoy sending him a copy of my book.

Chapter Nine

SOME OF THE PIECES FIT TOGETHER

– but not all

This chapter covers a period of a number of years – an undefined span of time which, at first sight, may appear to be an unsystematic method to use. Yet, this mode of coordinating my discoveries has been chosen with intent, partly due to possible pitfalls concerning confidentiality, but also because several chapters need to be recorded in a similar way.

In spite of the complexity of the setbacks encountered, my therapeutic journey had turned out to be a maturing experience. I had faced certain basic realities, I had begun to appreciate, to some degree anyway, my value and my potential as a person. I had a map and I understood some of the events and influences which had left an imprint upon me during my formative years. I was aware of some of the patterns which had evolved as a result of these heavy footprints. I was aware that I had missed out on many stages of normal development: I had a deep sense that there was a lot more for me to discover about myself and I doubt whether I would have felt safe and integrated enough to venture into this unknown territory without the security of this launching pad.

Once I had overcome my initial feelings of trepidation and nervousness, I found participation in groups such as Encounter, Psychodrama, Bioenergetics, Art Therapy, Seed groups, Transactional Analysis, Psychosynthesis, Primal Integration and The

Hoffman Process – stimulating, challenging, exciting and packed full of surprising adventures and discoveries.

In his book *Therapeutic Experiencing* Alvin Maher explains what he understands as the nature of experiencing. He writes:

"The process is of letting it happen more, more fully, more deeply: with greater depth and breadth and saturation...

"Those moments in which experiencing reaches the highest plateau are tantamount to a taste of what in existential-humanistic thinking is called 'actualisation'. That is, the person is sampling a little of what it could be like to fully experience in a good form what the person has available."

(*Therapeutic Experiencing*. Alvin R Mahrer.
W W Norton. 1986.)

A friend who read this chapter asked me why I had included this quotation and it took me a while to work it out for myself! During my childhood , my development had, to a great extent, been moulded and shaped by my environment and I am using the word 'environment' to draw together all the elements and influences which were incorporated in my upbringing. I didn't know 'what I had available'. I hadn't developed, grown, evolved freely from my own centre – spontaneous responses had been crushed, forbidden or had potential consequences which were too bewildering even to be considered.

Another quotation comes to mind from a book called *Healing in Depth* by Culver Barker which had a deep influence on my life during this phase. He refers to a patient called Eleanor:

"The fundamental fact about Eleanor's pattern of life, like many others, was that ever since she could remember she had never felt it safe, secure or right to live out of her own self, but 'was lived' under the authority of what was expected of her.

"To be in such a way 'lived' under the authority of an expectation I have found is one of the most crippling authorities for any human being to live under, because then you are counterfeiting yourself, you are living not your own pattern – but out of a desperate need to attain the minimum amount of security to survive, you have to shape yourself according to the expectations of parental authority which you feel, and it is often only too true, will not accept you unless you conform to its pattern. It can be a very serious situation. One is dealing with something which is inaugurated with the intensity, and is lived under the insecurity, of a life-and-death situation. Your existence is not your own unless you are received as the person your are."

(*Healing in Depth*. Culver Barker.
Hodder and Stoughton. 1972.)

That's exactly as it was for me as an infant, as a child and as a teenager: I was 'lived' under the authority and the edicts of a three-line whip – my mother, her Lord and my father. I was shaped by a combination of their ordinances, rules and decrees, their demands and expectations, and the repercussions of these influences upon the rest of the family. Added to this was the emotional manipulation of my mother's frailty. Quite simply, my existence was not my own. I was trapped in an atmosphere which blunted, twisted and distorted my natural development as a person who had a basic right to be herself. So, I had a lot of catching up to do: experiences in groups helped to fill this need.

It is logical and no surprise that at first I felt a bias towards adapting myself to the leadership of the particular group I was attending; getting the lay of the land, sussing out what seemed to be expected and then endeavouring to fit in and fulfil these expectations. But it was surprising how quickly this changed and more spontaneous behaviour began to appear: I seemed ready to clutch at any opportunity of expressing a new freedom, in whatever configuration the pieces tumbled out.

I was fascinated and intrigued to watch both men and woman opening up about their problems and sharing their feelings; a wide range of varied emotions, tensions and conflicts were revealed and such outspoken directness was a new world to me. I felt stimulated, motivated, and encouraged as I observed or became involved. I was helped to contact my own feelings by identifying people who reminded me in some way of my mother, my father, God, a member of my family or a playmate. This aided my recall of early childhood experiences and encounters and brought some of the hazy scenes more clearly out into the light.

One of the techniques I had used in childhood in order to survive was to divide myself neatly into compartments and in this new, free and easy environment I was always surprised when an inhabitant of one of these secret domains spontaneously sprang out of hiding and took part in the proceedings. This little escapee might shout, scream, giggle or roar with laughter, might risk using inappropriate language or open my mouth and find no words there. He/she might use body language to express my mood, be it slouch, stamp, sulk or skip, dance or flirt or maybe even to question, tease or mock when God-like authority figures seemed unconvincing or plain ludicrous. In this way, snapshots from the past were nudged out into the open and could be slotted into the jigsaw puzzle.

In my childhood, simple, ordinary ways of reacting and responding interactively were absent; they were not openly demonstrated within the family. There was no direct expression, no direct interaction – strong emotions had to be masked, concealed or twisted into a shape that was acceptable. Yet, at the same time the camouflage didn't really work – they weren't totally masked, concealed or hidden away – the vibes, the undercurrents were mysteriously picked up, experienced, felt to be present. This utter confusion of mixed messages still has the power to twist my guts. The net result was that in my family we did not learn how to behave and express ourselves in a natural way and as we grew up this put us at a great disadvantage socially. Helen seemed to get by, but as the youngest, who arrived at the most crucial stage of my parents' marriage, I was probably the one most affected and disadvantaged.

My experiences in groups helped to make good some of these aspects of my personal history which had been so neglected. Vignettes from the past were triggered and I became aware of how I had felt as a small child, as an older child, a teenager and even as an adult. There was ample opportunity to express some of the pain, angst, confusion, frustration and rage; these emotions were experienced in a re-vamp of the original context, which was both a relief and also bestowed a sense of satisfaction. I began to get glimpses of my many-sidedness: to discover aspects of my personality that had previously been obscure, undeveloped, unexpressed, ill-defined, lying dormant, waiting in the wings.

I found I could be warm and cuddlesome or cold and distant, say 'Yes' or say 'No'. I discovered that I could make choices, could be ridiculous or irrational, outrageous or provocative, be small and vulnerable or angry and destructive (provided, of course, that no damage was done to person or property). It was new for me to acknowledge jealousy, competitiveness or rivalry, to admit to anxiety, fear and even terror, to own up to rejection, hopelessness and despair, to confess that I felt shame and guilt about my body, especially my sexuality, and that I had such a profound problem with relationships. I was even able to acknowledge awareness of bottomless pits, deep crevasses and to admit the horror and bewilderment of not knowing who I was or if I existed at all. This is an area which will be covered in a further chapter.

It is difficult to describe exactly what happens and how things unfold in growth groups in a way which is meaningful and yet, at the same time, respects confidentiality. Each group is unique, not just characterised by the particular method or model used, the leader/leaders, the resources on offer, but also the mix of personalities present. But I will attempt to give a few examples of how group experiences were useful to me.

In one workshop we took part in some manoeuvres in pairs and there was an exercise in which we were instructed to pull each other in turn from one corner of the room to the other. We were encouraged to take careful note of how we felt in both roles – pulling and being pulled. When my partner attempted to haul me by the arms, I astonished myself by putting up a feisty resistance – there was no way in which I was going to be dragged ignominiously across the floor by this woman and finally she had to admit defeat. When the roles were reversed she came with me like a meek puppy on a lead; she put up no resistance whatsoever and I despised her and the part of myself that she represented. I found this extremely interesting because acting out this simple scenario had put me in touch with two conflicting aspects of myself.

I found role-play informative and illuminating – it often provided me with a ringside view of the interplay between various elements which comprised my inner world. I became renowned for being able to play the role of a dominant, possessive, manipulating mother figure, as well as the child who had been on the receiving end of such treatment, but there was another simple challenge that revealed aspects of myself of which I was previously unaware.

Working with a partner we were provided with a dish of food and a spoon and were told to explore the feelings around feeding and being fed. Once again, my spontaneous response was a surprise. When I fed my partner, I aggressively shovelled the food into her mouth, making her splutter and choke. She allowed me to continue doing this in spite of her discomfort – appearing to be unable to stop me. When the roles were reversed and it was my turn to be fed, I pursed my lips in stubborn refusal and whatever cunning tactics were used to coerce me into eating I wouldn't budge a millimetre. In fact, my resistance became quite belligerent and the food ended up all over me and all over the floor. The subject of food and eating disorders will feature in another chapter but I remember one therapist said that I had a tendency to 'bite the hand that fed me' and I was interested to observe how this particular role-play illustrated both a relentless, attacking, ruthlessness and also an equally relentless stubborn, intractability.

In another group we were encouraged 'to take a risk'. This could be anything we wanted to explore, and we could ask others to help us if we wished. I can't bring to mind how I introduced my 'risk' when I volunteered to sit in the centre of the circle and I can't recall how I set things up and got going. What I *do* remember very distinctly – and I don't recommend it as an intervention unless set up as a role-play – is that my very worst fears were realised when the assistant leader started to goad me by sneering that I was old and 'physically well past it'. This demolished me in one stroke. It epitomised my dread of ridicule, the discomfort I felt about my body, the weight of embarrassment I carried about my sexuality. I felt as if the lid had been lifted from my inner cess-pit and my shame was exposed for all to see.

But I rallied. As was intended, I became extremely angry. Instead of playing the victim role, I put up a valiant fight, which ended by me being pinned down to the floor by this bully of a trainee, who was obviously much stronger than I was. Caught in this deadlock, I looked around the circle of faces, most of whom were unsympathetic, and quickly spotted an ally – a macho, gladiator type who came to my rescue and dragged my assailant off. My rescuer was reprimanded for doing this more roughly than the situation required and it become apparent that he had a lot of hidden aggression. This didn't worry me too much at the time because I felt, rightly or wrongly, that justice had been done.

My reaction to men in general in workshops was worthy of note. A subtle, confused pattern emerged in relation to authority figures which was familiar in work situations too. I seemed very ready to 'put down' weak, ineffectual male figures who allowed themselves to be dominated by women, but I became exceedingly angry with males whom I experienced as blind, deaf or unperceptive. I could also be quite competitive, especially with arrogant 'clever clogs' who thought they knew everything about everything. Although there seemed to be something early in my life which had made my father into a blank screen, in groups, as with Philip, I often gravitated towards a 'good daddy' kind of figure and I enjoyed a snuggle in a corner provided there were no sexual under- or over-tones.

Where women were concerned, more prominent aspects of my attachment to my mother are going to feature in a more religious setting later on but in the phase I am describing, I often met up with someone who reminded me in some way of my sister Helen. Invariably such an encounter triggered confrontation and brought into focus an accumulation of uncomfortably powerful feelings like competitiveness, jealousy, fear, rage and vulnerability. I sometimes felt an impulse to attack or bulldoze this person out of my territory and once we actually arranged a wrestling match although I cannot recall the outcome.

On one occasion I suddenly became intoxicated with peals of laughter. *Something* was excruciatingly funny. I threw my legs into the air, bounced on the mattress, rolled across the floor. Never in my whole life has anything been quite so hilarious and to this day I don't know precisely what it was about, although I have an idea.

Sexuality came in for its fair share of attention and was explored from a variety of diverse angles. I was usually the only post-menopausal woman present and I was unbearably embarrassed at still having inhibitions in this area. But I persevered.

In any 'past-life' scenarios that unfolded I appeared to have much familiarity and know-how around this theme, which suggests the possibility of some riotous experiences on the sexual front but who knows? My niece who is editing my manuscript suggests that this is ambiguous and needs to be amplified or removed but I have decided to let it remain.

I hated, with a deep, unfathomable loathing, when the men and women were split into separate groups: if the women went upstairs and the men stayed downstairs my spontaneous choice would be to sit halfway up the staircase. In the event, of course, I joined the women but it reminded me that both my parents had wanted a boy. It also pinpointed the years I had spent with my mother in the marital bed. Once, just for fun, I strapped on a large rubber penis and danced like a dervish against a background of colourful psychedelic slides and seductive music. This was riotous but I soon tired of it. I cast the penis aside and decided that I preferred female genitalia. And thereafter, surprisingly, for a short while I was able to relish being a sexual, sensual woman: I flirted outrageously and earned the nickname of 'Red Hot Mama' which I thought was a compliment. Feeling so good about my sexuality was like crossing the Rubicon; I wanted to laugh, sing and drink champagne. I hoped that my mother could see me because I felt sure that she would now be in a state of enlightenment and would enjoy seeing the enlightened me. But, as before, the feelings did not last.

Another time I became involved in body painting and no words could be crafted together in a way which would adequately describe the unutterable feelings of shame that I experienced. Yet, with the shame came a sense of outrage. I kept repeating, "*Something* has caused me to feel like this." And the usual round-about would start up in my brain – the gypsy, my knickers, the teacher, the policeman? Memory? Fantasy? False Memory? Tormenting, unremitting questions circled in my head like a hamster caught up in a wheel in its cage. I even wondered whether the gipsy scenario could be some kind of smoke screen to put a veil over an incident or relationship with someone much closer to home – a sequence more in line with what actually happened with Philip.

This turmoil often culminated in feelings of being trapped, blocked, unable to move forward and this neatly introduces the subject of Frank Lake.

PART THREE

PRIMAL PAIN AND PRIMAL LAUGHTER

CHAPTER TEN

PRIMAL INTEGRATION

– *exploring the roots*

My *Collins Dictionary* (published 1986) and my *Roget's Thesaurus* (published 1987) are always at my side. It is amusing to observe that while the 'pieces' of my personal history have been slowly fitting together, the pages of my ancient volumes have been slowly falling apart through overuse. In spite of the short cuts provided by my PC, whenever I am sitting at the screen, these old 'friends' still come to my rescue! However, these days I find that many words in common usage are no longer to be found in my antique hardbacks.

In spite of its age, my Collins Dictionary gives a definition of the word 'primal' which I find clear and concise:

> "PRIMAL 1. *First or original.*
> 2. *Chief or most important.*"

This definition provides an adequate gateway into this chapter; a chapter which will include several personalities who have featured prominently in my personal journey. The first is the late Dr Frank Lake – a name which is a password to some yet may be unknown to others.

Frank Lake

When Frank was experimenting with the drug LSD in connection with birth traumas in 1967 I was one of his guinea pigs. In his research and in his writing, he was exploring the connection between religion and psychology and, as a result of my strictly religious upbringing, I was fascinated by this. My indoctrinated brain asked, "How on earth, in heaven or in hell can these two fundamental opposites possibly be connected?"

Who was this controversial figure? Briefly, Frank studied medicine in Edinburgh and pursued theological courses at the same time. He joined the Church Missionary Society and worked in India specialising in Parasitology. He served as a doctor in India during the Second World war and returned to Britain to train as a psychiatrist.

John Peters who has written a book about Frank, suggests that four images – one could say four subpersonalities – are pertinent to an understanding of his character: the parasitologist, the prophet, the psychiatrist and the priest. I resonate with this synopsis and also identify with the categorization expressed in Peters' book by psychiatrist Dr Roger Moss who first met Frank in 1966. I condense as follows:

> "Frank acted and breathed like a doctor, even though later he absorbed and shone in many other fields of activity. He had a very deep longing that his work be accepted by the medical profession, and I suspect he was disappointed that he did not enlist many more in the fields of exploration *he* opened up.

> "He had an unusually strong personality, so much so that many felt overwhelmed and invaded by him. In the personal therapeutic work I did with him, I needed that strength to anchor my own – I felt deeply secure in his

medical, Christian and fatherly experience... . He won the affection of many who allowed themselves to get close to him by his unusual capacity for love. His love undoubtedly made his insights and discernment therapeutic when it might have been destructive.

"He undoubtedly experienced a considerable measure of healing of his personality in the course of his lifetime, but both he and those around him recognised areas in his character which never fully aspired to the wholeness he strove to find in so many others.

"His mind moved quickly, sometimes rather abstrusely, though by no means always oppressively. He could call upon immerse knowledge, and increasingly used his right hemisphere to call on images and colouring in his talk and thinking. To a considerable extent, conversation tended to go in the direction he steered it. There was perhaps a sense that everyone he encountered was a kind of subject in his laboratory of life: this could be experienced as intense personal interest or being passively manipulated, depending on how you chose to take him. He stimulated many, angered not a few...

"As a psychotherapist, he became unusually percipient, skilful and successful. As a psychiatrist, he was eccentric and individualistic, and quite unlike the mainstream of British psychiatrists. Very few psychiatrists (as contrasted with psychoanalysts or psychotherapists) in Britain have remained anything like as psychodynamic as Frank Lake.

"As a scientist, he came under fire because he chose not to think in the accepted fashion. Actually, I think he strove harder than most to cope within the framework of basic scientific principles. For the most part, however, he did not present his results in the accepted journals or with impressive statistics, and although most psychiatrists would agree that these are not the only measure of behavioural scientist's professionalism, they are common yardsticks of acceptability. Moreover, the way he communicated his findings was a good deal too abstruse and verbose, and probably too laden with images for those used to the parsimonious and dehumanised communications of science. Overall he was very competent in the areas he concentrated upon. Simply because his effectiveness was not measured in conventional terms, should not detract from the help he gave very many people."

> (*Frank Lake – the man and his work.* John Peters.
> Darton, Longman and Todd. 1989.)

I have quoted extensively from this contribution by Roger Moss, whom I know personally and, with his permission, I would like to add a few words of my own to the last sentence,

> "Simply because his effectiveness was not measured in conventional terms, should not detract from the help he gave many people, '**nor should it detract from the rich legacy which Frank left; an inheritance which many still draw upon as they follow their life journey, as they broaden their understanding, do their own research, and pursue their own ministry, whatever form this may take.'**"

I first met Frank when he visited Lee Abbey while I was in the Community there; he had a link with Geoffrey Rogers through the Church Missionary Society. He had returned from India, had taken up psychiatry, and, in his new field of endeavour, he began to use LSD 25 in the therapy of neuroses and personality disorders. He was astonished to observe the regularity with which pre and perinatal traumas were relived and he later produced a massive tome called *Clinical Theology* which included details of the research he had undertaken into birth traumas using this drug.

At one stage of my therapeutic journey, I repeatedly touched into a sequence of experiences and feelings that seemed to be associated with a difficult birth and I arranged some sessions with Frank using LSD. What transpired was truly terrifying, because I seemed to relive the entire painful struggle of emerging from my mother's womb. The experience was, of course, intensified by the powerful drug and, during one session, I experienced coming to the surface and returning to reality for a brief spell. In those few moments I said, "How can the body survive such pain?" I am probably one of the few people still alive who worked with Frank in this way and, as I still have the notes and tapes from these sessions, I will quote a few extracts. Many of the phrases are repeated time and time again, indicating the profound complexity of the confusion and the seemingly endless, timeless quality of my journey through the birth canal. Repeated dashes indicate continual repetition of the same word or phrase.

> "Hammers in my head. Hammers, hammers…tighter, tighter…being squashed and twisted like in a mincing machine, a mincing machine…being squashed and twisted like in a mincing machine.

> "Everything breaking up, breaking up…swimming in my head, everything swimming in my head…all breaking up, breaking up.

> "Colours, all different colours swirling around, breaking up…

> "Crashing, crashing…crashing together, breaking up, breaking up, breaking up…tighter, tighter…being pulled

in two. Shivering, shivering…cold, cold…so cold…can't hold together anymore.

"All in different parts, different parts…not together any more…separate, not together any more, not together any more…split into different parts.

"The mincing machine is getting tighter, tighter…it's all breaking up…it's breaking *me* up…I haven't got *me* anymore…Betty not there any more. Hardly any air, no air, no air…being squeezed, horrible twisting, twisting…no air, no air…"

During the series of sessions, I went through this process a number of times, sometimes with additional experiences but always ending the same way. There was a crisis in which I felt myself fragment, then I became agonizingly cold, appearing to run out of oxygen and, without knowing how I did it, emerged from the womb. I arrived.

Once I touched into a wonderful sequence in which I felt feather-light – just like a fairy – dancing in a sunny glade full of bluebells. Frank steered me back into the mincing machine, which I regretted because my search was intrinsically focussed upon reuniting with my lost child self rather than the wounded warrior.

Some years later after the use of LSD 25 had been banned, in common with other pioneers in this field, Frank discovered that deep breathing alone was a sufficient catalyst for primal recapitulation and was, in fact, superior to using the drug. He started to run workshops in Nottingham, where he was living at the time, using this method; each workshop lasted for five or six days. People came from diverse walks of life, with equally diverse life histories and degrees of preparation for such a venture into regression. I think dear Frank was naively confident that all who came had been sent by the Holy Spirit, but maybe I was not alone in thinking that the

Holy Spirit would also expect a careful check to be made to ensure that all who participated were psychologically ready for such an exploration before diving into such deep waters. It was also advisable that each person taking part had a solid support system already in place when returning home and needing to integrate all that had been experienced. Such vetting is now taken for granted in all the recognised organisations that I am currently acquainted with.

In my own case, I already had a firm support system in place, and the deep patterns which were evident in the exploration of my birth were also apparent in the way I lived my life. I felt fundamentally split, not just in the sense of being divided into various parts or subpersonalities, but also I had met head on an invisible wall dividing one part of me from another part. This first became apparent when I was in therapy with Philip when I experienced those magical and mysterious sunny months of living in a different, 'other' world. Since then I had often fleetingly touched into this wondrous space, but without consciously knowing how I achieved the connection – what flicked the switch – how the transition had 'come to pass'. What a great Biblical expression. I like it!

One facet of this compartmentalisation tactic was that I loved mysteries, secrets, dark closets, tree houses, underground passages. I loved anonymity, hiding out of sight (reminiscent of my book and apples sanctuaries in my early teens, high in a tree or in the warm airing cupboard) but now, in adulthood, watching *the* world, *my* world, or my *inner* world pass by. What a vantage point, a secret nest high above involvement: "See but don't be seen, observe but don't be observed, scrutinise but don't be scrutinised, monitor but don't be monitored, detect but don't be detected, perceive but don't be perceived." It is a position from which to identify people's foibles and failings, to study behaviour, to make secret judgements; sometimes to chuckle with glee at the antics of the righteous, sometimes to laugh the laugh of a child's pure enjoyment when the mighty trip over their own frail feet and, sometimes, even to gloat with malicious venom at the fallibility of the so-called infallible. I really 'had it in' for my mother's Lord or anybody who appeared to fit into this mould!

These compartments have opened up very gradually over the years and have revealed a covert haven – a secret refuge from irreparable loss, pain and grief. During the process of journeying, characters have leapt out, as if released like a lion cub from a cage. They have surprised me as much as anybody else, especially if we have been sitting solemnly in a religious setting. It's only comparatively recently that I have come to understand, in some measure, the protective mechanism that lay behind this scheme of imprisonment. I owe many of these discoveries to the explorations I undertook during these courses at Nottingham.

Frank Lake was one of the pioneers in the field of Primal Integration and I consider it a great privilege to have attended seven of his workshops in addition to the sessions using LSD. I reaped the benefit of his experience and his genius. He helped me unravel some of the complex scenarios which were woven into my inner world: scenarios which subsequently and quite unavoidably were woven into my outer life.

I was also able to observe, over a span of many hours and many days, the unique quality of concentration that was an essential part of the way in which he functioned. He was so focussed: his eyes, his ears, his intuition, his medical training, his experience as a psychiatrist, his faith – each valuable component poised, ready to step in so that he rarely missed a clue. His mind was an ever-flowing spring of ideas, insights and practical, informative teaching. His perception and technical brilliance as he worked were an education; his use of imagery inspired magical fantasy journeys that I shall never forget. I loved him dearly and considered it a compliment that, when he revisited India towards the end of his life, he asked me to make his travel arrangements – he said he would feel safe in my hands.

Bill Swartley

Another pioneer in the field of Primal Integration was Dr William Swartley PhD who is said by Anne Jackson to have been Carl Jung's youngest student. He also studied with Emma Jung at the C G Jung Institute for Analytic Psychology in Zurich; with Roberto Assagioli at the Institute for Psychosynthesis in Italy; with Ernst and Wolfgang Kretschner at the University of Tubingen in West Germany; with Swami Swarupanandda in India and with Alan Watts, Fredrick Spiegelberg and Haridas Chaudhuri at the University of the Pacific. He had been the Senior Clinical Psychologist at a New Jersey Reformatory, an Associate Professor of Psychology at the Community College of Philadelphia and a management training specialist for the Radio Corporation of America. He was the founder of the International Primal Association in the USA and Canada.

Clearly Bill was a professional with awesome credentials and wide-ranging experience but, unlike Frank Lake, he did not write extensively about his work. I first met him in 1977 when I took part in a series of Primal Integration groups in London, in which he was assisted by Jean Snow. Having sampled the product, I enrolled in one of the Primal Integration Training Programmes which he was running in London and Reading at that time.

I vividly remember the first group that I did with Bill. All participants were given an opportunity to introduce themselves, share personal details, give a context to feelings that might be emerging and/or share a direction for exploration in the unstructured part of the group which would follow. In taking my turn I explained the predicament I had found myself in. A small child part of me had crept out of hiding only to disappear again when something went very seriously wrong. I was carrying the small doll that I had wanted to hide in Peter's consulting room before he had his accident. Bill's response, "I like her already", endeared him to me for ever and that's always how it was with Bill. He had complete trust in a natural process. His baseline was that any person whose early childhood had been fraught with trauma and/or a dysfunctional environment needed support in order to disentangle the muddled ball of string – *but* the only person who could monitor the process was the 'patient' for want of a better term.

Bill had implicit faith in my own knowledge regarding myself; he joined me in my search, he encouraged me and he helped me to pick up ephemeral clues. There was no good or bad, right or wrong, acceptable or unacceptable with Bill; you knew he was there to assist you in your task, to be 'alongside', to facilitate, to support, to give confidence. He was an 'ideas' man, innovative in suggesting ways of detecting and exploring. His groups were full of tears and pain, fun and laughter. He was quick to identify patterns of behaviour in the here and now which tracked back into early life experiences and equally alert to spot parts of the self that had never been allowed to surface and develop.

When we started the training, Bill clearly considered it an advantage rather than a disadvantage if you were a person who had encountered severe problems and deep traumas. It was necessary to the work. It meant that you knew the territory, you were fighting your way through your own jungle, you knew in your own experience feelings of terror, panic, pain, hopelessness, despair, blackness. You would therefore be able to travel alongside others on their journey. He did not expect you to be 'cured' or complete, rather he saw personal growth and development as an on-going process, a continual 'becoming'. The necessary requirement in his eyes was to be ready to take the next step – to allow the next unfolding to happen.

In Bill's groups it felt safe enough to allow parts of myself that had been blocked off for decades, to be expressed in an instinctual, spontaneous, creative way. I welcomed each weekend workshop with a sense of excitement, wondering what was going to pop up this time, what discoveries I would make, what secrets would emerge from my Aladdin's Cave. It had begun to dawn upon me that I was the possessor of a profound truth, an incredible secret about myself which I had guarded and defended with the utmost zeal and tenacity through the decades. *This was the ultimate primal laugh.* My mother and her Lord had not triumphed. In my innermost core I was still myself; in my innermost core I *was* the person I was meant to be. My mother had attempted to squeeze me into her cast-iron mould, but as her strictures had become more and more rigid, I had retreated more and more deeply into my own secret hiding place. *But* I had saved my own soul. My potential to be completely myself was there, intact; it was not a question of *changing – working things out* – it was much more a task of allowing, giving permission, letting happen, revealing, giving space to my true self. This was a liberating revelation, because I had always assumed that in some subtle way I was maladjusted, that something was intrinsically wrong, and by some unknown methodology I had to sort myself out, to make myself different, to change myself, to get myself right.

I enjoyed the family aspect of an on-going group, it triggered flashbacks to 'set pieces' in my childhood, but also gave me a new, positive, affirming experience of a different kind of family, where people were warm, accepting, tolerant, yet challenging; where one could be mischievous, outrageous, play tricks and have fun.

I valued the fact that although Bill and Jean worked well as co-leaders, they were complementary in the way they operated. Bill was active, innovative and in his element when a chain of diverse experiences were unfolding all around him in the unstructured part of the group. These enactments, all occurring simultaneously, yet safely, under Bill's watchful eye, could range from a quiet massage in one corner of the room to a screaming 'infant' in a hospital cot in another; a silent foetus in the womb could be curled up protected by a barrier of cushions, while opposite a dramatic reconstruction of a family row was re-enacted. A struggle in the birth canal could take place next to a noisy confrontation with Mother; and at the same time others could be completely absorbed in their own unfolding processes, quietly pondering, peacefully sleeping, absorbed in some colourful creation in paint or crayons or...so many variations, innovations or possibilities. Somebody might say, "How was it possible to undertake personal exploration in such chaotic surroundings?" Yet, in essence, it was not dissimilar to the basic environment which a foetus embraces or an infant, or a developing child experiences in a large, noisy family.

Jean, on the other hand, was more analytical in her approach, and we valued talking to her and drawing upon her interpretative skills. I liked this diversity – it was a pleasant eye-opener to me, in contrast to the inflexibility of my home background: it demonstrated that in team work there was room for breadth and depth, multiformity and multilateral opinions.

Our syllabus was far-reaching and included many aspects of primal work and personal development, but I would like to pin-point two subjects which were of outstanding value to me. The first was a weekend on the topic of 'Subpersonalities' led by John Rowan who, as well as leading this particular workshop, was also a fellow member of our training group. The many books he has written include an excellent one on this fascinating subject – subpersonalities. John believes that a person's defences can get into such a convoluted tangle that they are very hard to sort out. By eliciting the subpersonalities involved, it is possible to see more clearly how the internal parts are constructed and played out. I found this methodology extremely stimulating; in short, it gave me completely new insights regarding the management of my many-sided personality. The second was my introduction to Sandplay by Cecil Burney, a clinical psychologist – a pivotal experience which was going to deeply influence my future life. This will have a chapter of its own later.

William Emerson

The third person to have a special place during my explorations into primal work is Dr William R Emerson, PhD who is an esteemed teacher, writer, lecturer and pioneer in the field of pre and perinatal psychology. His CV is impressive: among many notable spheres of experience he is a former university professor for California State University and a European lecturer for the University of Maryland. He is the founder and director of Emerson Seminars and has been named an honorary fellow for the National Institute of Mental Health for his scholarly excellence and contributions to the field of psychology.

A contributor to the Emerson Seminars website who has worked with William writes:

> "There are few opportunities in life to train with a master – and William Emerson is a master clinician and a master teacher. His discovery of the differences in treating shock and trauma is a major breakthrough in psychotherapeutic treatment. His documentation of the profound and pervasive effects of pre and perinatal trauma, and the treatment techniques that heal those early wounds, provide a new structure for healing the deepest wounds and shifting the pervasive (and stubborn) patterns that traditional treatments have struggled with (usually unsuccessfully) for decades. The treatment methods developed and taught at Emerson Seminars are the future of emotional healing. Emerson's deep, personal experience in the techniques he has pioneered and now teaches allows him to walk his talk more thoroughly and consistently than any teacher, guru, mentor or visionary I've ever known. He is the work."
>
> (Emerson Seminars. Praise & Comments. Terry Larimore, MSW)

I echo the sentiments of this writer. Although I was unable to do many of William Emerson's workshops because he didn't visit the UK very frequently, each one stands out for me. He worked in an entirely different way from either Frank Lake or Bill Swartley but there was something about his relaxed, quiet, confident presence which created an atmosphere of safety, spiced with a spirit of excitement and expectation.

He held a group of participants together in a way which made every person's exploration, intervention or contribution part of a whole experience. Spirituality was an essential part of the structure but it wasn't cluttered with complex jargon – it was an essential part of what we were all experiencing together. He liked and appreciated me and I shall always be grateful to him.

Richard Mowbray and Juliana Brown

Sadly Bill Swartley died in 1979 at the age of fifty-two and this was a grievous loss. After his death, members of the training programme, including Richard Mowbray, Juliana Brown, John Rowan, myself and others, formed the Whole Person Cooperative to offer workshops in Primal Integration and to organise further professional development. This organisation lasted for about two years. In 1979 Richard and Juliana started a comprehensive Programme of Primal Integration at the Open Centre. They have been in practice there ever since and are loved, respected and revered by very many people who have travelled primal pathways with them through the years.

Founded in 1977, the Open Centre is one of the UK's longest established centres for self-development and personal growth and its practitioners have many years of experience in their particular fields. In the latest brochure Juliana Brown and Richard Mowbray describe what they offer:

"We do group and individual work in Primal Integration and Bodywork. Primal Integration involves an exploration of our deeper levels of experience with a view to being more alive and living more authentically. This process fosters 'growth forces' which can help splits in our being to heal and blocks to our 'doing' to resolve. Traumatic and other experiences in early life may interrupt the wholeness of our development. Such experiences may have occurred during childhood, birth or before. Integrating these experiences into consciousness – acknowledging them as memories – reduces the confusion between what was then and what is now and releases more of our energy and qualities for life in the present. Primal Integration is concerned with both the recovery of the self one has apparently 'lost' and the discovery of the self one has yet to become.

"In our groups and individual sessions we endeavour to create an environment conducive to this process of connection, expression and integration and one which allows both the freedom to 'stretch one's wings' and the security to explore one's most vulnerable and fearful states of being.

"We also facilitate the process in a variety of ways including 'Primal Bodywork' and work with feelings, dreams, fantasies, thoughts and words. Self-direction and self-responsibility are particularly emphasised.

"The work we currently offer is a synthesis that we have evolved over the last thirty years since our training with Bill Swartley, the original developer of Primal Integration. Other major influences include work and further training with Frank Lake, a pioneering explorer of pre-and peri-natal experiences and the configurationally psychology of Francis Mott. Richard has also trained in bodywork with Jack Painter (Postural Integration) and Curtis Turchin (Pulsing and Postural Integration).

"Our comprehensive programme of Primal Integration – monthly weekend groups, weekly ongoing groups, periodic residential group intensives and regular individual sessions – has been running at the Open Centre since 1979.

We are co-authors of "Primal Integration" for *Innovative Therapy – A Handbook (OUP, 1994)* and "Visionary Deep Personal Growth" for *What's the Good of Counselling & Psychotherapy?* (Sage 2002). Richard is also author of *The Case Against Psychotherapy Registration – A Conservation Issue for the Human Potential Movement* (Trans Marginal Press, 1995) and various other publications in that area including *Controversies in Psychotherapy and Counselling* (Sage, 1999). (The Open Centre Programme <www.opencentre.com>)

In the early 80s' Richard and Juliana invited me to assist on their groups at the Open Centre, and I worked with them for about eighteen years, an extremely rich experience for which I shall always be grateful. I was a very late developer in a number of ways, so this was a period in which I was finding my own feet, formulating my own opinions and discovering my own creativity. I think they often found me difficult to communicate with because, as I have already explained, communication was a skill that I only started to learn very late in life. I thank them most sincerely for all that I learned from them, for their tolerance and forbearance, and I thank all the clients who, over the years gave me so much love and appreciation.

Most of all, I thank Richard and Juliana for giving me time and space to develop facilitation skills with both groups and individuals, and time and space to develop my Sandplay and other creative outlets within the group setting. This has turned out to be an exceedingly important and significant phase of my journey – a development which I shall enjoy writing about later on.

Reading this chapter again just before going into print, I am wondering whether I have any pertinent reflections around Primal Integration? Yes, I do. I am glancing up at a collage which I made around this time – it will be included in my book – it depicts the wonder of life in the womb and the miracle of emergence into life.

I believe that, for some of us, spending time delving into these deeply formative areas can be richly rewarding. The opportunity offered to observe emotional patterns that are profoundly imprinted and severely affect life in the present and allowing a natural unfolding into pivotal root experiences can be vitally significant. A unique breadth of freedom is offered to hidden child selves to emerge and express themselves – be it in pain, joy, rage, laughter, tears, irritation, frustration, action, interaction. Another picture in this book depicts some of the selves which I uncovered!

*But, as with any other therapeutic or personal growth model , **we are on a journey** so I suggest that it is unwise to get stuck and bed down in this fascinating area of discovery. We are extremely complex individuals and need to explore widely and make use of every aid to further enlightenment that is open to us.*

CHAPTER ELEVEN

OUTBURSTS FROM A SECRET HIDEAWAY

– *a child emerges*

The Jesuits claim that, if they have a child until it is seven years old, they have that child for life – such is the impact of powerful imprints during those early years. I can well believe this to be true, because, in spite of a prolonged process of revising and modifying my views on religion, time and time again, in the innermost recesses of my being I have found a child who is still confused about the doctrines and dogmas inculcated directly or indirectly during the budding of her life, and reinforced throughout her formative years.

I continue to marvel at how deeply implanted these beliefs were, how tenacious was their hold, like spectres casting threatening shadows into the murky, subterranean nooks and crannies of my underworld; whispering warnings of condemnation and judgement and forecasting an impending, punitory encounter with Nemesis. When the ghostly images weave their way to the surface and see the light of day their credibility crumbles; yet the images still bring feelings of fear, dread, guilt and shame, and face me with the terrifyingly ominous alternatives of life and death, heaven and hell, survival and extinction. The kind of emotional blackmail that urges a child to deny self and surrender to the pressure of authority.

I truly believe that there is something morally flawed and evil in the presentation to young children of doctrines and dogmas that can have such power to shape and colour a child's life and thus become enmeshed and entangled in the already complex imprint of parental influences. It seems to me that, in general, the Church is unaware of this danger and the probable repercussions and reverberations in the life of a child who has already been made to feel guilty, bad and unacceptable. Such a child will *already* have a scene set for serious personality problems, but this underpinning will be reinforced and intensified by the additional weight of religious culpability.

If, in addition to this infusion of inflexible rules and precepts, the child is also made to feel that it is too risky to talk, to question, to doubt, to want to know – all the spontaneous signs of a child's natural curiosity and thirst for knowledge – then a serious blockage in the development of that child's mind and, consequently of the whole personality, occurs. I am referring here to the effects of religious indoctrination but, obviously there are other systems of belief which, if imposed in a similar way, will have an equally damaging effect.

These paragraphs were first written many years ago and I find myself wondering whether I dare express myself this strongly. And yet, although on a rational, cognitive level I have grappled with the mystery posed by the Christian faith, the journey itself has been a deeply painful mental and emotional struggle, and I can echo Stevie Smith's heartfelt cry:

"Oh Christianity, Christianity
Why do you not answer our difficulties?
If He was God He was not like us,
He could not lose.
And sin, how could He take our sins upon Him?
What does it mean?
To take sin upon one is not the same

As to have sin inside one and feel guilty.
Oh what do you mean, what do you mean/
You never answer our questions."
(*The Collected Poems of Stevie Smith*, Allen Lane 1975.
Permission of Estate of James MacGibbon.)

Frank Lake was a convinced Christian and, retrospectively, I think that the religious atmosphere at Lingdale, where his workshops were held, had a significant bearing upon some of my experiences there. In my childhood, intimate things were never mentioned and the door was firmly closed against any discussion of sexual matters, or anything to do with procreation. The edict was simplicity itself – your body is a temple of the Holy Spirit; lust and passion are of the devil. On an adult level, I had sorted these things out decades ago, but in the deepest enclaves of my being there was a child who was activated into a vociferous response in the hallowed precincts of Lingdale.

Frank always used a guided fantasy to lead us into our exploration. We had permission to call a halt at any point on the journey if deep feelings were stimulated, and might take over in a way that suggested a need for further investigation. Other people, exploring alongside in the same room, were able to continue their voyage of discovery at whatever pace their own individual process dictated. An experienced person facilitated each of us, a helper scribed notes and another kept an eye on a recording machine.

The fantasy journey started by picturing our father and our mother separately, against the backcloth of their own early environment, then we imagined them meeting, marrying and setting up home. We gave careful consideration to both of them, as individuals – the 'colouring' as it were of their personal lives and also the 'climate' between them, as a couple, at the time of our conception. It was suggested that we pause a moment to capture the feelings that we experienced as we pictured them coming together in sexual intercourse.

We were also encouraged to identify with the special sperm which was going to win this splendid race and with the 'ovum of the month' which was moving up into the fallopian tube within our mother's body. When the eager sperm plunged through the cell wall of the ovum, Frank encouraged our awareness of a precise happening – a new beginning; **a unique recipe for each one of us individually.** The process of development had already commenced, the division of cells would continue inexorably as the Blastocyst moved towards implantation into the wall of the womb. Were we being welcomed by our mother's body or was there resistance to our presence?

We were escorted through the developmental stages of growth in the womb including the mysteries of the first trimester when mother was unaware of our presence. Particular attention was allotted to the third month, when the placenta took over and we started to draw nourishment through the umbilical cord. We were encouraged to pause at this juncture and sense this direct link, this two-way flow between the mother and the foetus. What were we experiencing? Were we being nourished on every level? Were there mixed messages? As the programmed development continued it was suggested that we might become aware of movement and sound: of having less space to move without restraint until finally we reached our actual birth; our journey into life, our arrival into the world and the welcome we received.

Enacting this journey linked the 'now' with the 'then', using a technique which allowed an engrossing, enthralling experience to unfold. In a unique, subtle way it was possible to be present in this re-living of the past in a three-dimensional way – in body, mind and spirit. Yet, at the same time, one had the advantage of an observer's knowledge, experience and even emotions – rather like a modern commentator in a TV documentary.

Like many others, I found it exceedingly difficult to picture my mother and father having sexual intercourse; for me there was something about their incompatibility that was extremely disturbing and terrifying. There was a turbulent intensity about the act –

something about dangerous component parts that *must at all costs* be kept apart; must not be allowed to come together ; of pulsating, invasive, explosive energy penetrating an actively resisting, muscle-bound, rigid vagina. My father had been reared in a macho, male-dominated household and, although I am sure that he loved my mother deeply, he lacked sensitivity and tenderness. My mother, with French blood in her veins, was, I believe, a sensual, passionate woman. But at the time of my conception she was gripped by obsession and was hidebound by strict Pauline doctrines about bodily pleasures. Intimate sexual contact with my father must have been purgatory to her – a dreaded, on-going torture with undertones that cannot even be envisaged.

It appears that I may have picked up this ambivalence throughout my development in her womb, especially when I was directly connected to her body for physical and emotional sustenance through the umbilical cord. I seemed to sense an eternal conflict in her body; her instinctual, human sex drives clashing with her inhibitions. Rather like enemies on the battlefield: colourful troops on horseback, facing a formation of black-coated, equally powerful aggressors; a battle that somehow, whatever energy might be required, had to be deadened. In my mother's case I presume this resulted in depression.

I recognise that I was 'experiencing' on many levels during these fantasy journeys: my life in the womb, my life as a child and the conditioned structure of my personality but this is what made them so enlightening. I had a sense of being filled and totally enveloped by a degree of physical, emotional and spiritual conflict which had a quality of life and death urgency. I seemed to be in touch with her continual pain and distress, her deep grief and desolation. It was like a dark, bottomless pit of extinguished hopes and black despair, from which there was no escape. Where did the feeling commence that it was all my fault? 'IT' all seemed to be *my* fault...all *my* fault...the 'grey cloud' feeling, which was so familiar in later years.

On one occasion I seemed to plunge into real madness and craziness – a deep terrifying space which I suspect lurks, secretly hidden away in many of us. Strangely enough, on more than one occasion, I spoke a kind of gobbledegook which resembled 'speaking in tongues', sometimes heard in charismatic religious meetings. The impression I had at the time was that I was imitating the sounds of muffled voices, as heard through the walls of my mother's womb.

Reliving my birth produced similar sequences as when using LSD, except that the slower motion of deep breathing allowed other recurring successions of movements to unfold, such as finding myself in an awkward position, being pushed around, moving in the wrong direction. This seemed to lead to a bewildering experience of confusion. My instinctual urges and programming seeming to be in conflict with my physical position in relation to the pelvis. It is possible that the doctor may have tried to re-position me.

This revelation had occurred when exploring with Bill and also when I worked with Dr William Emerson. They both had the same impression as Frank, that I might have been a breach birth, and on the journey into life I may have experienced an entanglement with the umbilical cord. Due to lack of oxygen there may have been a brief moment of unconsciousness as I emerged. In one of Bill's groups I had a very strong reaction to the smell of ether.

I shall never know but Frank *was* able to pinpoint a recurring component which he had observed in many of my early experiences – that of a fathomless depth of **confusion**. He perceived this at my conception, when I was developing in my mother's womb, during my actual birth, suckling at my mother's breast, listening to her endless prayers, in the sequence with the gipsy and sharing the marital bed. I found this observation extremely helpful. It placed 'confusion' in a category of its own, an extremely disturbing, frightening experience *in itself*: something that had an endless quality to it, had been relentlessly endured and could never be unravelled. This insight was a revelation; it gave a context to the 'experience of confusion itself' and released me from the illusion that *I would understand the feeling if only I could unscramble it.*

I have no way of checking the facts about my life in the womb, my birth, my experience at the breast, but the value of reliving these sequences is the way in which they link to patterns in my life: the repetition of negative scenarios, the compulsion to put myself under pressure, things going wrong, continuing to get stuck, difficulty in finding a way through, not trusting my instincts and perceptions, dividing myself into compartments and, above all, the power of shame itself. I was conceived and nurtured in shame and conflict.

There were also many hilarious sequences. Amusing scenarios about penises and vaginas, a small child's voice obviously enjoying making observations to Frank and the whole room, that wouldn't have been allowed at home; utterances that sometimes sounded quite comical even within the hallowed precincts of Lingdale. I quote from the transcripts:

> "I'm an all-conquering sperm. The world's all mine. Colours, lots of different colours, swishing sounds, endless possibilities, excitement."

> "The baby is all right. It was conceived by a jolly good penis – not by the Holy Ghost. No Holy Ghost for me."

> "Penises are the funniest toys God ever made. You don't know just how funny they can be very, very funny indeed. They can be all soft and gentle and flabby but when you play with them they grow bigger and bigger. Real magic toys they are."

> "I hid in a very funny place – an exceedingly funny place: the one place where my mummy would never find me – in my clitoris; she would never look for me there. It was my real self I hid there."

"I'm a marble of colourful energy. There's no need to restrict that colourful energy any more."

I often reminded myself that my parents were the product of their own individual upbringing and I imagined how they might have developed had they been truly themselves. Once I set out on the fantasy journey identifying with the free, fun-loving child in my father, my mother and myself. This proved to be an hilarious and enchanting sequence in which a cheeky, chipper sperm out-swam all his squiggling rivals to win the race and dance around an ovum of delicate, mysterious quality, totally different from the heavy, grey, doom-laden egg which usually appeared at my conception.

There was joy in the union of sperm and egg, magic in the sensation of cells dividing, and a brilliantly coloured Blastocyst was wafted along by softly waving cilia towards implantation in a welcoming uterus. Later, a joyous foetus kicked, turned somersaults and cartwheels in oceanic bliss in a spacious womb, thrived on a plentiful supply of physical, emotional and spiritual nourishment through a magical cord of many colours. Harmonious voices could be heard singing through the chapel walls and a flexible, acrobatic little person limbered its way through a slithery, cooperative birth canal and emerged shouting:

"The baby is all right. I am all right. All of me is good. Tell all of Lingdale. Tell all of Nottingham. Tell the world. I thought I was bad. I have always thought I was bad but I am good. I am good. I am a smasher."

I thought I was bad but I was good. It is hard to explain to anybody who has not been afflicted with a lifelong conviction that they are intrinsically bad, essentially unacceptable, 'not right' in some fundamental way, just how merciless this feeling can be and how inexorably and relentlessly it can persist. You can carefully and diligently create a new self-image, you can understand intellectually and prove in your everyday life that you are good and acceptable;

you can utilise visualisation, positive thinking, and meditation techniques and yet, in the very core of your being, the child can still experience itself as being bad and unacceptable. So, there was a glorious, spiritual triumph in finding in those hidden depths of my being a core person who knew herself to be good. I wanted to proclaim this wonderful discovery from the housetops.

As I write I still feel enormously enriched by these 're-formative' experiences, which have been 'built in' and which have reconnected me to my true source of 'being'. I grew to love Frank and admired his quicksilver brain, the wide range of his knowledge, his versatility, the quality of his listening, his unfailing interest and caring. I know he was a sleuth, hot in pursuit of knowledge yet, I, myself, the person, wasn't lost sight of in his quest.

I felt a deep sense of loss when he died on 10th May 1982 after struggling with illness for some time. Yet another of my special people had gone.

After his death I decided to take part in one of the two-year seminars on Human Relations, Pastoral Care and Counselling, organised by the Clinical Theology Association, a body founded by Frank in 1961. The organisation is now known as the Bridge Pastoral Foundation; it is flourishing and still organises seminars, modules and conferences. These courses incorporate Frank's profound knowledge and experience. They include insightful, experiential opportunities, cunningly designed exercises and role-plays, extensive teaching about personality types, and much more. When I signed up I was aware that I already knew one of the tutors, Tony, from Lee Abbey days.

Chapter Twelve

MORE OUTBURSTS

– the child becomes more confident

Most people on the Clinical Theology Course were practising Christians and, for me, this added a useful dimension. When I met up with Tony, we started to reminisce about the old days at Lee Abbey: in particular about a house-party to which he had taken a group of young people from his church. He vividly recalled one evening when a picnic supper had been arranged round a camp fire, way up on the headland, looking out to sea above Lee Bay. He spoke of the closing Epilogue at which a young woman had given her testimony. He said how moving and inspiring it had been. He hesitated: "What *was* her name? B...? B...? Betty! That's right, Betty, daughter of Pop." Then he looked at me and the penny dropped. It was me!

This put me in a quandary because at this stage of my life, Lee Abbey seemed light years away, and I was now in a very different position in relation to the Christian faith, and didn't know how I was going to bridge this gap. However, I decided to be open, honest and spontaneous during the seminars and to deal with any questions and interactions as they arose. It proved to be a good exercise in having the courage to be myself, especially as it felt rather like being back in the family again – much more so than other growth groups because of the religious dimension. Even so, connecting back over the years to a spontaneous self that had been forced into hiding was a strange position to be in and when I dared to open my mouth I could never be quite sure how the words might tumble out. Any direct link to these sensitive areas automatically results in an emotional disturbance that requires attention.

The experiential exercises that Frank Lake had devised very cleverly triggered deeply buried scenarios from early childhood. Often we were able to share together packages of confused and painful experiences which were waiting to be eased out into the open. On one of these occasions, in an honest attempt to bring comfort to deeply troubled souls, Tony said something like this, "How wonderful it is to know that Jesus came to this earth and lived an ordinary life. This means that He can feel with us in all the distress and anguish of our early experiences and traumas. He can fully understand all the agony and grief, and will help us to bear the pain." As I listened I became more and more tense – like a pressure cooker about to explode – and then a voice burst through the barriers, "That's absolute nonsense. Jesus doesn't know what it is like to be a woman and He certainly doesn't know what it feels like to be sexually abused as a small child." Whoosh! Nobody seemed unduly upset but it was important for that child me to speak from her heart and to have her truth accepted.

While attending the seminars, my attention was drawn to the flier publicising the forthcoming Clinical Theology Annual Conference. The subject was "And what about Father? An Exploration into Father-Child Relationships. This year's Conference offers opportunities to discover, or maybe re-discover, aspects of an important and yet neglected relationship, and the impact which this neglect may have had on our personal development."

I was intrigued by this title and felt it was tailor-made for me. I reserved a place. Once again, I knew I would be in a large group of Christian people and made another contract with myself to be open and honest and to cope with any ripples which might result. I had explored my relationship with my father in therapy, and in groups settings, and was already in touch with a lot of the negative material associated with him in my early history. So I was interested to find that I was eager, excited and energised at the Conference, looking forward to each session with a sense of expectancy – I knew that I was going to discover something new and that it was going to be important.

The programme included Psychodrama workshops led by Jenny Biancardi. I was familiar with this technique and was particularly intrigued when members of the conference were invited to work on some aspect of their relationship with their father. In one session Jenny invited us to set the stage for ourselves and, "Say something to Father" – something we needed to say, something we would like to have said as a small child but hadn't been able to do so. I was sitting on the edge of my chair with eagerness. I knew that I had something vitally important to say to '*my daddy*' and I was the first to volunteer. I had no idea what would tumble out but I allowed the scene to unfold. I chose a tall, robust man and sat him in a chair reading the *Daily Express*. I crept towards him slowly like a small, nervous child might, tapped tentatively on the newspaper, caught his attention and launched into what seemed to have been waiting to be said for all these years. Briefly, it went something like this:

"I need you to listen, Daddy, really listen, Daddy. It's important, Daddy, very important, Daddy. It's a secret, Daddy, a heavy secret, Mummy wouldn't understand, Daddy, she would never understand. She'd say I was bad, very bad, very bad, never to be forgiven. I couldn't tell her, Daddy, but I might have been able to tell you if you had had time. I'm going to tell you now, Daddy, because I know you love me even if you couldn't show me that you did, I knew you loved me. It's a secret, Daddy, a heavy secret but it wasn't my fault, he shouldn't have done it."

My father had been dead for many years but at this moment I had a strong sense of his presence, of feeling his arms around me, of being warmed, comforted and blessed. All the warm feelings I had had for him as a small child came flooding back. I had rediscovered my father – but I hadn't said what the secret was.

Soon after this conference I decided that I had some ghosts to lay at Abbey and I planned a return visit.

Chapter Thirteen

LEE ABBEY REVISITED

– *With Great Trepidation*

While my father was still alive I had paid a few short visits to Lee Abbey to see him but I had not been back as a guest, taking part in a conference or house-party, since I left the Community about thirty years before. I booked a place at a conference on the subject of caring for needy people and became increasingly apprehensive as the planned visit drew near.

Lloyda, who had also been in the Community, was coming with me, and she came to stay for a few days before we left for Devon. It was 16 October 1987, the night the great storm hit the south of England. At that time I lived on the fourth floor of a large block of flats, situated in an elevated position, high above the town, facing straight out to sea. We had settled down for the night when the hurricane hit us and a mighty force of wind shook the building. It felt as if the windows would splinter into fragments and the walls would cave in at any moment. We were terrified. It reminded me of when I was a child; whenever there was a heavy storm with thunder and lightening, I feared it heralded either the end of the world, or the Second Coming of Jesus.

We dressed with the utmost speed. Lloyda collected her belongings together and I enacted the question, "What would you take with you if had to leave your house at a moment's notice?" I shoved my most precious possessions into a bag – just in case the whole block collapsed. Should we stay high up and have a chance of being on the top of the pile or should we go down to ground level? That was the question.

All the lights went out – darkness without and darkness within, relieved by torches and candlelight. Sounds of breaking glass, splintering wood, falling debris added to the roar of the raging storm. We decided to stay with our neighbours, cowering in murky corners, drinking cups of tea in the fourth-floor lobby. It was reminiscent of bombing raids during the war and we trembled as even more earth-shattering, ripping and tearing noises came from above. Someone ventured up to his penthouse to investigate and was visibly shaken when he returned to tell us that his flat was open to the sky – large sections of our roof had lifted off and been flung in all directions at the mercy of the storm. A second penthouse resident found that his roof had also been lifted off.

When dawn broke we went to investigate and we were dismayed at the extent of the damage. Trees were down, cars were damaged, two portions of our flat roof had been whipped off. The lounge of the penthouse above my flat was completely open to the sky! Later in the day, when the heavens opened again, the inevitable happened – the flat above mine became a reservoir of trapped water which started to seep through my ceiling like a sprinkler.

We became galvanised into action. Lloyda gallantly ferried my most precious possessions across town – by criss-cross routes due to fallen trees and debris – to the houses of kind friends for safe keeping. Supplies of any kind of waterproof covering had run out, so I hastily contrived covers for my furniture from black rubbish bags, put everything into the middle of the room swathed in a massive sheet of plastic which had been sent from London to my rescue by Richard and Juliana. It was no longer safe to live in my home, so I warned the occupants of the flats below me that nothing could be done to prevent water from penetrating their domains. Then we set off for Devon. By carefully negotiating fallen trees and debris we managed to reach Lee Abbey just in time for the conference.

It was a weird feeling re-entering those portals and so many memories came storming back. But most poignantly, I remember the strange mixture of excitement and trepidation as we took our seats in the Octagonal Lounge for the 'Epilogue'. We opened our hymn books for the first hymn. This room has a unique atmosphere for me and, I suspect, for many others. This is where, as a Community Member, I had listened to high-powered, emotional exhortations and low-key persuasive declarations of the love of Jesus and to clever intellectual expositions of the eternal truth about God and His Universe. It is where I had taken part in so many activities, both religious and social. This unique room enshrined so much of my struggle to be 'good' enough, and the ever-present anguish of blaming myself for falling leagues short of the required standard. There was even an irrational, superstitious murmur of fear lest ghostly spectres from the past might still have the power to invade my precious, new-found inner sanctuary.

The next day we went exploring and marvelled at the transformations which had extended the old buildings to provide additional accommodation and facilities. We rejoiced that these improvements had been undertaken with love, care and sensitivity, to blend comfortably with the original structure in its beautiful setting. I could picture my father leaning on his stick, looking with pleasure at the herd of cows grazing contentedly in the lush pastures, and could see him give a nod of approval at the thriving gardens, still providing fresh fruit and vegetables for use in the kitchens. And that new kitchen, with all its modern appliances – light years from the days of the old coal range with its ovens Mathew, Mark, Luke and John.

We trod the woodland walk to Jennifred's Leap and the zigzag path up to the tower and wondered whether a fox might still be observed frolicking with golden, bushy-tailed cubs on the grassy headland below: the very spot where certain Community members had sunbathed in the nude and where some of us, against all the rules, had staged a barbecue at dead of night.

Lloyda and I had chosen a conference entitled 'Towards More Effective Caring' and, as we listened to the talks and discussions, we were pleased to note that things had moved on since our time. Developments in pastoral care and counselling over the past few years had percolated through to Lee Abbey and were incorporated into the tone and content of the lectures. There were a few die-hards, of course.

The experience of being back in that familiar setting, breathing in the atmosphere of the place evoked so many memories for me and, with the memories, came the pain and, with the pain, came deep sorrow – the agony of the empty womb. It felt as if vital years had been stolen from me – years in which I might have met a partner, married, settled down, and had a family of my own. At my present stage of life I could be enjoying grandchildren. Yet, I was still alone...why? The ever present why?

John Perry was Warden at this time (later to become Bishop of Southampton and later still Bishop of Chelmsford) and my first encounter with him was pivotal. When I introduced myself, the immediacy of his perception of my pain will remain with me for ever. We had a number of talks together but it was that first encounter, the spontaneous acuity of John's insight and discernment and his generous warmth and understanding, that reached that fugitive child and brought healing. It was like being handed a magic key which opened a secret compartment: in that compartment a child had been barricaded and gagged for all those decades. Utterances had been emerging for some time, especially whenever I found myself in a religious setting, but on this occasion it was as if a dam had burst its banks!

Fortunately, I had a tape recorder with me and was able to catch most of the flow which was couched in a child's voice and language:

"I'm muddled about my mummy's God, and it isn't as if there's just one – there are so many. Her Lord, the Messiah, the King, the Master, the Word, the Creator, the Lamb, the God of

Abraham, Isaac, and Jacob, Jehovah, and he sounds a bit of a monster, that one. Then there's the Holy Spirit and the Three that make One, the Father, the Son and the Holy Ghost. There really are a lot of them. I don't think much of my mummy's Lord. He didn't seem to do much for her anyway – she was always so sad, always crying, and if He is her Lord then who is my daddy, he doesn't get much of a look in?

"And these Gods, they are supposed to be such 'clever clogs' – almighty ones, able to do anything – **absolutely anything**! Move mountains, count every sparrow that falls to the ground – and there are a lot of sparrows even in our garden. But they are as blind as bats these Gods – they don't see anything that's really important like a little girl's troubles.

"And all those words. I hate words, specially words from that book [the Bible]. My mummy is full of words, they pour out of her. Often she kneels by her bed and talks to her Lord in a loud voice – you can hear her downstairs – she weeps and wails in pain and in misery, and when she comes downstairs again it doesn't look as if He has made it better. He doesn't seem to make her happy and I sit on her lap and try and iron out the deep furrows on her brow. She feels so heavy and burdened, as if she were carrying a huge sack on her back, like Pilgrim in that other book The Pilgrim's Progress, *except that I thought **his** burden fell off when he got good enough. But my mummy **must** be good enough with all that crying to her Lord and all those things she **doesn't** do 'cos they're bad. We sing, 'I am h a p p y' or 'Joy, joy, joy, with joy my heart is ringing', but if her heart is ringing then why does she look so sad? It must be my fault – I think it must be **my** fault.

"I hate that book [the Bible] – every single word in it is supposed to be true. My mummy and all those funny people who *come to stay with us, go on and on and on and on talking about it, just as if I wasn't there and didn't matter. So many words and then explanations and translations and interpretations of the words – it goes on for ever and ever. And the prayers – they go on for ever too, and you have to crouch down on your knees on the hard floor, with your face in the tickly seat of the chair. It isn't as if the words were nice words – they are long dreary, heavy, burdensome words like justification, condemnation, sacrifice, righteousness, sanctification, redemption – if they were light, bubbly words like Daffodowndilly, Hiawatha, Rushing Water, Minnehaha, that would be different.*

*"And those therapists, they're a bit full of words too. They drown you in words and you have to pay them for doing it. **And** they ask you tricky questions – you just say something innocently and back comes a question; that's not fair – making you pay them to ask you tricky questions. They're supposed to understand about little children and they should know that children don't always have grown up words for things. Some things don't have any words anyway. They are quite like those gods – they can be blind and deaf as well. Quite like my mummy and God. And I don't need those therapists to be like that – I need them to be different.*

*"But that Jesus was a bit different. He took little children and put them on his lap, so he knew a thing or two. And when he went to look for that lamb that had lost itself, he took his crook and went searching for it in the bushes, up hill and down dale, on and on until he found it. **And** he put it up on his shoulder so that it could see everything as he took it home.*

"Yes, that Jesus was a bit different – more like that John Perry. He didn't know anything about me, how bad I was and that

I had a big muddle about gods. He wasn't blind – he saw that I was in big trouble; saw without being told and I shall never forget that. He was such a dear father kind of person – you could have told him anything. Jesus would be more like that – if there was a Jesus.

"But that's not the end of the muddle. There's the Holy Ghost – the Bible says 'conceived by the Holy Ghost' – Jesus was the only one who was good enough and He was conceived by the Holy Ghost. But if God made the world – all in six days – if he made the people and the animals and everything was good – then why did he have to use the Holy Ghost for Jesus? There's nearly a whole chapter in the Bible about begetting, so it can't be that bad. And how did Joseph feel about it as he stood at the manger? A bit left out I guess, rather like my daddy. But the animals don't seem bad and they do ever such naughty things that I'm not supposed to look at. Really there are very funny things they do – they have those magic toys – interesting toys and they all play the game. The bull and the cows, the ducks and the drake, the white rabbits – they all do it but I'm not supposed to look – that's very, very, very naughty, a great big sin frowned upon by my mummy and her Lord.

"But to get yourself all right you have to be born again. Does that mean that you have to get yourself back inside your mummy? That's not going to be easy. Do you have to find a Holy Ghost to help you? And if you do get back inside, you would have to come out again through that rude place which has to be washed with a special flannel because it is so dirty. You're not supposed to know that that place is there, and certainly you mustn't touch it, so I don't know how a child is going to get itself born again, and they say that is the only way into the Kingdom of God. There's no other way – no other way at all, so…

*"And there's another thing – the Second Coming of Jesus – it's just round the corner – it could happen any day, any hour, any minute. The heavens are going to open and the Lord will come down with a mighty shout – like my daddy calling the cows from the top field. The graves will open: all the earth and tombstones scattering in every direction – and the good dead ones will go up into the air first, then the good live ones will join them, and they'll all join Jesus in the sky. But I'm bad – I feel very bad and I haven't solved the muddle of getting myself born again, or have I? And what about my daddy? He does a lot of bad things like shouting at the cows and at me – so perhaps he won't go and I can stay with him. Yes, I'll stay with my daddy. Ah yes – my dear, dear daddy. I had a big, big secret and I lost my daddy but I have found him **again**."*

I had been a dutiful daughter to my father all my life. I knew that he loved me, yet for so much of my existence he had been a blank screen. This had always puzzled me, because I felt that as a small child I may have been close to him. Some trauma had changed this fundamentally. The Psychodrama, recounted in the last chapter, provides a missing link. Something had happened – this child had become split off – a burdensome secret still blocked the way forward. But now my father was a blank screen no longer: it was if time had stood still. He had slotted back into his own special place and all the warm, close, loving feelings had come flooding back. *Yet the child still does not reveal the secret.*

Equally meaningful, some of the child's muddled ideas about Christianity had been emptied out and I felt more whole, more in touch with my central core. I went to each of the wooden benches, that had been placed lovingly 'In memory of Pop' on the lawn in front of Lee Abbey, and along his favourite walk to Jennifred's Leap. I sat for a while on each seat and thought about my father.

As I write these feelings are still with me. I treasure them and a sense of my father's presence, his interest and his encouragement lighten my step. Sometimes a shock has the effect of releasing closely guarded memories. The terror of the hurricane just before leaving for Lee Abbey, most amazingly followed by the meeting with John Perry, did this open secret doors?

PART FOUR

HIDDEN TREASURES

Chapter Fourteen

AFTER LEE ABBEY

– the world starts to turn the right way up

I am writing this chapter just after my birthday which reminds me of another very special birthday celebration. My niece Nikki, who always says that I am treated like the Queen when I travel abroad, describes the occasion in her usual jaunty style:

"The landmark anniversary

"The edict went out: 'Important birthday – one with noughts – to be celebrated in Somerset in May. Everyone to cancel all other engagements and attend; B&Bs all arranged.' The invitation was exceptional in that Betty's friends and family had never been gathered together before and it presented a unique opportunity to discover who fitted into which period of her life.

"The weather was kind and after a visit to Lee Abbey and my grandfather's grave in the Valley of the Rocks, a pleasant pub lunch, and a walk on Exmoor, al-fresco cocktails at sundown on the beautiful lawns of Selworthy Farm were much appreciated. Our second landlady at Selworthy Cottage produced a feast of fresh food and family and friends dutifully moved places at the table at each course. Come the dessert, my elder brother – who has inherited our father's gift to amuse by way of a funny story – stood up to speak. His phone rang; this was strange as none of us were getting a signal in the valley. He listened and we listened in to his conversation. As I remember it went rather:

" 'Hello sir! Yes, your highness! I'll certainly pass on your regards to my aunt for her birthday…and best wishes from your mother, too? Yes, they have been likened to each other, at least on our side. It's kind of you to call, Prince Charles, thank you!' and rang off. It was obviously a spoof but one so cleverly contrived, down to a perfectly timed ringing mobile, and so apposite – it IS, after all, sometimes much like being part of a queen's entourage – that no one will forget the quality of that evening or the rest of the celebrations that followed."

Nikki is right – this was such a special occasion. It was the very first time in my life that I had decided to celebrate my birthday. My friends and family had never met each other and the setting around the green in the centre of Selworthy village was quite perfect. Everybody still talks about it. *That was my eightieth birthday and it feels strange, as I run through this MS for the last time before going to print that I am now planning my ninetieth!*

But back to the story. In total contrast I had spent this birthday in a totally different way – out of doors meandering among the primroses, the wood anemones, the violets and the bluebells; savouring the coming of spring, marvelling at the way in which nature reveals its hidden treasures. The drama of sticky buds on a horse chestnut tree – new tacky buds already fully formed before the dead leaves fall away. I had watched a tree creeper, caught two fleeting glimpses of wild deer and happened upon a troop of horses – thundering hoofs, mane and tails floating in space – galloping round a grassy meadow just for the fun of galloping round a grassy meadow.

I had enjoyed a sense of a continuum. I had felt deeply connected to the child who had her happiest times out in the fresh air savouring the mysteries of Puckwell Wood – this small child at Broadmead Farm who loved to escape from the confines of the house into the freedom of the outdoors. I had tapped into a wonderful feeling of just 'being' – being totally present, completely absorbed in the moment; full of eager curiosity, alert and attuned to nature, optimistically expecting a new discovery to be around the next corner – feeling close to the beauty of the earth, revelling in the freshness of the air, the warmth of the sun. Listening to the silence is a spiritual experience. It creates a sense of awe and wonder – provokes a deep sense of belonging – of being in tune with God and His universe.

A few days later I was driving down to Devon and took a familiar turning off the A303 which led me into the village of West Knoyle. I drove slowly past Broadmead Farm and parked at the edge of Puckwell Wood. Time stood still. I meandered at leisure. As a child I knew all our cows by name and found it especially exciting when they were let out of the barn after the long months of winter. I stood on the very spot where I had watched them gambolling up *that* hill, throwing up their back legs and swishing their tails as if they could smell the succulent new grass in the nearby meadow.

As a child I had always watched eagerly for the first pussy willow, the first snowdrop, the first primrose, the first bluebell, all sure signs that winter was nearly over and spring was on the way. I had loved searching for the very first nest. I counted each egg as it miraculously and mysteriously appeared – especially the blue tit's nest: it was such a snug little home with its neat round entrance hole and soft, downy interior.

I had eagerly awaited the first lambs and liked to mimic their team games as they jumped over little hillocks, contorting their agile bodies as they frolicked around. I had absorbed from animals something primordially basic about the validity of being embodied, having the freedom to express, to follow natural instincts, to exhibit and display, to allow expression of exuberant energy. This was the antithesis of my mother's rigid inflexibility regarding feeling, experiencing, and revelling in the sheer enjoyment of the body. It was as if, at a profound, primal level, I had always known that if God had created everything and it was GOOD, then our bodies must be good, not bad. **I must be good, not bad.**

This was my core self and it still amazes me how authentic this voice is when she is allowed to speak – the sheer authenticity of this small child before splitting due to trauma, layers of imprinting, conditioning and adapting sculpted her into a false shape – moulded from without instead of naturally unfolding from within like a flower gently opening up. Her ability to extract gems of insightful consistency in spite of the constant indoctrination with which she was flooded is as if she was an observer, a secret onlooker sitting on the sidelines, carefully monitoring, sussing out, making up her own mind and filing it away.

This was so humorously illustrated at Lee Abbey when she expressed her views of the Bible! And this is where I link to the last chapter. My experience there marks a change. Miraculously, late in life, when things are expected to slow down, my creative energy started to surge to the surface. My 'tree of life' started to grow new shoots.

Until now, I think my therapeutic journey had been concerned with 'sorting out'. 'Getting it sorted' had been my goal. "If only I could find a way through all the clutter. If only my head wasn't so full of confusion, arguments, contradictions, obsessions and compulsions. If only I could sort it all out I could start to live." This had been my constant endeavour. I felt that I couldn't really start to live until the tangled ball of string had been unscrambled.

But now some daylight had started to penetrate – something crucial had shifted. I began to get a glimmer of what, right at the commencement of therapy, Phillip had referred to as depersonalisation – splitting off due to stress and/or trauma. I had clearly become divided into separate selves: not only were there different selves, manifested physically, emotionally, mentally and spiritually but the lines of communication between the different parts had become intricately twisted, intertwined and interlinked with immense complexity. These parts, in turn, wove their individual tangled webs in the form of transference: not only with therapists, group members and the family but also with the world in general.

I had already started to have glimpses of a different way of experiencing myself but at this milestone a shaft of light lit up my scene. I recognised that the core of my true self was still there, intact under the load of conditioning and experiencing that had deeply affected and shaped me. There was a **'before'** and each time I touched into this primitive **'before'** energy I experienced myself in a renewed way. This 'touching in' gave a different dimension to following the path, because it put certain packages of feelings and certain patterns of behaviour into perspective. I could see and understand how they had come into being and become part of me and this new perspective seemed to make room for new developments. One of these developments was the way in which a workshop in Bill Swartley's training programme – using the technique of Sandplay – grew into a unique resource which I am still using thirty years later.

Chapter Fifteen

SANDPLAY

– *a magical alternative to words*

When I was describing my explorations with Bill Swartley I mentioned that we were introduced to Sandplay in a workshop led by Cecil Burney. This was a momentous landmark for me.

He had brought from the USA a large suitcase containing 'just enough' objects from his extensive collection to give us a taster experience. He demonstrated the way in which pictures, enactments, dreams, and fantasies could be created in a tray half filled with sand. I was captivated…fascinated…excited…spellbound. Here at long last was a way of expressing some of the inexpressible thoughts, confusing imagery, intangible ideas, wistful longings, shadowy ghosts, vague wonderings that defy verbal expression. Here was a way to fill some of the gaps in the confusing preverbal areas when we were fed words yet did not ourselves have this tool at our disposal. Here was a world in which a child could say, "Look! This is *me* – this is what I want to show you – this is what I am trying to tell you."

I knew immediately that I was going to get a sandtray and start my own collection of objects. At the end of the training programme this resolve was deepened by work in Zurich with the late Frau Dora Kalff – known worldwide as an expert in this field.

Sandplay has its origins in the 'World Technique' which Margaret Lowenfeld developed in London in the late 1920s. It was picked up by Charlotte Buhler in the USA and further developed in Switzerland by Dora Kalff, a student of Carl and Emma Jung. In the prologue to her book about Sandplay, Harold Stone, President of the C G Jung Institute of Los Angeles in 1970 writes:

"Personality is seen as having in it a capacity for growth and healing that needs to be freed and allowed to grow and evolve...

"Mrs Kalff brings us a way of objectifying, in the form of symbols, the energy of the unconscious, through the medium of sandplay. This creative evolution of symbolic expression is encouraged to evolve in the child or adult in as free and untrammelled a way as possible. The effect is healing in the traditional sense, but, even more importantly, it leads to the deepest connection to the centre within which is the source of the human spirit...

'The unconscious knows a friend, and Mrs Kalff is a friend to the unconscious as well as to the patient himself. The great need of our time is for people to be connected to the spirit: for people to be connected to a core of feeling in themselves that makes their lives vital and full of meaning, that makes life a mystery evermore to be uncovered."
(*Sandplay*. Dora M Kalff. Sigo Press 1980.)

I was wide-eyed at Dora Kalff's collection of objects attractively displayed around her special room and I immediately recognised a friend of the unconscious. From very deep within myself I responded to her quiet, attentive presence and her sparkling eyes which conveyed the message that everything you revealed would be welcomed, honoured, respected and valued. She gave you confidence to trust that there were deep mysteries waiting patiently to be uncovered and that you yourself knew how to allow this to happen. She was another person, like Bill and Frank, who positively affirmed my search for my whole self and I am grateful to her.

Who can translate into words the meaning of a Sandplay? It is an enactment, an experiencing, a happening, an event, an actualisation. As with drawing, painting and fantasy journeys, Sandplay unlocks doors, opens up new worlds, allows expression to ideas, inklings, whispers, traces, footprints, skid marks, unfoldings – clues that are not yet sufficiently formed to be shaped into words. We are talking about gaining access. Access to our deepest fears and horrors but also to the Aladdin's Cave of treasures which we all have hidden away waiting to be discovered. It is not an instrument of magic but a creative means of manifesting levels of inner knowledge that are not readily articulated. It opens doors, reveals hidden connections, unblocks perception, unveils possibilities, discloses pathways into deeper experiencing.

For me this medium had a natural appeal and even before the training programme had finished I set about starting my own collection with imaginative zest. It included figures of all shapes and sizes – dolls, babies, animals, houses, letters, signs, mythical figures, gods, religious emblems, monsters, dinosaurs, etc. Nowhere was safe from my search. I scoured lanes and bridleways, I trailed along the shoreline searching for interesting shapes, textures and colours; pieces of driftwood, bits of gnarled root, a sinister black glove, the arm of a doll, a battered toy, a child's shoe, an iron ring, tangled rope, seaweed – anything that might possibly fire the imagination and be meaningful in bringing the mysteries of the inner world out into the daylight; anything that might assist a further unfolding to take place.

I developed Sandplay over many years within the setting of Primal Integration groups run by Richard Mowbray and Juliana Brown and I know that the technique can assist this emergence. The joy of Sandplay is its potential for multiformity and improvisation.

One can set out a life panorama or a family constellation, open up a relationship, look at a pattern of behaviour, stage a confrontation, set out the pros and cons of a decision. Subpersonalities, alters, selves – whatever term we care to use – can be explored, choices can be reviewed, dreams or nightmares can be re-enacted pictorially for observation at a safe distance. Rational and irrational behaviour can be examined and the complexity of transference phenomena can be appraised. One can experiment with life on the surface and life under the surface by utilising the drama of hiding objects in the sand or representing a vague sense of something hovering in the wings. The whole spectrum of feelings, moods, fears, anger – in fact any emotion, can find creative expression.

Alternatively one can 'let happen what happens'. Perhaps this is the most exciting way of using Sandplay. Simply give one's fingers permission to pick up whatever captures interest and attention – pause a moment and then allow the selected object to find its place within the tableau. Each choice is a happening – an event – and as successive objects take up position an unfolding takes place – an unfolding which encompasses both the conscious and the unconscious.

There is room for surprises, for dramas, enactments, fantasies, the unknown, the unexpected. Sometimes the sand itself will be contoured to create hills and valleys, lakes and rivers. The scope is enormous. It ranges from clear representations to intricate, complex compositions, from simple peaceful scenes to the ghoulish horrors from which nightmares are made: from jam-packed dramas to the pathos of a solitary figure standing alone in a barren wasteland.

Whether we like it or not – whether we acknowledge it or not, we all have an underground system – an inheritance; our genes and our early environment have influenced our development. Many of us are troubled and concerned about the root problems of mankind. Most of us want to grow to our full potential so that we can most usefully play our part in this deeply troubled universe. Finding out more about how we tick – how we hang together – can help towards a greater wholeness. For some an exploration may reveal trauma, tragedy, horror: others may observe signposts – locations where, for some reason, development has been halted. There can be surprises, hidden talents, unexpected delights, child selves waiting in the wings for playfulness and adventure.

Harnessing positive symbols and anchoring positive experiences assists the release of new vitality – dawn energy in the present. Observing active parts of our personality demonstrated before our very eyes can reveal how we still restrict ourselves or tie ourselves in knots in the here and now. Detecting deeply entrenched patterns helps to free us from their grip. We perceive how the blueprint hangs together, how the system works, which parts of ourselves are engaged in the repetition of familiar negative scenarios. This provides access to allowing an alternative structure to be developed. When a picture, a symbol, an incident, an unveiling, connects directly with our core self, it becomes built in at that site and stays with us forever – a reminder at the deepest level of our being.

An important facet of using Sandplay is to share the completed scene with somebody else, to talk about it, explore it, allow it to speak to you, give permission for deeper layers to unfold, allow feelings to be expressed. Objects that have been considered, but finally discarded, are always worth attention. Why didn't they fit in? Walls, fences and cages are obviously informative and 'so called' accidents, like leaving a gap in a fence or placing figures close together or further apart, tell their own story. Watch for figures or objects buried in the sand and keep track of 'missing objects'.

Eagerly searched for items that I have *not* provided in my collection are usually meaningful and can open up scenarios about deprivation. If this happens, it is always interesting to note whether this leads to initiative and resourcefulness in creating a 'good enough' substitute. One lady was frustrated because my supply of female characters was so limited. She undertook the task of carefully watching girls and women of every type as she travelled back and forth to work and then she created a cross-section of figures, each one beautifully crafted and individually dressed right down to the underwear. After that I wished that someone would find that there were not enough interesting men in my collection and would then take similar action!

Sometimes attention is riveted upon one figure or one area of the tableau and the possibility of change offers a choice. Add something and create a new dimension? Move something and risk the challenge of a chain reaction? Follow the energy and see what happens?

Objects can take on a unique significance, they can embrace magic, convey secret meaning, be messengers, informers, moles, harbingers, heralds; flags marking a spot, secret passwords, connections, watermarks, codes, emblems, clues, logos…

I well remember a series of scenes created over a period of some weeks by someone we will call Molly who was the second of a pair of twins. She had been a breech birth, emerged three months prematurely and existed in an incubator for some weeks. She was often ill as a child and was frequently in and out of hospital. She suffered many traumatic experiences, including sexual abuse. When she relived some of these events, she feared becoming violent or self-destructive. After completing the first sandtray she did not want to talk about it – she just had a powerful urge to break it all up which was, in itself, a significant experiencing. Later she revealed that the foetus attached to the cord and the tiny baby in a stone crib were especially meaningful; also the collection of figures flanked by an ambulance which were buried under a large plastic dome. In the cage were more objects including a mysterious black box.

Molly became distressed as she talked about the second scene in which she had placed a font, some angels and a Bible. It transpired that she had often spent time alone in church as a child and had wandered around gazing at the magnificent colours of the stained glass windows and enjoying the flickering of the candles. She was right back there as she talked, trying to sort out the confused, mixed messages she was receiving. "Something is very wrong but you can't tell anyone," she said. "I am the only one who knows. It all looks so beautiful but how can it be so beautiful when something so bad is happening?" Once again, in the sandtray, objects were hidden: under a raised platform this time. She continued, "The church can't cope with these things, the lid has to go on everything. Everything has to appear how *they* want it to be – it has to fit in like everything else. It has to be neat and tidy – it has to be good." In the tray a heavy iron weight was 'keeping the lid on things' and there was a well, which might have been a symbol of drawing up the water of life but instead, when you peered into its depths, you saw a tiny baby and a large knife. Securely walled in and weighted down under the platform, we found a collection of figures, including twin babies. One had no arms and Molly said this represented herself. The other was her first-born sister. She was different. She got what she wanted – she made her mark by throwing tantrums which amused her parents so she was always able to grab their attention.

At this time Molly was also painting a picture which she was unable to finish, but it was completed by the time she created her next Sandplay scene. The theme of buried objects continued but there was less confusion. Two black authority figures were weighing her down and underneath them a pile of bricks and a giant snake protected a deep cavity. In the cavity, hidden away, for safety, was a delightful little girl with long flaxen hair. She looked quite perfect and her picture gave Molly encouragement for many years.

On another occasion someone we will call Mary had arranged to use the Sandplay corner but after a very long time the sandtray itself was still completely empty. I glanced around at all the display boxes and trays which contained many hundreds of objects. To my complete amazement, all the figures were standing up rather than

21-23 These pictures date back to when I started my Sandplay collection – every day was exciting, searching for unusual objects.

24 (left) This is one of my very early sandtrays when exploring creativity was a new adventure. I am intrigued by the space in the centre where objects have been buried deep under the sand. I like the old well, a symbol rich with potential, and the open paint box.

25 (left) This is Molly's first sandtray. She hated it and had a frenetic urge to smash everything to smithereens. A collection of objects was hidden in the cage and under the dome.

26 (above left), 27 (above right) & 28 (right) Molly's second scene was carefully crafted. In the centre a deep pit had been hollowed out in the sand, skilfully walled in with bricks – a container for secret treasures. A mask was placed on top: "To keep the lid on things," she said.

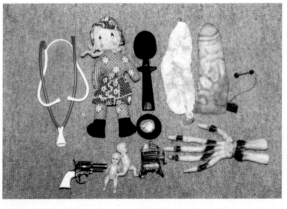

29 (left) It was a long time before Molly was able to lift the treasures out – slowly – one by one. Each told its own story. She was the baby without any arms.

Nos 30 (above) & 31 (right) Lucy says, "Sitting behind bars, yet, the way out is there. This is a familiar figure who has appeared in many sandtrays. Betty had to point out to me that one bar was missing!"

32 (below) Whose eyes?

33 (right) "These figures were a bit like 'Job's Comforters' – people who encouraged me to have an abortion. 'Too many people already in the world,' they said."

34 & 35 "Walking into the workshop that Spring day, I had little idea that I was about to embark on a journey of self-discovery, of expression. Surrounded by shelf upon shelf of miniature figurines, stones, crystals, flowers, pieces of driftwood, lichen, moss, shells, gems, houses, postcards, buttons, everything imaginable. I wondered what I was letting myself in for.

"Running my fingers through the sand. Cool, constant, connecting, calming my racing, pounding heart. Stillness wrapping itself round me, protecting me. Grounded, secure. Time stood still. Safe. Betty's gentle invitation — "see what speaks to you, trust what happens."

"Lost in some timeless internal space I examined the pieces, gently placing any which 'spoke' to me into my tray. Not 'choosing', but reaching for those which reached out to me, placing them without any real purpose in the sand."

"Some screamed at me — too vile to even gaze upon. Wrestling/needing to pick them up but being unable to do so. NO! Other pieces glaring sickeningly, daring me. Buried them — dead, buried."

"It had begun. Much later, my work complete, I gazed at my tray. And wept."

36 "Silent, remorseless tears. Gazing without words.
Stories there, in the sand. Pain – such pain, what agony I felt, allowed myself to feel.
Stories of such unfathomable grief and pain, shameful, sad. I wanted to scream and scream
but not a single word came out."

"But there was not only death and destruction in the tray that day.
There was also birth."

"There's a butterfly symbol of the mind. A
broken mind. A mind that fell to pieces, which
couldn't comprehend, which absorbed the
shame, the filth, which couldn't make sense of
the world as it fell apart.
And all around her illness and death took its
toxic hold.
And of course she was to blame, as she too was
toxic and evil beyond measure.
But beneath her wings, hidden below the sand,
lies a figure.
A tiny little girl.
Her cheeks are red with shame, she scarcely
looks my way."

37 "I stared incredulously upon this child as I gently uncovered her and
the grief which had overwhelmed me, frozen me over the years, began
that day to thaw."

38 (above) This sandtray marked a significant staging post during my journey with Sarah.

39, 40 & 41 (above) These characters all play a significant role in the unfolding of the final chapters of my book.

42 This is the 'Stranger' who appeared during one of my sessions with Sarah and then disappeared for months on end.

43 (above) The same sandtray in reverse (photograph by Trevor Skeates).

44 (right). The nun, symbolic of my mother when she ousted my father from the marital bed and put me in his place.

45 (above) There was nearly always a nativity scene in my Sandplays. I think it represented a secret hope of being born again as a perfect baby!

46 (right) DEPRESSION.

The figure set in stone.

48, 49, 50 & 51. *Every sandtray is unique and it is fascinating to watch the variety and ingenuity of the ways in which the sand itself is contoured.*

Choosing objects is frequently an experience in itself. Placing each item in its chosen position often requires serious deliberation. If one figurine changes place then a chain reaction frequently follows.

lying flat in their boxes. All the male and all the female figures, all the children, all the animals, all the gods and goddesses, all the traffic signs and even the tiniest babies were sitting up and taking notice! Clearly a 'fun child' had been at work – a fun child who had no intention of being conventional but meant to be noticed in her own very individual way.

Rachel has given me permission to include her story. The illustrations in the colour section on Sandplay are of poor quality but this is more than compensated by the moving way in which she reflects upon the complex, disturbing scene which she had crafted in the tray. There is a sense of diverse images having been thrown together in the sand, yet, as she quietly meditates, each miniature plays its own part in an unfolding drama. In gentle, perceptive stages Rachel allows the scene to tell its own story: the unconscious slowly emerges into awareness and enables her to explore in depth through many months of therapy and group work. Much later she was able to reflect upon this important journey as follows:

"What was it that made this work so potent, so revealing?

"Before the sandtray I had never looked at my life it in its entirety – I chose to compartmentalise it, breaking it up into manageable little pieces – that is what survival does. The boundaried sandtray allowed me to see it in its entirety, to face, embrace and conquer, and that brought understanding, as well as permission to be 'me', and the beginning of healing and growth. The sandtray facilitated a process which allowed me to begin to speak, to finally express and tell my stories. It gave me a whole view of my story. I saw it in a new light. It became manageable to see, to deal with, and, most importantly to share. Making the unconscious conscious, both tangible and *visible* was probably the most significant point for me.

"In subsequent therapy and group work I explored the unfolding themes of the experience. Such themes unfolded gradually and naturally during the course of the work; **grounding and silence in relationship, abuse, grief, healing and growth, and rebirth**. My aim throughout this work has been to bear witness to *my own* process, to illustrate the significance of the work *for me* as an adult client, but clearly framing my own story with general notions as to what this might mean for other practitioners is relevant and important.

"Letting the sand slowly move through my fingers had been relaxing, soothing. I remember a peace descending in the silence, and feeling steadily calmer. Sifting the sand somehow took me into a trance like state, where the silence of the room was essential.

"Though silent, I was acutely aware of Betty's presence in the room and this was important – she was the 'silent witness'. It was not necessary for me to share my narrative, but I welcomed her presence. It represented a simple, collaborative view of the client-therapist relationship, which relates with my own person centred approach. There was no need for words, only the silent knowing as we gazed upon the scene. Betty did indeed become a 'midwife', welcoming into the world a part of me I thought was lost. She provided freedom, protection, and empathy so the twin urges toward health and growth could activate healing and individuation.

"Being psychologically held in this grounded, safe space, and the expression of *my own* meaning was significant for me in my work, being simultaneously mindful I was not alone.

ABUSE

"There were objects that day which I found too difficult to even pick off the shelf. Some were so abhorrent I had to leave them there, but that was therapeutic in itself, as it gave me a choice I had never had. Others I transferred to the sand as quickly as I could, afraid that others in the room would see. These I buried as deeply as I could, knowing only one other person, Betty, would ever see what lay there. And it was ironically important to me that someone else saw. Not to discuss or worse, interpret, that would come later, but certainly someone whom I trusted to witness my stories

"It was significant that in the process of my sandtray I *buried* many of the miniatures associated with my abuse. There was for me something liberating in this, as hiding them was associated with both my deep shame, and the emotional burying of those painful memories. It felt reparative to physically bury the figures I had the courage to pick up. It felt as if burying them gave me a means of expressing anger, sadness, disgust and shame. Also, I felt powerful, as if I was taking control for myself.

"This hiding and burying of things and people associated with my own abuse was a significant act for me. Strangely, their power over me seemed to lessen when I could pick them up and put them out of sight. This reminds me of the feelings of dissociation I made sense of even more after my sandtray experience. And though these had indeed been previously explored in therapy there was also something for me about 'seeing' in the sand what I was doing in my life—burying, hiding, covering, 'going somewhere else'. I was also hiding away the many 'little

147

girls' within, who quite clearly were frequently activated. The entire process allowed me to understand this even more.

"For me there was something empowering about being in charge, even if, at this early stage, it simply meant putting symbols of my abuse out of sight.

BEREAVEMENT

"Seeing that pain in the tray, and seeing the reality of the major losses in my life, in some way gave me permission to grieve. There was no getting away from it – the losses through death and abuse were immense, tragedy upon tragedy. But strangely, I also remember the sheer relief of seeing them there – and somehow, in the safety of the tray they became less able to hurt and shame. I could finally allow myself to cry, to grieve.

"Recognising the complexity and harshness of my journey through life and grief was important. I began to make links, rather than compartmentalise events.

"It was as if I finally acknowledged the impact of the grief in my life, and allowed myself to *feel*. In some ways I couldn't continue to deny these monumental events in my life. I *had* to see them and face them, untangling them in subsequent therapy. My grief had never had a voice; I had grown up learning to wear a smile on my face, burying anything that hurt. Again, seeing the representations of those I had loved so deeply somehow allowed me to give my grief expression both in therapy and group work. I was aware of so much grief in my tray, and the sheer relief of being able to express this. Seeing it there gave me permission to do so, for which I was infinitely grateful.

It appears to evoke the deeper places in the body where trauma and grief are stored. Expressive sandtray psychotherapy provided a safe arena for me to process my losses in a number of ways. I recognized how grief and trauma had made me shut down, totally denying my feelings, and in subsequent therapy I was able to express both grief and incandescent rage at my abandonment.

HEALING AND GROWTH

"For me, the entire process of Sandplay and subsequent work in therapy has brought healing and growth. It has been my *experience* that has healed, rather than solely an understanding from the therapist, which fits very well with my person centred philosophy, and the concept of self actualisation. The sandtray has shown me how to cope with distress and pathology but I regard it as the *beginning* of a journey, in fact of many journeys, certainly not the end point.

REBIRTH

"The burial of the little girl, separate from everybody, and interestingly far away from the abusive figures, allowed me to access the separateness I have always felt, and the associated loneliness. Finding and significantly 'seeing and holding' that little girl in the sand was totally astounding. I had 'met' her, and others like her, in therapy before, in moments of deep pain and vulnerability, and she had started to write too, though tentatively. Yet my feelings for her had mainly been those of contempt, no matter how I tried to be compassionate and understanding.

"Here though, buried in the sand, was a tiny child, and as I silently revealed her to Betty it felt like a birth. Together we dusted the sand away and gazed upon her, looking into her eyes in a way I had never done before, never been able to do. Maybe I feared what I would see in those eyes. Perhaps I was afraid she would hate me, hate me for letting her down, for not protecting her. But here she was;

"Tiny, innocent, imploring.

"Lifting her out, and tenderly caring for her, was immensely therapeutic. The impact this had on me was astounding. I found I couldn't part from her, she was so symbolic of something so tender, so beautiful, and so innocent. Her innocence struck me more than anything, an incredibly important part of my healing. I remember wrapping her up gently in a tissue, carrying her as if she was newborn – which of course, she was. I still carry her with me, wherever I go. She was innocent. I had never allowed myself to believe that before.

"The experience somehow opened up other avenues of communication. I cradled something tangible in my hands, and was able to take her into the safety of a growth group at the same conference, where others gazed upon her tenderly, and understood. Having her 'welcomed' both by the group and in subsequent therapy was vitally important to me. She was finally 'gazed upon' in a healthy, healing way.

"The embodiment of someone I knew existed, but could not connect with, was deeply significant and healing. This was a profoundly illuminating stage in my therapy. It was as if gradually things began to make sense, explaining why at times I couldn't speak, couldn't find words, felt 'strange', wrote as if I was a child at times. It all made sense. I don't know if this would have happened without the sandtray anyway, but clearly this was a transformational time for me."

Another client, Matthew had been exploring extensively in the Primal Integration groups. He was born in England and soon after birth developed severe medical problems involving hospitalisation. He went abroad with his parents at six months and returned aged eight to go to boarding school. Here he felt abandoned – a complete misfit. He was also bullied. He understood that, although his mother loved him dearly, she was an inhibited woman who was unable to hold him, cuddle him and fulfil his basic emotional needs. Yet, in spite of much searching, a piece of the jigsaw still seemed to be missing – until he did a Sandplay. This depicted a scene in East Africa where he spent his formative years. As he set the native figures and animals in place, the memories came flooding back. He recalled the affectionate, friendly African servants with whom he had been left for long periods as a small child. They behaved towards him in the same warm, spontaneous, intimate way in which they treated their own children. He, a white child, was totally accepted as one of their race and, as he relived the scene, a cheeky fun-loving Matthew appeared and spent the rest of the weekend beating an African drum.

I asked Lucy if I could use pictures of a sandtray which she had created two or three years ago at a BPF Conference. At the time there was a deep sense of urgency about the scene that she had created: she was aware that these memories were haunting her; they were painful and damaging. The scene in the sand had some vitally important information to impart to her. This slowly unfolded as she observed the tray and led to further exploration.

Lucy's response to my request to use her sandtray in my book was extremely interesting. She had created this scene a few years previously but as she considered the photographs very carefully she had no recollection whatsoever of its meaning. She remarked casually that she only had three children and wondered about the eyes peeping out of the sand. She was disturbed by the small figure crouching behind the bars of an open cage but the core issue upon which the tableau was centred still eluded her.

However, after a few minutes another 'self' suddenly recalled the full impact of the scene. This sandtray had drawn her attention to an event in her life which she had hidden deeply out of sight – an abortion. Tragically, it was the eyes of the lost child which were gazing up at her out of the sand. Lucy decided that the little person in the cage might be asking for her attention and she wrote some captions for the pictures.

More stories could be told but in the next chapter I would like to return to a Sandplay which I crafted around the time of my return visit to Lee Abbey.

CHAPTER SIXTEEN

THE PAINT BOX

– *seeing the world in colour*

I am looking at the Sandplay scene which I referred to at the end of the last chapter. At one end of the tray I had staged a scene depicting many of the key essentials of my personal history – the sources and roots of the early years. But, and this is extremely significant, I had left plenty of space for a mountain range of beautifully shaped pieces of wood, reaching into the sky and beyond. Three boats representing body, mind and spirit were sailing the seas, there was a deep well from which to draw the water of life, a paint box was on hand to symbolically enliven and energise the scene with all the essential colours of the rainbow. A large glowing sun and a cup full to the brim and running over completed the scene.

I still find this panorama heartening and stimulating in its impact. I am inspired and encouraged by the space deliberately designed to depict affirmative, colourful developments and transformations in the future: in particular, the paint-box draws my attention. I have never been clever at drawing or painting but I have often longed to find a way of conveying the beauty, interest or novelty of what I see, feel, or imagine. While I was developing my Sandplay equipment I also discovered that you did not need to be clever at drawing in order to paint – you could just dabble with shapes and colour with gay abandon. You did not need to be able to write in

153

order to tell a story – you could do it in pictures. Or you might even find that you could write! This gave me access to a completely new world of expression and I started to play with paint and collage in a way which was an enchanting pastime.

One of my early pictures depicts the significance of imprints in the sand. Another illustrates a path running through mountainous terrain. This was a collage and I had to fit the sections of the path together in a way which created an unfolding walkway. There was a simplicity about this task that helped, in itself, to sweep some of my clutter out of the way. We arrive in the world with our precious crucible of aliveness – this essential essence of ourselves. We encounter whatever environment awaits us and this environment deeply affects our development during our early years. We are moulded and shaped by it – we carry imprints that cannot be rubbed out. From then on maybe the task set us is to accept our humanity and follow the path; growing and developing within the given situation and attaining whatever degree of wholeness and maturity we can manage. This thought gave new meaning to the undertaking and put 'sorting out' into a new perspective.

When I had completed the picture of the path a child's voice burst out quite venomously and said, "*My path wasn't straight forward!*" So, with incredible energy she scrambled pieces together into another collage, depicting a convoluted trail with all kinds of hazards around every corner. And a third voice chipped in and said, "Perhaps there could be an easier way through," and a picture with steps, doors and windows appeared with comfortable places to sit and rest

I had become very tired of words as a means of communication and exploring in pictures was a revelation. In the past things had *not* been sorted out – they had been undergone, lived through, endured – in fact the past was 'unsortable' but the act of giving it shape and form helped to develop a pathway through the confusion and a growing awareness that I was more than these feelings: I was a person not just a mishmash of responses and adaptations.

I found tremendous satisfaction out of using an alternative medium to words. It was as if my diet of words as a child and again in therapy had built up a resistance to verbal communication. I now found a new world of expression which mysteriously provided me with a more immediate contact with my sources of being. I found myself sorting through old photographs and pictures to create representations of chapters one to four of this story: child selves enjoyed finding illustrative pictures and giving them a voice. An intriguing image in both these collages is a little girl and a little boy sitting side by side looking puzzled. He looks resigned or perhaps numb. She has a small finger up to her mouth and looks puzzled. They can also be spotted in some of the later collages.

It was such fun playing with colour with a freedom that allowed pictures to happen without any preconceived plan or to put pictures together in a way which gave shape to something that had previously seemed intangible. Some of my interpretations were raw, crude and basic; gaping voids, distorted images, and the materials nightmares are made from. There were attempts to express the agony and desolation of unmet needs and the sheer confusion caused by mixed messages laid down by authority figures. But there was also clear identification with the world of the small child: a sense of eager expectation, wonderment, imagination, whimsy – the very essence of 'becoming'. There were pictures depicting vulnerability, fun, colourful energy, the search for truth and meaning.

Looking at the collection now, I can see open portrayal of destructive, violent, ruthless parts of myself, warring, contradictory selves and also wistfully wondering selves who were lost in the fracas. Sometimes I used photography, which was another new interest, to catch my facial expressions – these often portrayed the fathomless depth of my hopelessness and despair, the ferocity of my wrath and the spiteful destructiveness that I had turned back upon myself in self hatred. The play technique helped to link the past directly with the present and helped identify patterns that were still enacting the original scenarios.

I became intensely interested in trees, studying and taking photographs of root formations and the way in which trees grow and adapt in response to location, environment, etc. 'Every tree tells a story' and 'the family tree' generates for each of us the ground work of our personal history. I found it fascinating observing the close link between the root system and the shape and structure of a tree as it developed. I enjoyed creating the collages that form the end papers of my book.

The sequence started when I found a picture of a huge tree trunk with widely splayed roots, set in a forest among bracken and foliage. I had enormous fun cutting out shapes and miniatures and slotting them in among the mass of intricately entangled roots: spooky faces, ghostly images, secret inhabitants of somebody's underworld. Mine? Who knows? However, I have just noticed that the pensive figures of the little boy and little girl are there although they are not sitting together.

What happened when I reversed the foliage and the collage? Lo and behold I saw what could well be a representation revealing all the evidences of environmental influences and deeply imprinted conditioning in this person's life.

I pondered gently upon this picture and found myself imagining a long journey into awareness. Light, colour and energy appeared among the roots' secret inhabitants as their voices were heard and they responded to enlightenment, care and nurture. And, in the upturned version, I found that this surge of awareness had a life force of its own. Something was happening. A secret two-way communication had been re-established. Vibrant dawn energy was being released – more colour, more activity, new images, a sense of being more alive.

Another tool that I found extremely useful was drawing and painting with the non-dominant hand. There is an amusing story of an incident that occurred in a group who were learning this technique. One participant turned to the leader and said, "I don't believe in this nonsense," but as he said it, his left hand was stabbing the pad with his pen and jagged, spiky black lines began to fill the page with venomous, angry strokes! This technique, which uses another alternative means of communication, is useful if something is puzzling you and you are unable to come up with an answer. Asking a question with the dominant hand and answering it in words or pictures with the non-dominating hand can often break the deadlock and provide unexpected responses.

Discovering my creativity and finding an alternative to words removed a jinx. Choosing a selection to include in this book has been a torture. Some of my favourites do not lend themselves to reproduction!

Chapter Seventeen

KODAK INSTAMATIC TO SONY DIGITAL

– an exciting adventure

During this eventful period of my life when I was linking to the springs of my creativity I started to develop a lively interest in East Africa. I had had a taster of the safari scene when I was a travel agent but there was something about this fascinating part of the world, its people and its wildlife that captivated me.

My first snapshots, taken with an old Kodak Instamatic camera, were a bitter disappointment. I clicked away with great enthusiasm but when my snaps were developed I was filled with acute disappointment; they bore no resemblance whatsoever to the wonder of my safari experience. This disenchantment was quickly replaced by an exciting surge of energy and determination. I recognised immediately that the quality of this motivation was inspirational – it came from my roots – the kind of dawn energy that brings projects to life. I had a goal.

Many trips to East Africa and one to South Africa followed. The South African trip was quite an adventure as I hired a car and devised my own itinerary. I started off in Johannesburg, dawdled along the Panorama Route in the Transvaal, visited a private game reserve where they had a hand-reared giraffe who met you at your tent and escorted you to meals, then on to the famous Kruger National Park. A short tour through the Drakensberg mountains was spoiled by continuous rain and mist and, by this time, I was ready to hang out on the beach at Umhlanga Rocks for a couple of days before a rendezvous with an old friend at Port Elizabeth. Then I drove alone down the Garden route to Cape Town and explored this magnificent area with no mishaps of any kind. I loved South Africa but it is East Africa that draws me back time and time again.

I started my photographic project by experimenting with a range of cameras and lenses. I slowly built up a tool box which was adequate for the task I had set myself – to become a good wildlife photographer. I found that professionals were always upgrading their gear and excellent second-hand bargains were on offer in good stores.

Many of us are enthralled by programmes like *Big Cat Diary* and we are aware of the hours of watching and waiting involved in acquiring such perfection, not to mention the kind of budget that allows for miles of film to be binned. So what standard can an ordinary holiday-maker hope to achieve? I was going to find out!

On safari, sharing a minibus or land-rover with fellow travellers, manoeuvring for the best angle, changing lenses and reloading film at critical moments presents a challenge in itself, but it's not just the problem of camera shake, its the frustrating limitation of available options. A perfectly composed scene presents, but the sun is coming from the wrong direction, a brilliantly coloured bird perches on a branch in the sun but flies away just as you have adjusted the focus, a rare animal gazes at you for a split second then deliberately turns and stalks off, or film runs out just as lions are about to mate.

But there were wonderful rewards and it was a great thrill when my first photographs were published in a magazine called *Wild about Animals*. Thus encouraged, I decided to write a feature about wildlife photography called 'Capturing the Wild'. It was about my own experiences on safari and was supported by my own pictures.

Venturing into writing was a strange yet exhilarating experience. All my life I had carried a sense of vulnerability about verbal expression. It was a handicap which had negatively affected my learning ability at school, especially in relation to grammar, literacy and other quite elementary skills. My niece, Nikki, who is a photo-journalist assisted, challenged and encouraged me along the way and the article was finally completed, edited, submitted to a publisher and was accepted first time round. The feature was so successful that it inspired Nikki to accompany me on safari on two occasions and now she is as much in love Africa as I am! In her own inimitable way she describes her first trip:

Travelling with my aunt

"Betty had been making trips to Africa for many years before I joined her for the first time. I'd previously spent years in Southeast Asia and had edited her first Kenya wildlife photo-essay, so I had an idea what to expect. I thought!

"On arriving in Nairobi on her special itinerary, I was soon to discover that travelling with Betty was a bit akin to travelling with the queen. Everyone knew her...or of her. Wide smiles blossomed, favourite rooms were found and luggage was magicked away. I quickly learned the rituals: the first Tusker beer by the pool at the Serena, regardless of the time on the clock; the swift shopping trip to the supermarket for supplies; the writing of postcards. All on Day One and every other day thereafter just as crammed with high energy activity.

"I still think Samburu is my favourite game park, but I'm open to being convinced by the Mara or Amboseli. My favourite snapshot is of the two of us enjoying a picnic safari lunch – with Tusker! – under a Masai Mara tree.

"Like Betty, I am enthralled both by the variety of the

game and the wealth of photo opportunities; the indolent leopard looped over a branch, dappled young lionesses snoozing under a thorn bush; the bright rollers and shy mousebirds. I was overwhelmed when my own camera broke down one time, but Betty generously allowed me access to one of hers. Digital photography has, of course, changed so much and camera cases are, thank goodness, no longer back-breakingly heavy. When Betty discovered the camcorder, everything changed again and now family and friends are treated to unforgettable film shows every year while the staff in each game lodge delight in seeing the footage of themselves even before we do.

"But it's the 'travelling with the queen' aspect that remains clearly with me and probably always will. And, every January, when I get that first postcard from Kenya, I can picture exactly where she was sitting when she wrote it, surrounded by friends and loyal 'subjects' at the Serena poolside."

Needless to say, the publication of my work gave me a great sense of achievement. It was a bit late in the day but I felt as if I had triumphed over all the influences that had put me down, closed my mouth, restricted me and made me feel lacking in ability and intelligence all through my long life.

Another development followed similar lines. Ponies had featured in our childhood and my pony was my closest friend and confident; much nearer to me than the humans in my life. I have always maintained an interest in equestrian events, specially show jumping and eventing and I was commissioned to write a feature covering the thirtieth birthday of the All England Jumping Course at Hickstead – a sporting spectacular which attracts famous individual and team riders from all over the world. Nikki edited this and the photo-essay was published in the prestigious glossy *Singapore Tatler* with a satisfying spread of my pictures. Other opportunities opened up.

The pleasure generated by these achievements was out of all proportion to the events themselves – an outlet had been uncovered for the development of parts of my self that had been nipped in the bud in childhood. Back then, early shoots of essential development, progression and expression were not nurtured, encouraged and affirmed, so did not flourish, bloom and reach maturity. Now I was catching up – establishing another outlet in which I was directly connected to the child who had loved the outdoors and had been fascinated with all living creatures. I quote from my photo-essay:

> "Watching exotic animals against the backcloth of their natural habitat – spectacular scenery which changes from hour to hour – is the most fascinating adventure. Attempting to capture the magic of these experiences on film can only be exciting, exhilarating and rewarding.

> "You never know what may be lurking around the next corner and an ongoing sense of expectancy keeps you perched on the edge of your seat. It may be a pride of lions lazing in the dappled sunlight, or a herd of ambling elephants. A timid dik-dik may gaze at you curiously for a split second before disappearing into the undergrowth, a flash of colour may be a Lilac Breasted Roller alighting spectacularly on a nearby tree."
>
> ('Capturing the Wild' by Betty Hughes. *Choice Magazine* 1992. Copyright Betty Hughes)

Over the years I have come to love East Africa, especially the warm, friendly Kenyan people who always welcome you with a smiling 'Jambo'. I receive an affectionate welcome in many places and have become especially interested in the Samburu culture where I have watched with great interest the slow development of educational opportunities. I admire the integrity and honouring of life that has been passed down from generation to generation. I respect the dedication of individuals who have worked their way to university level, yet have retained a deep loyalty to their traditions and a determination that this culture will be honoured and respected in the future. I love the wide-eyed joy of the children who need no encouragement to sing proudly to you their latest song and the friendly politeness of those who look after your well-being and comfort with so much grace and charm. I sometimes wonder whether in a previous life I may have lived among the wild beauty of the African bush but who knows? I do know that Africa will never lose its magic for me.

I am adding a note as I do this final check of my manuscript. In the light of the final chapter of my book I am smiling. The comely black child who played such an important role in my exploration could, so easily, have come from Kenya!

Way back in my sixties I had decided that learning to use a computer was way out of my range – even the thought of mastering the technology made my mind boggle. My latest photographic venture was the purchase of a digital camcorder which involved learning to use a PC, and mastering the mysteries of editing software. This has enabled me to capture the magic of Africa in a form which is easy to share with others. And it is such fun! Not only can you capture the whole sequence of a lion tearing the carcase of a wildebeest to pieces, but you can also hear the actual crunching of the bones! I was elated when a major British tour operator decided that I had captured the spirit of the safari scene so well that they would like to use my movie in training sessions for their African sales staff. My video brought the safari scene to life in a way that enabled them to market this rather specialised kind of holiday more successfully.

Chapter Eighteen

GIVING OUT AND TAKING IN

– *a two-way flow*

Exploring in all these creative ways, including Sandplay, over many years meant that I had accumulated a wonderful collection of resources that I now use in what I believe to be unique workshops. When I stopped assisting in groups in London, I started, with the help of colleagues, Tim Brown and Susan Jordan, to run workshops under the heading of 'HIDDEN TREASURES – a journey into awareness'. It has been a source of great pleasure to have other people delight in all the treasures that I have accumulated.

Hidden Treasures lie within all of us and a spirit of curiosity and wonderment can sometimes unlock doors which may not give way to more direct pressure. The workshop programme has an easy flow and the space is designed to allow child selves to play and explore. The innocence of relaxed, unstructured playfulness, which is such a pivotal phase in a child's development, is something that many of us were denied. Instead, our energy became intrinsically engaged in basic survival, adapting to our environment and scratching a living.

These workshops have now developed and expanded and I believe that they will continue after I have moved on to pastures new. Susan, a Core Process Psychotherapist, who is also a Focusing teacher and a writer, made a brilliant contribution in the early days. She is still closely associated with us but just at the moment she is too fully occupied to take an active part in our programmes. She has been replaced by Anna Clarke who is trained in expressive art therapy and has worked with individuals and groups, including children, for twenty years. Anna is very widely experienced and is an excellent group leader. I am happy to say that she is slowly allowing my leadership mantle to fall upon her shoulders. Her wide experience, her enthusiasm, her delight in the sheer magic of creative materials makes her an invaluable member of the team.

Tim Brown is well known for his expertise in the field of music, dance, authentic movement and bodywork: he is a leader who can create atmosphere. He combines light and shade, drama and comedy – all laced with humour and a delightful sense of playfulness. As a bodywork facilitator clients experience a solid, rocklike quality in him which is combined with acute perception and sensitivity.

We offer a wide selection of resources – Sandplay, artwork, including paint, collage, clay and a range of exciting decorative materials, toys and masks, and even a play pen that presents an opportunity to view the world from the perspective of a toddler.

The atmosphere is quite unique in the way in which it is possible to flow quite naturally between all the different resources at will. The energy released in crafting a picture might find further expression in dance or bodywork. A scene in the sandtray might develop into dialogue and role-play and there are always other people who are willing to join in and play a part. Focusing on an interesting image can increase awareness of its significance and this often leads to a further unfolding. In fact, it is the multiplicity of the resources, the interplay between them and the deep bond which develops between the participants that makes the workshops unique.

Appreciative group members have written:

> *"Hidden Treasures offers the very rare opportunity for grown-ups to play like children. The resources available are rich and varied, the facilitators present, available yet unobtrusive. It gave me the chance to connect with a deep and rarely accessed place of colour,*

shape, energy and joyousness which was life-changing. The mixture of music, movement and visual and sensual stimulation worked a kind of magic for me which gave me a brighter and wider view of my life and my relationship to it, I will never forget my first encounter with hidden treasure."

"I like the atmosphere in your workshops – the environment feels safe – there is no pressure – just freedom to explore and 'let happen'. The diversity of your vast collection draws me like a magnet."

"I sometimes move on to collage (all those boxes of cut-outs – a world of possibilities just there for me to choose from) or I might dabble with clay or muse among the remarkable display of pictures. The rich collection of Art Materials encourages adventures in colourful daubing or artistry."

"I enjoy the special interludes of music, movement and dance (especially with all the toys and masks lying around inviting playfulness), but it is so unusual to find oneself absorbed in some kind of creative activity and then, spontaneously, just like a child, sprint across the hall and express my feelings in music."

"All three facilitators are on hand to listen, to support, to encourage, but, what is equally important, there is an easy sense of freedom to talk or not to talk. To open up or not to open up, and this is one of the things that makes it safe to experiment, or to venture into new territory."

"Hidden Treasures it certainly was. There was

room for joy, sorrow, anger, grief and indeed every aspect of human experience was skilfully welcomed with loving awareness, explored and expressed through an amazing array of resources, which had been lovingly collected, collated, arranged and offered to us to provide a cornucopia of abundance of colour, texture, shape, and, most of all, of exciting possibilities to stimulate the creative imagination."

"Coming from a 'hard core' group therapy background where people go through big catharsis and emotional expression I never thought that this softer format could uncover so much depth. But I have to say that it was one of the most powerful weekends that I have ever been on, the quality of energy prevalent in the final closing circle was very rich and loving."

This is clear evidence that people have been stimulated and inspired by what is offered in our Hidden Treasures days and weekends and this gives me deep satisfaction. It makes me feel that my journey has paid off. But it is also important to mention that I have found it imperative to look for interesting and stimulating experiences to further my own growth and development. One of these was The Hoffman Process, a unique course devised by Bob Hoffman. This process is distinctive in a variety of ways and *distinctive* is the right word to use: in particular because people seem to find it equally valuable when they are totally new to personal growth or if they have been journeying the path for some time. Some individuals find it a 'Damascus Road' type of experience because such a remarkable change takes place: their way of being themselves in the world has changed so radically. Others experience a less dramatic outcome but I defy anyone to come away being exactly the same person as when they arrived.

I found the Hoffman an adventure – there was always a surprise around the next corner and this was exciting. The unique format for looking at one's family constellation gave me a new angle on my early childhood. It underlined, with deeper significance, my early experience: I had seen 'my mother's Lord' as a member of my family. It was 'Mother and her Lord' and my father – a grouping that left me no option but to compartmentalise my relationship to them. It still moves me deeply to catch the deeply puzzled look on the face of the small child as she ponders, "If Mother is married to her Lord then who is my father?"

Another aspect that was highlighted by the unique structure of the programme was the sheer depth at which I was enfolded – as if by the tentacles of an octopus – in shame. *Shame* had me locked in its grip from the beginning of time and there is something indelibly awesome about the power shame has to mould a child's view of herself and her world.

It was a delight to find that child selves were warmly welcomed during the unfolding of the process however they might decide to make their presence felt and 'my lot' were not slow to take advantage of this opportunity – especially to rebel! Every therapeutic model has its own descriptive language and my child selves were puzzled by the terminology used in the Hoffman Process to express both psychological and spiritual aspects – so totally different from my mother's Christian vocabulary and other personal growth models but equally bewildering to my child participants! But this was useful because a very determined character decided to stick to her own path and this was totally accepted without question.

In fact, it was this total acceptance of me, in my many parts, that made the most lasting impression upon me. Because of my history the word 'love' has been deeply contaminated and distorted both as a verbal expression or as a manifestation of true affection and caring. In the Hoffman Process, expression of an extensive range of emotions was encouraged, each person was respected, supported and nurtured, child selves were welcomed, honoured and accepted. Spirituality was an essential ingredient and there was something about the quality of the total experience that gave me a sense of being generously loved, affirmed and sent on my way with a bounce in my step. In fact, as a result of this experience I found that I could dance without feeling inhibited.

It is now more than twelve years since I did the Hoffman Process but I often go over to Florence House in Seaford to share 'Closure' with new graduates as they are about to emerge from their eight-day marathon. I am familiar with the unique journey they have undertaken and I love to share in the bond of loving care which pervades the group and their teachers. I receive such a warm welcome and as I am probably the oldest person to have done the process I am often asked to chip in and say my piece! It is always received with applause and I leave with added enthusiasm for the journey ahead.

When Tim Laurence published his book You Can Change Your Life *in 2003 he wrote on the fly leaf "Dear Betty, thank you for being one of the most playful young-spirited people that I have had the joy to meet. Onwards! Love. Tim"*

Another encouraging venue for me has been the Bridge Pastoral Foundation Annual Conference – a residential, five-day event in which a well known guest speaker introduces a given topical subject which is opened up for discussion and debate. A wide choice of workshops is available but the most significant feature is when the large group splits up into small gatherings in which deep experiential exploration can be undertaken. Each small group is led by two skilled facilitators who are supported by experienced supervisors. This is a system devised by Frank Lake and is of tremendous value. A deep atmosphere of trust and safety develops in each group and space is offered to each individual to explore in wide-ranging ways. I am amazed at the depth and breadth of the work undertaken in this unique setting. In some other growth groups or even in individual therapy one sometimes senses a resistance to venturing too deep into ones primitive roots but this is not the case with BPF. One feels safe and supported in following the path wherever it goes.

I find that growth is an on-going process – the journey of life is never completed and I treasure this resource. As already recounted it was in this setting that I re-discovered my loving relationship with my father.

For several years now I have taken the Sandplay to the annual conference and this was where Rachel created her sandtray, which is described in Chapter Fifteen. It has been an optional extra, a facility which participants have been able to sample during the afternoons. This works really well because when the scenes that have been created are quietly observed, insight often dawns or emotions rise to the surface. Sometimes particular objects are found to be of special significance and all these aspects can be taken to the small group setting and explored further. In 2008 Anna Clarke enjoyed taking the Sandplay to the conference ably assisted by Kitty Willis.

BPF Conferences are going to feature again later in my story.

PART FIVE

DOES MY STORY HAVE A CONCLUSION?

CHAPTER NINETEEN

WHO AM I?

– I face the ultimate question

It is a challenge for me to embark upon this chapter and I have resisted settling to the task. Why? Because I see myself as a contender who has run a marathon over many decades: run a marathon as a dogged personality made up of a motley collection of colourful 'hangers-on' who trail behind, boosted by a dogged determination not to give up, yet still able to toss a cheeky quip to curious bystanders.

My resident observer often gives serious consideration to where I am on the path of life, yet it is no simple task to span the years and remain totally impartial and non-judgemental. A spiteful critic is one of the squatters in my inner sanctuary – with an age-old voice that always pulsates with self-blame, condemnation and dismissive judgements – a voice that not only gratuitously hands out a never-ending commentary but is also partial to 'should be, could be, might be, ought to be' remarks that serve no useful purpose whatsoever.

Slowly, over the years, the tone of this voice has softened and mellowed. It has been outwitted by the light of truth. Insight regarding my personal history has opened up deep understanding regarding the intricate complexity of my inner world. Immaturity, disharmony and the dissonance of deeply warring factions have been exposed and this illumination has revealed the degree to which I have been at the mercy of deeply imprinted, profoundly entrenched influences. A power on the throne of my life has manifested itself in repetitive patterns: has deceived me into thinking that I have no power to choose and has left me with deeply rooted trigger points that have the muscle to colour my feelings and distort my responses in the present.

This insight and understanding has revealed the way in which conditioning throughout my early years has shaped and moulded my development – an insidious, unrelenting influence during the most formative period of my life. There is a merciless, implacable quality to this kind of indoctrination; a tortuous twisting of reality, an insemination of doubt that eats away at the trustworthiness of perception. When a child has not bonded with her mother and subsequently receives mixed messages; sees, hears, feels and perceives things that do not add up, the senses are battered by a cacophony of invasive data which is beyond the child's power to process into any kind of order. This results in a distortion of truth during the most formative, 'becoming' chapter of the child's life: a phase during which she or he has a vital, foundational need for good role models, life-giving nurture, affirmation, support and encouragement.

It is challenging to put into concise, simple words just how fundamentally this brainwashing penetrated to the very core of my being; how deeply ingrained this distorted image of myself became – just how basically it obscured my view of my true self. An image of a whirlpool comes to mind representing a source of energy mysteriously emanating from a centre far below the surface and visibly revealing itself in ever-widening circles.

Yes, much essential enlightenment has dawned and this illumination has not only resulted in more wisdom, tolerance and acceptance but has also opened up a deep fascination and curiosity about the mystery of life itself. It raises legitimate questions: when we accept that we have been affected both by our genes and by the imprinted experience and conditioning of our early years, how much do we have the power to change in significant ways? How much can we make good? How much re-learning is achievable? History cannot be rewritten but how much of our original potential can be recouped, reclaimed and what assists this reclamation? I remember Phillip telling me very early on in my therapy that radical personality changes did not take place in people after the age of fifty years. Very encouraging news when I was already in my late forties at the time!

There is a wonderful prayer that often comes to mind when I mull over these weighty matters:

> "Grant me the serenity to accept the things I cannot change, to change the things I can change and the wisdom to know the difference."
>
> (Attributed to Rheinhold Niebuhr. 1936.)

I ponder deeply upon the profound question, "How can I develop the wisdom to know the difference?" Sometimes I do a review which goes something like this:

"I have diligently studied my personal history. I have had many years of individual psychotherapy with (with one exception?) well established, well respected practitioners and I have also benefited from participation in a diverse range of models of growth work. Exploration has opened up the area of 'The Primal Scream' – wide-ranging fear and dread of the unknown, obdurate frustration and intense rage, pain, emptiness, loss, the blight of deadness, the dreariness of guilt and the heavy persistence of shame.

"Further careful study has revealed the plight of a child deprived of essential nurturing – a child whose development was shaped by her environment – a child who continued to use the safety device of splitting when the 'elastic' holding body, mind and spirit together was overstretched. Above all, a child who, with dogged determination, in spite of all odds, in the most secret fortress of her being, has managed to protect herself and keep herself intact. In spite of traumas, indoctrination and unrelenting conditioning. truth has revealed the area of 'The Primal Laugh' – the amazing discovery of this core self which, at the beginning of my therapeutic journey I didn't know existed. An essence, an essential life-force, a fundamental source of sentient energy and motivation, a flow of just 'being' instead of merely existing – an ability to live in the present. An Aladdin's Cave of hidden treasures.

This is a way of experiencing myself that has all the essential know-how for a late blossoming; a self who is much younger than my years, one who thinks that the word 'wonderment' is one of the most precious words in the dictionary. One who loves to dance, an earth mother who knows how to mother and support, an artist who loves playing with colour. A fun self who can mix socially without misery-making self-consciousness and angst. A self who wakes up with a sense of wonderment and excitement about what may be around the next corner – a light-hearted expectation that what has to done can be accomplished without a weighty sense of pressure. Days filled with a vibrant feeling of being alive instead of poised upon the edge of death – that dreadful state in which an overshadowing sense of doom and gloom lie in wait around every corner, every minute of the day. In this remarkable experience of resolution I am remarried to my past – continuity has been re-established."

This is the end of my soliloquy!

Yet the bitter truth is that I am unable to live in this space all the time. Why? Why? Why? A chemical imbalance? Who knows? There is so much that even the experts do not know or understand about the workings of the human brain and the question intrigues me and fascinates me; tantalises me and frustrates me.

This pivotal experience, after the revelation in therapy of the abuse by the gipsy, in which I enjoyed being truly alive for the very first time lasted for about three months. The experience has remained in focus – it represents a mainstream event ; a highlight of truth – nothing has the power to render it null and void. I was reconnected to the source of my being, I was no longer living through a grey fuzz, I knew who I was, I was attached to my own

176

Travels with a camera

52 (above left) Cheetahs are one of the most
spectacular, yet elusive animals one may be lucky
enough to see on safari.

53 (above right) I like this picture because his royal
highness clearly posed – just for me.

54 (right) Possibly everyone's favourite lion picture
from my collection of hundreds; my nephew has even
made a fantastic oil painting of it.

55 This is the dream elephant picture: seldom does one have the family, the matriarch, the
dust **and** the mountain all in shot at the same time.

56 (above left) My niece Nikki and I on safari in Kenya. Nikki's caption for this one reads: "This picture always reminds me how well-loved my aunt is in all the game lodges she visits. Queen Betty gets special treatment with a cold lunchtime Tusker smuggled into the wagon by our favourite driver Maina."

57 (top right) The quintessential hippo shot; they spend most of the time underwater but it is eerie to meet them when they come out of the water at nightfall and feed on the lawns of your lodge. This picture was taken while eating eggs and bacon beside the Mara River at Governor's Camp.

58 (above) Driver guides love quizzing their passengers and a favourite topic is antelopes; there are so many varieties. The Beisa Oryx, with its handsome face and elongated polished horns is one of the most elegant of the species.

59 (left) Possibly one of the rarest of giraffe photo opportunities, taken, I seem to remember, in Tanzania.

60 *(left) This rather tattered copy of* Choice *contained my first illustrated article on Kenya and it often travelled with me. The staff at The Intrepids in Samburu were excited when they recognised family members – in print – in an English magazine!*

61 *(below) I always debate whether this is a good picture to include in all its gory splendour, but it is Africa and African wildlife can be raw.*

62 *(above) A lilac-breasted roller in full song. A pity the picture is badly framed.*

63 *(above) It is not hard to guess which of my 'selves' likes taking pictures of animals mating, but often the most comical of expressions occur when the subjects have their minds firmly on something else!*

64 (left) Cows are an integral part of the Swiss landscape and the annual Spring procession of the cows from the lower pastures to the higher alps is heralded by the sound of cow-bells. Everybody gets out of bed to cheer them on their way.

65 (right) A stunning view in the Bernese Oberland looking towards the Wetterhorn and the Grosse Scheigegg. The Spring flowers lured me there year after year and often family members too.

66 (left) When I think of all the gentian pictures I have taken over the years I am disappointed not to find a better one. The first gentian spotted on the first Swiss walk each year is always a cause for celebration.

67 (above) *What a sunset. For many years I watched every mood of the setting sun from my balcony.*

68 (above) *The Bank at Hickstead, the All England Jumping Course; truly the most terrifying of fences requiring consummate skill from horse, rider and photographer. This is how it should be done! What you don't see is the fence only fifteen metres from the bottom of the bank.*

69 (above) *My niece Nikki tells me she always stops here, halfway down the toll road above Porlock Weir in Somerset. I know the exact spot and if you are lucky Exmoor ponies will be grazing nearby.*

70 (right) *I took this photograph to show to Sarah the first time I saw her. It describes depression perfectly: a black cloud descends and blots out the sun – as if for ever.*

First adventures into creative artwork

71 I can still recall the excitement of making my first collages: sorting out the old photos,
finding the old copy of Pilgrim's Progress with the pictures that were still vividly alive to
my child selves. This is where we first glimpse the little girl and little boy who were to
reappear regularly, puzzling over the ambiguities of life.

72 My 'selves' derived much pleasure from writing their chosen captions! Seen from this vantage point I am awestruck by the collection of boxes labelled 'Failsafe Security Systems'. What an ingenious way of describing Dissociation!

73 When a child is relentlessly presented with mixed messages, spontaneous communication is out of the question: survival depends upon endeavouring to read expressions, trying to decipher what eyes are telling you, picking up deeply secreted vibes. There is no secure resting place – anywhere.

lifeline. Yet, without warning, within the space of a couple of hours, the heavy oppression returned like a thick grey cloud drifting across the sun. I was back in the deadness – the familiar greyness in which my spirit does not flow and everything is an effort – as if to get anywhere I have to push my own car.

Since then my life has been a strange mixture of living in the light and living in the darkness. The contrast is clear cut. When the light is switched on it feels that the darkness can never return. When I am in the darkness it feels as if the light can never return. This applies to the whole house of my being. Yet, as truth has slowing unfolded, the light switch has turned itself on in certain clearly defined areas – travelling, creative writing, the Sandplay, Hidden Treasures and being privileged to be alongside people in their life scenarios.

So where is the mains switch? I am aware that trauma stops the chronological clock. I am aware that this trustworthy device, scientifically designed to cut out when overloaded, came into play at the time of my birth and at several subsequent sites of trauma. And yet, locating these areas of splitting, reliving, re-experiencing the packages of emotion involved has only given me temporary respite. Why?

This is where time and time again I get stuck. It has taken me decades to come to a place of rest and accept myself as I am and an additional aspect that is especially intriguing is this – **deep shame about still getting stuck persistently dogs my footsteps and adds weight to the burden.**

In a strange way being involved in personal growth work has made the affliction seem particularly shameful. Even my enlightened inner critic can still say, "Surely you should have moved on by now – you should be more whole and no longer afflicted with these mood swings." But I suffer from depression and have to learn how to live with this problem. This is the simple truth. At long last I acknowledge that I am a normal, fallible human being whose intricate system has reacted in a logical way. I recognise that

I have achieved a degree of 'wholeness' involving recognition, acceptance, and delicate balancing of certain component parts – emotional, intellectual, physical, and spiritual. But I still suffer from depression.

This is where my book goes into hiding once again.

Chapter Twenty

MY BATTLE WITH DEPRESSION

– and what a battle!

When I am depressed, feelings of dread and darkness claim the right to define my reality. Rather than being *part* of my truth, with a distinctive contribution to make to the whole, these feelings envelop me. I disappear. For no apparent reason, although I am aware that at some level that there must be a logical explanation, when this switch is activated I find myself in a greyness that has the power to extinguish light – to blank out colour and distort truth. It is misery-making. It is a 'forever' state of not being fully present, feeling detached, not operating from my core.

Life becomes a wearisome, tedious effort to do simple things. It involves never-ending lists of tasks to be undertaken; lists that are repeated the next day with ceaseless repetition. It makes every day seem a lifetime. It involves doing all the simple things that you know give pleasure but doing them almost as an observer. It makes sleep the only refuge, yet even this sanctuary becomes a troubled haven of anxiety in the early hours of the morning, shadowed by the dread of waking up into a repetition of the on-going dreariness.

There are also obsessive, compulsive sidelines to depression that are equally dreary and frustrating: in my case the monotonous tedium of eating disorders – the fatal attraction of comfort eating and drinking, a pattern fully understood at cerebral level but totally dismissed in the mindset of a deprived child who still insists upon getting *something*.

I have already mentioned how useful I have found the small groups at the Bridge Pastoral Foundation Conferences. During one group I set up a very revealing sculpture. It arose out of a confrontation with the two female facilitators who were leading the group. I perched one leader high up on a chair to represent my mother's Lord; the second leader was cast as my mother, kneeling humbly at His feet, looking up at Him adoringly and bound by a solemn promise to do His will whatever that might be. She was offering me up to Him. I sat on the floor beside my mother, clinging on to her even though her face was turned away from me. I was highly dependent upon her and deeply concerned when she turned towards me and I felt the full weight of her sadness. My little fingers gently tried to smooth the furrows from her brow.

On the far side of the room I put my father, comfortably relaxed in his armchair, reading his newspaper. The scene unfolded and I became increasingly troubled, tormented, tortured – yes, torture is the right word – desperately needing to stay close to my mother, yet also wanting to move over to join my father. I was physically and emotionally wrenched apart – agony twisted my guts. I was caught between the three of them with a force that wrenched my arms out into the form of a cross – a position of never-ending push and pull. Occasionally, in small child mode, I would break free from my mother, creep over to my father and tap on his newspaper to gain his attention. But, in no time at all, a compulsive wrench deep in my innards forced me back and I was clinging on to Mother again, with occasional looks of pure venom directed towards her Lord.

I have expressed pictorially, with great satisfaction the on-going battle which developed between my mother and myself around the fundamental, basic essentials of life. In individual and group work I have found a safe environment in which to give expression to extremely primitive desires to bite, to draw blood, to tear apart with my teeth, to destroy with murderous rage, my mother's tantalising breast. These primitive instincts then became turned back onto myself and my own body; hate turning into self-hate, loathing into self-loathing. Wanting to draw blood has been experienced as a frenetic impulse to tear my own skin into shreds. I am reminded of a quotation from a book by Melanie Klein in which she writes:

"One of the most fundamental and far-reaching discoveries ever made in human history was Freud's finding that there exists an unconscious part of the mind and that the nucleus of this unconscious mind is developed in earliest infancy. Infantile feelings and fantasies leave, as it were, their imprints on the mind, imprints that do not fade away but get stored up, remain active, and exert a continuous and powerful influence on the emotional and intellectual life of the individual. The earliest feelings are experienced in connection with external and internal stimuli. The first gratification which the child derives from the external world is the satisfaction of being fed. Analysis has shown that only part of this satisfaction results from alleviation of hunger and that another part, no less important, results from the pleasure that the baby experiences when his mouth is stimulated by sucking his mother's breast. This gratification is an essential part of the child's sexuality and is indeed its initial expression. Pleasure is experienced also when the warm stream of milk runs down the throat and fills the stomach.

"The baby reacts to unpleasant stimuli, and to the frustration of this pleasure, with feelings of hatred and aggression. These feelings of hatred are directed towards the same objects as are the pleasurable ones, namely, the breasts of the mother."

(from *Love, Guilt and Reparation* by Melanie Klein, Hogarth Press. Reprinted by permission of Random House Group Ltd.)

But, looking back, I can see that there was also a secret undercurrent of conspiracy in my life with my mother. A sly, furtive contest in which I gained points with subtlety and deviousness. I drew great satisfaction from playing this game. It had many ramifications, and, needless to say, I have continued to play the same game with myself in my inner and outer world.

Mother was dead set on keeping me clean and I derived exquisite pleasure from getting as dirty as I could in the shortest possible time. I can easily picture the look of disgust on her face as she turned her nose away from a particularly smelly nappy. I can also imagine the look of glee on my small face when, as soon as possible, I soiled the freshly scrubbed nappy with the fragrance of my own precious essence.

I used to creep secretly into the dining-room, stealthily open the sideboard cupboard and then delight in sticking my little finger into the honey jar. I even pinched pennies from her purse if she left it lying around. At meal times I liked to crouch over my plate, sorting out and hoarding the most tasty morsels – keeping them till last. If I had an iced cup-cake I would very carefully slice off the top, eat the sponge and then, at the very end, relish the gorgeous, sugary stickiness of the icing. But this was strictly forbidden; it fell into the category of self-indulgence or gluttony.

I loved scrumptious goodies like fresh, warm bread which I held close to my face when I fetched it from the bakers, crumpets dripping with golden, creamy butter, cakes, biscuits, chocolate, clotted cream and jam, crispy bacon, cheese on toast – all rich delicacies high in calories and cholesterol. I still find it rather mean that these foods should be bad for one's health and leave unfortunate rolls of fat on one's figure.

In theory I had identified some of the usual connections with eating disorders, bulimia, etc. such as compensating, comfort eating, filling up the void, a need for perfection, giving myself a reward, an investment in not looking my best, a need for sustained conflict, an issue of control, a substitute for sex, etc. One could go on – I am sure there are even more aspects that have been drawn to my attention at some time or another as I have battled through the years with the never-ending ding-dong of putting on weight and taking it off again.

My stuck place included many aspects: depression, an underlying murderous rage which had the power to explode like putting a match to the touch-paper of a firework, an ever present battle regarding food, the complete defencelessness and vulnerability of a helpless infant and, sometimes piercing through the ether, a small piercing voice echoes down the ages, *"Look, I am stuck here for ever, push/pull between Mother and her Lord and my father. I've been denied so much – allowed so little. I will have something nice. I deserve it. I have a right to it. To hell with the lot of you. I'll have it now!"*

It still amazes me that I continue to remain stuck in this pattern. I was going to say that I have tried all of the countless useful devices on offer to help with depression but that would be an arrogant presumption. But I haven't sat idly by. I have made gigantic efforts to find a solution, and, strange as it may seem, at long last, an answer presented itself.

I went to see my GP one day. He didn't know much about my personal history but I have known him for a long time and was able to sit in his chair and rant on about my weight problem – in particular the fact that it was such a battle ground. I was intensely angry and frustrated because I always end up in this stuck place and in spite of all the years of personal growth work I couldn't find a solution.

And then, to my great surprise, I found myself briefly disclosing the fact that many years ago I had been sexually abused by a psychotherapist. It is deeply significant that I shall always remember the spontaneous reaction of my GP as I started to tell him about this relationship. He immediately moved away from his computer, sat face to face, leaned forward in his chair and listened. There was something special about this simple gesture that touched the heart of a deeply wounded child. It was similar to her response to John Perry on her return visit to Lee Abbey.

After listening to me with rapt attention, he gently closed the subject by saying, "There's nothing you can do after all these years," to which I had replied with a surprising burst of energy, "I shall do *something*." Then, taking me totally by surprise as I uttered those very words, my right arm suddenly shot out across his desk as if to grab hold of something. It made us both jump – my GP instinctively pushed his chair back!

On reflection, I think that this spontaneous physical manifestation was pivotal to the opening of a new chapter. In the telling, in that particular setting, I think it dawned upon me for the very first time that Philip had committed a criminal act for which he could have been sent to prison, and, by extremely odd coincidence, immediately after leaving the surgery I happened to go into a newsagent and caught sight of a front page headline in our local paper:

JAILED SEX CASE DOCTOR
WOMAN OF 47 COMMITS SUICIDE

Yes, I thought, that could have been *me*. I had lived with the ever-present thought of suicide for decades.

During the night that followed it dawned upon me exactly what this powerful, autonomous gesture with my right hand indicated – **a repressed impulse, way back when I lay on Philip's therapeutic couch, to grab his penis and destroy it!**

Time for action I decided – some kind of symbolic gesture to mark the end of this tyranny of shame. I made another appointment and asked my GP to witness the end of an era. I stood up, drew a giant carrot from my bag, attacked it with venom with my teeth, broke it in two and threw the pieces in his wastepaper basket. I got up to leave with a polite, "Thank you very much," and added one final quip from the doorway, "How are you going to write that up in my notes?" He replied, "I'm not."

Next day, I walked round the supermarket with a spring in my steps and tossed a broad smile in the direction of the carrots. To celebrate this triumph I assembled a meaningful collage which included pictures of some of my selves! Something had shifted. Shame had lost some of its power. I was dancing in the light again. My book came out of its closet and was updated. But you all know what I am going to say: the sun disappeared again behind the clouds. I found myself back in doom and gloom, and my book went back into hiding.

CHAPTER TWENTY-ONE

THE DAWN OF RESOLUTION

– can this be true?

I made another appointment with my GP and he suggested referring me to a psychiatrist. I accepted this offer because I have never followed this route and felt I had nothing to lose and might have much to gain. I prepared a Case History which I have condensed as follow:.

BETTY HUGHES – BRIEF CASE HISTORY

Date of Birth – 17 April 1920 – the youngest of four children.

Parents Father – a farmer – a workaholic with little time for his children. He took the line "Do what your mother says" or "Don't upset your mother". He had a loud voice and was often touchy and irritable. Mother was obsessively religious – Plymouth Brethren orientated – extremely narrow and restrictive, devoted to her Lord and to the Bible, every word of which was true in a literal sense.

How did this affect me? I was brought up in a parental triangle – 'my mother and her Lord' and my father. I conformed and became mother's 'good little girl'. I was very closely attached to her and emotionally dependent upon her. I also lived a secret life – outside, around the farm, close to the animals and to nature, often shadowing my father and daring to approach him if after careful consideration I thought he might notice me. My pony was my closest friend and companion.

We moved house when I was nine. A change in the sleeping arrangements occurred in the new house. My father slept alone in a double room at one end of a long corridor; I slept in a large room at the opposite end of the corridor, spoon to spoon with my mother. She died when I was eighteen. I experienced both sadness and relief.

After that? I spent about thirty years trying to sort myself out. Late forties, when I was working in Switzerland I started psychotherapy with a highly recommended psychotherapist. This went extremely well: I was able to unravel some of the confusions of my childhood – schizoid and depersonalisation were among the terms used. A very vivid re-living of a traumatic experience of being raped as a small child occurred. My psychotherapist gave careful consideration to whether this was an actual memory or a fantasy.

What followed? A period of about three months during which I felt myself to be truly alive for the first time. The ever present dark clouds of depression disappeared. Everything changed, especially my relationship to my body, sexuality, communication skills, being myself, self-esteem, feeling pleasure. But, quite suddenly and for no apparent reason, the sun dimmed and I was back once again under the dark clouds of depression.

Back to the drawing-board. I continued my sessions. I trusted my psychotherapist but disastrously he fell in love with me and sexual abuse on the therapy couch followed ,which led to an intensely complex personal liaison lasting about five years

The result? I was more confused and fragmented emotionally than when I had first started out on the therapeutic path. Thoughts about suicide were around for many years.

Since then? Finally I went to another psychotherapist for about ten years and dipped into diverse models of personal growth work. At various times, for varying periods and in varying degrees, I touched into the experience of wholeness described above in which the sun bursts through the clouds. This pattern persists. What causes it to happen is a mystery to me. The dark clouds of depression are never far away, and at these times the flow of my natural energy is blocked and it takes a huge effort to perform normal tasks of living and fulfilling my commitments.

How do I cope? I no longer have a problem with self-esteem. I am deeply loved, valued and respected. I have accessed my creativity and use these talents. I still have eating problems which ease when the depression lifts. I recognise and accept my true identity which, incidentally is the person perceived and experienced by the outside world. I think and act from that centre but this becomes extremely tedious and dreary when I am depressed.

After some delay, I found myself sitting in front of a young, rather puzzled-looking psychiatrist. She was studying the two-page document which I had compiled. I had sent it ahead, anticipating that my personal history, spanning a trek of many decades (years not devoid of note-worthy incidents) would not be the most simple assessment she had undertaken! Fortunately she took refuge in a safe list of questions and passed me on to the Psychology Department suggesting that they put me forward for Cognitive Therapy.

Here I met an exceptionally skilled and perceptive clinical psychologist, who after three assessment sessions, recognised dissociative symptoms, diagnosed Post Traumatic Stress Disorder and offered me twenty sessions – open-ended. She happened to be free to see me immediately. What is interesting to note is that her diagnosis of dissociation matched the original opinion given to me when I started therapy about forty years previously. Obviously, at the beginning of my therapeutic journey I had embarked upon a sound route but my progress, in the present, had become diverted due to abuse by the therapist.

The psychologist – her name is Sarah – and I met regularly for about fifteen months. We enjoyed a brilliant relationship. She gave me freedom to present myself in my own way and was totally accepting of whatever means I chose to employ. She not only accepted, she also saw that it was imperative that I present myself *in my way*.

I always made notes for Sarah and it is intriguing now to look back to the beginning when I wrote:

"I think that over the years, since I started therapy, I have gathered together most of the pieces of my life-sized jigsaw puzzle but the information has come together in separate clusters. I need help in assembling these clusters into one picture in order to understand more about how my brain processed my early experiences. You asked me how I needed to be helped during our sessions. I would like to be free to think aloud so that you can observe what is going on in my brain."

In the early stages I gave Sarah extracts from my book describing pivotal events and this saved considerable time. The extracts incorporated my therapy with Philip, including the encounter with the gypsy, the abuse on the therapeutic couch and the scene in my GP's surgery. As our interaction continued I gave her the account of my extreme vulnerability at the time of Peter's accident, my return to Lee Abbey, the crucial encounter with John Perry and key episodes at the Bridge Pastoral Foundation Conferences. One of these was the all-important 'push/pull' crucifixion scene described in Chapter Twenty which aptly illustrates that oil and water cannot be mixed – I couldn't have my mother *and* my father.

I summarised some of the clusters of the jig-saw puzzle. I had no valid parenting. There was no cohesion between my parents. Mother's message was loud and clear and was backed up by her behaviour. Father stood aloof, he didn't get involved, his message was, "Do what your mother says", "Don't upset your mother". This was him toeing the line – he wasn't expressing his own opinion. Indoors he conformed – outdoors he led his own life on the farm as a workaholic. **God the Father** was an awesome, authority figure, distant yet ever present – closely related to my mother – a person with whom she communicated constantly. **His** voice couldn't be heard. **My father** was flesh and blood and had a very loud voice. **God** – all powerful, always present – could see everything but remained unseen. **My father** – seen, heard, and felt to be real and human yet blurred in his relationship with my mother, especially in the bedroom.

Rock bottom, basic, instinctual needs and desires were involved in my conflicts over what was good and what was bad, what was true and what was not true, what was fantasy and what was reality. There was no reality check – nothing added up – nothing made sense. Yet somehow, like a squirrel storing nuts, I managed to stockpile my nuggets of perception in a secret compartment.

I shared with Sarah a sense of my brain feeling scrambled – suffering from on-going persecution, never-ending torment, perpetual torture. Rather like a royal mail sorting machine: letters never ceasing to flow, always 'sorting', no completion.

Right from the beginning I jotted down random thoughts, feelings and flashbacks that occurred after the sessions and also through the silent hours of the night. Later I typed them up and gave them to Sarah. It is going to be extremely difficult to decide how to condense our interactions while at the same time maintaining the essence of how the trail unfolded but these are a few extracts from the earliest sessions. Italics indicate a small child's voice speaking from a regressed space in which she still seemed to live (there is always an immediacy to her utterances – a feeling, a reaction, a response which expresses her 'now'): the point at which the clock stopped ticking:

- Comfort eating fills a gap. Putting on weight reinforces my hatred of my body.
- My depression has nothing whatever to do with the present. It feels like being caught up in a scenario – living in a loop. A package of feelings and a chain of reactions which cannot be undone.
- *It happened to somebody else. I'm outside looking in and inside looking out. Shut in and shut out. Perhaps I could talk to Sarah about IT.* (There was no explanation of what *IT* might refer to)
- *There's somefing I have to live with – somefing not nice.*
- *I did once have a daddy. Now I don't have a daddy. I have a drudgery – just a drudgery.*
- *I live in this drudgery place with my mummy. She has her Lord (Jesus) but I don't have anybody. I'm not special to anybody – only special to my mummy because she wants to keep me pure for God.*
- *I was once special to my daddy – once I was.*
- Mother used to say to me, when I was quite small, "Men can be very cruel." Who had been cruel to her? My father? My mother would have been completely innocent and inexperienced at the time of her

191

marriage. His roots were in the farmyard. He didn't know anything about gentle tenderness. I can't imagine them being sexually compatible.

- I was conceived, nurtured in the womb and born during the period in which my parents were facing all the adjustments required by the move from London to the farm. Three small children were already in tow. What an onerous time that must have been for them both.

- For some reason my mind recalled a scene in a recent TV programme where a woman was waiting to give birth. The baby was overdue and she was expressing frustration and impatience to her husband. A friend said, "They say that having sex hurries things up," at which point the couple disappear upstairs. My immediate thought was, "What would that have felt like to the baby?"

- Could the persistent thought about my father raping *me* be my mother being raped by my father when I was in her womb?

- Vignettes of being in a cot in their bedroom, of them grappling in bed, my mother resisting being raped, pictures of them fighting over me. Mother took me into her bed when I was nine years old. Did she take me into their bed for protection when I was a baby?

- I live very close to all that I am writing down – especially in the early hours of the morning.

- *Do I have an outside? Did I fly out of the window? Is there anybody in my body? I got out so is there anybody inside? I seem to have to do it all from the outside and that's dreary.*

- I started to touch my body after saying these words but it felt like a carcase – dead and very unfamiliar.

- *I hear a voice saying, "Where have you been?"*

In these early sessions I touched into many diverse areas including the ever present subject of sexual abuse. The issue of False Memory Syndrome had confused my trust in my own perception. Jumbled thoughts and pictures kept on recurring around my father, the cowman Bertie, the gypsy, and evangelist Jonah. Was I abused during my childhood or wasn't I?

CHAPTER TWENTY-TWO

SARAH GETS THE PICTURE

– at last I feel fully understood

I explained further basic things to Sarah:

- I clung to my mother a lot but I had to be outside my body when I was close to her. When I was being tickled by my father I was *in* my body. I think I opened up my heart to my father as a small child but things went wrong...

- There is a feeling of innocent fun about the child who played with magic toys, even about being tickled by father. I can imagine innocent fun with Bertie, our favourite cowman. I recall naughty, funny games – magic toy games – up in the hayfield. He was a very dear one.

- I have always felt ashamed about my reaction to being kissed on my mouth or even sharing a glass with somebody. No mixture of body fluids for me! I remember being kissed by a man in my late teens and hated his tongue in my mouth. I also remember being hugged too intimately by an uncle. I loathed 'pleasuring' Philip during intimate moments in our long relationship; the very word 'pleasuring' still fills me with revulsion – especially having a penis in my mouth…I have very diverse feelings about male sexual energy – a mixture of magnetism and repugnance.

- Eating and drinking link directly to 'something nice to look forward to'. Eating alone with an absorbing book or TV programme is the nearest I come to 'a baby at the breast' – but it brings torture with it. A meal shared with others is a totally different experience – it drains rather than nourishes me.

- The **'I will have'** voice started to be heard way back in the early days of therapy and it is still extremely powerful. There is a degree of determination, even ruthlessness about it that overrides other voices. My fist went to my mouth as I shared this observation with Sarah and my heels dug into the ground. I seemed to move to the other side of a great divide as I said, **"I won't ever…"**; I won't ever what? I wonder what might have followed.

I continued to comment upon 'Catch 22' situations. Sometimes it seems to be 'Catch 23' – triangular – not just Mother and Father but 'Mother & God' and Father. Mother, with her dynamic issue about cleanliness and purity, backed by God, versus Father who thinks that pigs are the cleanest animals. When authority figures disagree it blows a child's mind.

During the night that followed my sharing with Sarah of my feelings about the 'Catch 22 and Catch 23' situations I described a lot of contortions going on in my body. I had to keep putting the light on in order to jot down the dialogue that flowed in my head. I transcribed it like this:

- I want to go to sleep. Cut it out…not remember it…break the link…go to sleep…not have it…not be there…not be *me*…not see…not be me. Anything else but being me. Go to sleep…be dead, dead,

dead…I want to be sick…want to vomit…want my body to go back where it came from. Can't breathe. Can't breathe. My head in an awkward position. Something over my face. I can't breathe. I'd like to pass out…go to sleep…not be there…not be there any more.

- *Perhaps I don't have to sleep.*
- My whole body is sick. My body must remember.
- *I could ask my body.*
- A certain look in a man's eyes. Saw it once in a group – such intensity – more than normal sexual desire. If I can sleep perhaps I can rest.
- *Can I rest? My mouf knows something.* (My mouth was trembling in the same way that it starts to quiver in the dentist's chair.)
- I would like to scratch my eyes out (My fingers desperately wanted to scratch my eyes out in the here and now – I wanted to tear my skin to shreds.) *Do you think I could go to sleep now?*
- He might come back.
- *Do you think he might come back?*

It was then about 4.15a.m. and I decided to get up!

As I continued to work with Sarah I found that my thoughts would wander round and round, backwards and forwards traversing the path I had lived as a child and observing ways in which those experiences were still being reflected in my life in the present. Time had stood still: I was both in the past and in the present. I reflected that my head (brain, mind?) in the here and now seemed to be stuck in a loop. It carried material that could not be sorted out – could not be processed. It was forever on red alert, always active, never at rest – always stressed, never at peace. It had too much to carry.

I was unable to lay the burden down. I lived in a 'floppy disk' of perpetual discomfort – always in turmoil about something that could not be alleviated. My brain had to jump over gaps – it couldn't get things together. It was utterly exhausting because the situation didn't change, the tension did not let up, couldn't be assuaged: it was controlled by a machine set in a fixed groove – for ever. I frequently found myself holding my head in a kind of despair, as if to say, "Poor head, you have had so much to cope with. More than you could manage."

I was always fighting to control what was, by its very nature uncontrollable – an eternal torture in my head which throughout my long life had always found irrefutable expression in the present. Unconsciously a system, ingeniously devised, eternally replicated the repetitive arguments, the confusion, the frustration, the rage, the despair, the hopelessness. **The confusion was excruciating.**

In my younger days at Lee Abbey the impossible demands of religion were the dumping ground for this package of feelings: on the continent it was the continual pressure of work; running a large hotel single-handed was like living on the edge of a volcano. After things went wrong with Philip therapy became the battle ground – the goal was to sort things out. **The bitter truth is that they cannot be sorted out.** Light began to dawn when Sarah pointed out, "The part of the mind that contains the trauma exists in a 'separate file' that is not integrated with other non-traumatic memories."

Our work together seemed to flow in a very natural progression. Sarah made her notes and I recorded the hand-outs offered by the my all-star cast of players – as varied in voice, tone and uniqueness as in any top-notch drama. The following extracts give a hint of the diversity, the individuality and the piquancy of some of the offerings that toppled out.

- *Don't like this place where I am – don't like it at all. Don't know how I got here. Don't know what happened. I don't know but I do know.*
- *Was it something with my daddy? I was unhappy about my daddy. He didn't get much. I wanted to comfort my*

daddy like I wanted to comfort Philip. Wanted to give him 'warmy' like I wanted to give to Philip.

- *Bertie was a nice one…he was so nice…I had fun with Bertie…used to play games with Bertie…naughty, funny games…magic toy games…up in the hayfield. He was a very dear one.*

- *Helen, my sister, used to let the Colses' boys play games with her…rude games…touching where you weren't allowed to touch. That's dangerous…not like the fun games with Bertie about magic toys. I wonder whether my daddy had one of those magic toys.*

- *I had to get out of my body. That wasn't very nice. I had to get out…just like that…no choice.*

- **It is shut. The door is shut. Shut for ever…SHUT…FINISHED…DEALT WITH.**

- *Not happy. I'm not happy.* (Tears, pain, choking, mouth trembling followed these thoughts.)

- **It can't be true. I must have made it up. Must have. It can't be true. It's silly. Rubbish.** (This was repeated many times. A frenzy followed. Clawing my head. Trying to get rid of something. Trying to get something out of my head. Incredible energy in this.)

- *No place to put myself. When I first went to see Peter I was always looking for a place to put myself.*

- *Perhaps I could get back in there (my head) – perhaps I could get back in.*

- *What 'you'* (referring to another part of myself) *are doing up there* (in my head) *is a bit out of date.*

- *There's a hymn we used to sing, 'GOD BE IN MY HEAD AND IN MY UNDERSTANDING' – does He still rule up there? If so, He thinks he controls everyone and everything. He made out he was all for peace and love but He was really all for conflicts and battles. He's a great big windbag with nobody inside.*

- *My daddy has somebody inside.*
- A voice describes somebody else: *"You see through everybody. You are a fun one. You know things. You suss things out. Even God hasn't got away with anything with you. They don't know you are there. You are puzzled about some things sometimes but when that happens you know that its something to be puzzled about. You are a very wise one."*
- *I hide behind my eyes – between my eyes and my brain. I have to monitor what I see and what I don't see.*
- *"THEY argue over my things, my body, what I can have and what I can't have. Sometimes I sneak in and get things anyway. I don't like this place. I don't like waiting and waiting…waiting…waiting for what?"*
- I don't like being controlled by you. Damn and blast you. I hate you. I hate life. Damn and blast from my roots to the top of my head. How dare you play games with me – use me as a chattel? I still do it to myself damn you.
- Get away. Get out of my head. Stop doing it to me.
- I'm shut out of life. I might as well be dead. I must be doing it to myself but I don't know how I am doing it.

These utterances led to much serious thought about my father. My mother didn't give him very much on any level. What would he have done with his sexual drive? I have an image of feeling his erect penis when he was tickling me. What would have been the expression on his face? How much would I have been aware of his sexuality? These questions were haunting me.

As my exploration with Sarah continued I became very aware of what was happening in my head and other parts of my body – the physical discomfort, the twisting and turning, the choking, the terror, the murderous rage. It reminded me of some of the painful and terrifying experiences with Frank Lake, Bill Swartley and William Emerson connected with getting stuck during my birth.

In my life in the here and now these feelings of rage often attached themselves to everyday tasks. Sometimes I want to lash out and destroy everything in sight. Once an explosion of anger was targeted at the trapped child within and blasted out in words:

- *These thoughts are driving me mad – doing my head in. My head is full of madness. Kill my body then we won't feel anything – I want to be dead.*
- *I'm angry at still being in this situation. Why can't she come out with it and be done with it? I'd like to kill her…strangle her…she has ruined my whole life. This torture in my head…I've had enough of it…enough of it. End it. End it for ever. I'll kill myself. That's what I'll do. Finish it.*

In complete contrast, I did my weekend workshop, which went extremely well. In this area of my life I seemed to manage to bypass the trauma blockage and tap into a source of freed-up energy. Somebody emailed me afterwards:

Dearest Betty

THANK YOU, THANK YOU, THANK YOU for your love, generosity and wonderment at all that is and is to come – you are the greatest treasure, an inspiration, showing me that life is fun and full of possibilities at any age.

Much love

It is strange that the 'Betty' referred to here is truly 'me' and the 'Betty 'who wakes up in the morning and does not want to live is also 'me'. After the workshop I went to Devon for a family reunion and I stayed with a friend for a few days. I coped but felt very stretched.

On the drive home I spent a couple of hours in the village where I was born. I looked with interest at the old house and the farm buildings. I walked through the bluebell woods and felt the sheer weight of the tortuous burden that I carry with me. I talked to myself. I affirmed the facts. "I actually lived here. Every year I used to seek out the first primrose in *this* wood. I jumped *that* stream on my pony. I searched for bird's nests." A small voice said, *"I did live here – that's the trufe."* But I couldn't sense any 'feeling' connection to that child.

When I got home I was deeply into depression. I was very aware of the load I carried around. It was all too much. I wanted it to end. I wanted to die. Nothing had any meaning. Simple things would always be a weighty task to be endured. This would go on for ever. The torment in my head would never stop. Part of me would never stop torturing the rest of me. There wasn't any hope. Pleasure was totally absent. Even at the time of year when the countryside was so beautiful I felt empty – my eyes saw it but it didn't touch my senses.

I allowed these thoughts to ride. If I awoke in this tortured place I sometimes checked into my body; it twisted and turned without any connection to any other part of me. A kind of mechanical sexual arousal happened but without any feelings of any kind. No sense of connectedness. I looked on with interest. I seemed to live in a very small space in relation to the whole of me.

A number of sessions passed alternating between depression, explosions of rage, puzzling about my father, getting angry with Sarah because she was ill and couldn't see me one day, and general irritation because I couldn't get things sorted. Once a new voice spoke in the night and said:

"Betty, you don't even see me. (I got up and looked at myself eyeball to eyeball in the mirror.) You fight over me

201

but you don't see me. You just don't see me. Why? Are you afraid? What of?" There was interested curiosity in the eyes that looked at me in the mirror – interested because I couldn't see her.

In the morning I was intrigued by the link between 'blind fury' that wanted to kill and a child who said I was fighting over her but didn't see her.

Sometimes when describing my feelings to Sarah I tapped into intense fear. This would escalate into total frenzy, reach a climax and would then slowly evaporate. At this point my energy would gradually seep away and my body would slowly collapse down towards the floor. The terrified person would then completely disappear – not be present any more – I would start to speak from another place. Typical voices caught during the early hours around this time were:

- *Don't push it in my mouf...I don't like it...when you put it in my mouf I have to get out.*
- *I'm frightened...I'm curled up in a ball...I'm without myself...it's bleak...I don't have an outside.*
- *I'm touching a dead face. (*I was touching my own face.*) It's a **thing**...I tell it what to do. I have to get it up in the morning...shut it up...keep it going...drug it.*
- *I don't know who I am but I bully that body and I like bullying it. I tell it what it can feel and what it can't feel. I keep it down. It has to think what I think. I'm totally detached from it.*
- *I seem to live with it – or perhaps it lives with me. It's someone else who bullies it. It's not me. I'm more curious about it...I wonder who it belongs to. I hold on to my mummy. That's what I do.*
- **I am in pain.** In a place of black nothingness with my head clamped. I have to live my life from this place.

This is the truth. It's arranged like this in my head (my brain?) It's fixed. It can't be changed. My body twists and turns...squirms...trembles...shivers...twists and turns – and it is going to do this for ever and ever.

- *I'm frightened. My body is frightened. Is part of me shut up inside my head?*

As my journey with Sarah progressed, independent characters slowly identified themselves by sitting in different chairs when they wished to speak.

1. A child who loves secrets, loves holidays and delights in hidden treasures. She chose the turquoise chair.
2. A child who knows things but is still too frightened to tell – the green chair.
3. In a black chair a burdened child who is full of blind rage and never wants to face the day. For her, every task is a heavy burden and a never ending trail of tasks stretches out into the future. Even Hidden Treasures tasks lose their magic and get translated into burdens.
4. A rust-coloured chair suited the chairperson who tries to work it all out. She fluctuates between hope, resignation and acceptance. She feels shame about being depressed yet is aware that depression does not represent her true self. She has a secret fear that she might reach a place where she's unable to cope in the present.

At this stage I pondered and asked myself, "Do I live with this degree of fear and anxiety all the time? Is this what I have to shut out constantly?"

In one session I finished up sitting in the black chair and experienced an intense concentration of depression. "I'd like to die. There's so much **nothingness.** I have no connection to life. No attachment to **anything**. My head feels strange. Blanked out. Zonked. Blotted out. I sleep. I eat. Nothing has any meaning.

DEAD – I AM DEAD

Death. An absence of life. No energy, no response, no arousal – **totally zonked**. Nothing of any interest. Heavy head. Drugged. All connections cut. A total **'black chair' feeling – an absence any life.**

I'M BACK WITH MOTHER
ATTACHED TO HER – TO HER BODY

I'm not in the 'push/pull, crucifixion' position. I'm totally zonked. The child who had a daddy doesn't exist any more. Intellectually I know that she does exist – that child who is full of life and energy is somewhere but I have no access to her. I don't know how to set about finding her. Whatever the 'connecting gismo' is, it is out of my range.

I seemed to be totally stuck in the black chair position and decided to move to another chair. Looking at the deprived individual in the black chair I started to get angry:

> *Did you do it, Daddy? Was it Bertie? The gypsy? Jonah, the evangelist who stayed in our house at Broadmead? I was deprived. I was left with an existence in which I was scavenging for crumbs – fighting being a zombie – a nothing person – scratching a living – denied my essence, my energy, my beauty. I was denied simple pleasures. Who did it? DID YOU DO IT?*

That night I spent a lot of time feeling terror, curled up tightly in a ball, shrinking into the smallest possible space – utter terror.

My body was twisting, thrashing, scratching, pushing away, kicking. I felt a very strong urge in my hands and fingers to rip flesh to shreds. Fury. My body jerked suddenly and violently. Breathlessness. Choking. Wanting to vomit. An unpleasant taste in my mouth – wanting to spit it out.

This sequence happened on a number of nights – each time with greater intensity.

I have read the proofs of my manuscript twice and each time I read these dialogues describing my work with Sarah I find myself thinking – and even saying aloud, "How tedious – how laboriously tedious these pages must seem to people who are not acquainted with this type of very complex exploration."

*So to readers who have found this part of my journey hard-going, boring or deadly wearisome: if you have had to skip pages, I am not surprised! Living the journey was all of that, yet it was underpinned by a relentless undercurrent of determination: **somebody** within me knew that this path had to be travelled.*

Chapter Twenty-three

THE JOURNEY CONTINUES

– toiling up hills and down valleys

At this stage I went to another Bridge Pastoral Conference and offered to do workshops there using my Sandplay. Before the main programme started there was time for me to use my own resources – a very rare opportunity and a particular delight. The scene I created proved to be central to a further unfolding of my exploration with Sarah.

I have mentioned before the method Frank Lake devised of working in small groups at regular intervals throughout a conference. Once again, this proved immensely valuable. When we met together I asked for time to describe the scene that I had created. I explained the farmyard setting and the figures representing my mother and her Lord. He had his foot firmly on the head of a figure crouched beside Mother – crushing any expression of sensual pleasure. There was a celluloid doll with no arms, lying in a state of helplessness. I pointed out the fun child who had enjoyed playing with magic toys and they picked up on the pure innocence of that child and were delighted by the quality of her colourful energy.

With hindsight I find it interesting to note that there were objects in the scene that I *didn't* allude to. These included a small black baby enclosed in a cage and a large double bed on which a fully dressed nun was lying on top of a another celluloid doll.

However, I did draw attention to a thin, spindly teenage young girl who said **she needed to tell her mummy something important.** She was exceedingly distressed and distraught as she crept into the centre of the group and asked each person in turn whether it was all right to 'tell her mummy'. When each person looked at her with loving acceptance and gave her an affirmative response she was clearly very moved and deeply comforted…but…she did not reveal her secret and right up to the end the teenager still denied that sexual abuse had occurred.

Just before the small group closed for the last time I happened to undo the cap of a large bottle of sparkling water and it exploded all over the place. Out of the blue someone remarked, "Magic toys explode." I laughed with everyone else and took no notice of this comment but about twenty-four hours later, when I was back at home I found myself in a state of severe shock. This lasted for several days. Clearly the remark had reached its target The paralysing state of shock was familiar – I had felt like this after breaking off my relationship with Philip and also when I heard about Peter's accident. It linked to a sense of fragility – a feeling of being held in life on the end of a gossamer thread. I found myself searching out the little blue doll which I had wanted to leave in Peter's therapy room and she accompanied me to my sessions with Sarah sessions for a while.

From then on different figures from the Sandplay began to come with me to see Sarah. The first to present themselves were the little girl who was still denying that she had been abused and the black baby in a cage. The former started a revealing dialogue:

☆ "You have to stay in your cage."
✳ *"Why?"*
☆ "It is too dangerous to come out."
✳ *"Why? I don't like it here."*
☆ "We can't come out…ever."
✳ *"I might as well be dead in here. I want my daddy."*

* ✶ "We both want Daddy but we can't have him."
* ✳ *"We used to have him."*
* ✶ "I know. Something happened."
* ✳ *"What happened?"*
* ✶ "I can't tell you what happened."
* ✳ *"Why not? Why are we cut off?"*
* ✶ "I shall never tell anybody ever...never ...never...never."
* ✳ *"But we have all that wonderful colour but can't enjoy it. Shall we take it into our grave?"*
* ✶ "You can't have that colour in heaven."
* ✳ *"Perhaps hell would be better than heaven."*
* ✶ "The gypsy was bad but this was worse."
* ✳ *"Why was it worse?"*
* ✶ "Because it was with Daddy but I don't know what happened."
* ✳ *"You don't know or you don't want to know? It's ridiculous if we have all that colour but can't enjoy it now. It's a waste. It makes me angry."*
* ✶ "It's locked away somewhere in my head...that's what it did...it went off in my head and it's still there...inside my head. I can't ever get rid of it. There's a horrid taste in my mouth. I don't like it. The Devil's in my body."
* ✳ *"All that colour belongs to me and you have portrayed me as BLACK."*

I produced coloured sketches of penises in my head and then the two characters who had been in dialogue were inserted into a new edition of a picture which already encapsulated my family constellation.

This session was followed by severe flashbacks during the following nights:

74 *This picture reminds me vividly of the fantasy journeys with Frank Lake: confusion
interlaced with moments of oceanic bliss.*

75 & 76 *These two pictures remind me that the original title of my book was going to be* The Primal Laugh *as a reply to Janov's* The Primal Scream. *The driving force which has kept me 'in life' has been the tenacious nature of the human spirit.*

77 & 78 *With my mother's milk I imbibed the precept that Jesus was* **the way, the truth and the life.** *This was absolute, unqualified, there was no other path. To piece together this collage and ask the question, "Is there a path –* **for me?**" *raised a cacophony of doubts, fears and horrors.*

79 & 80 Inconsistencies, contradictions, and dubiety, coupled with deeply buried traumas, filled my head with a tangled maze of unanswered questions. It felt as if my brain was being tortured and that the persecution would continue until the end of time.

81 I love this character. He takes on many disguises. In one of his masquerades he was cheeky to Sarah and then disappeared for many months! He doesn't suffer fools gladly, refuses to be used unless in a good cause, can be extremely nasty and even ruthless but is full of zest for life. He is articulate, his brain moves with the speed of light and he is a great asset on a committee.

- Terror...long sequences of struggling...strange sensations in my head...trying to lift a lid which had been shut down...Breathlessness...choking ...something being pushed into my mouth...more struggling than ever before.
- *I'm not here, Mummy. I'm not here with my daddy, Mummy.*
- A prayer to the Universe, **"Tell me the truth, God – please tell me the truth. Something is still happening now...happening in the present...I'm still here in this terror. There is still something that I know but I don't know...something that I can't get hold of but it has hold of me."**
- Another voice: *"Look, I want to connect to you. I don't know how to do it. Perhaps you can connect to me. Can you?*

It was strange hearing this voice. It was a positive voice which seemed to be working for my good. After that session a tiny window opened up for a second and I had a glimpse of a world that had turned the right way up. Yet, back in my flat – in my inner world – the situation remained the same. I lived each day in this deeply depressed place, experiencing the extreme drudgery of fulfilling routine daily tasks. The 'for ever' quality of the darkness shut out the light – the tedium of ongoing arguments in my head, as persistent as the bickering of a never-ending committee meeting.

I took an enlarged picture of my Sandplay to a session and Sarah and I focussed upon the figures lying in the double bed which had been placed in a 'gateway' position on the edge of the farmyard – a black clothed nun was squashing the plastic figure of a small girl. Evidence was piling up to confirm that I was suffering from trauma. In addition to my birth and the rape by the gypsy at perhaps aged seven or eight years old, all the flashbacks I had experienced while working with Sarah seemed to indicate that an additional trauma of some kind had occurred at a very early age. Undoubtedly these experiences would have thrown me back onto my mother – she would have been my only refuge. I would have been completely dependent upon her. Yet, the irony of the situation was that clinging to her for safety would have involved an alternative abusive situation.

I had studied this area of my life many times before but I now began to experience the full significance of the change in the sleeping arrangements. My father was banished to the far end of the house and I took his place in my mother's bed. I had to sleep, night after night, in close proximity to her body – 'spoon to spoon' – during those formative teenage years. This must have not only severely restricted my natural development and must have reinforced the conviction that it was dangerous to live in my body – much safer to live outside. I am describing a degree of retardation which, would insidiously have affected fundamental facets of my personality. Shame must have been my nightly companion as I experienced the complex changes involved in developing into a teenager.

We are all aware of the ways in which the unconscious finds expression in dreams and body movements during sleep and in such intimate proximity to my mother's body I must have picked up – in a very direct way – some of my mother's ambivalence about her own sensuality and sexuality. Even her innermost secrets?

It is extremely interesting. I was editing my manuscript and the night after reading the above paragraph I tapped into a flashback of sheer terror associated directly with this intimate closeness to my mother.

This stage of my journey with Sarah established just how tenuous, unbalanced and profoundly confusing my basic connection to my mother had been. Her obsessive belief system and her narrowly restricted attitude to sensuality and sexuality deprived me of the freedom of self expression. I recall picture books that we played with in those days. They had clear blank pages but, it was exciting, because when you brushed over the sheet with water a picture gradually appeared out of the nothingness.

A small child's life is a bit like this, bursting with all the potential of natural growth. All the elements are there in waiting. The stage is set for normal development – waiting to be nurtured, encouraged, given expression and affirmed; or, alternatively to be negatively imprinted with doubt, confusion, conflict and bewilderment. Certainly, in my case, the stage was set in a way that completely denied essential affirmation. There was absolutely nothing to confirm that it was good to be alive: that sensual and sexual pleasures were gifts from God, that close relationships were a joy, that the world was a safe place. Instead I existed on scraps, had a precarious foothold on life and lived on the edge of disaster.

In one of our sessions around this time Jonah, the Sandwich-man evangelist gave me much food for thought. He was a creepy individual. Even as I write my guts twist and I cringe at the thought of him touching me. He often stayed in our house so would have had easy access to our rooms without being observed. Mother would have trusted him completely. The message on his sandwich-board in large letters was:

YOU MUST BE BORN AGAIN

This gospel injunction became deeply imprinted upon my brain. Not just the inescapable, implacable directive, '**You must be born again**' but also the hymns we sang so vigorously about, 'being washed in the blood of the lamb – being washed white as snow'. The very words 'being washed white as snow' suggest that you must be unclean to start with, yet how can bright red blood make you spotlessly unsoiled?

I spent some time in sessions sitting in the black chair and I clearly recall an immensely strong impulse one day to roll the chair backwards – not just backwards but right out of sight – through the wall into the room on the other side. A return to my mother's womb? A hope of being born again? A glimmer of light? Might I be conceived by the Holy Ghost and come out good and untainted like Jesus?

The depression which I experience – the 'shut down' feeling, coupled with acute anxiety, clearly derives from this vast area that I have been exploring with Sarah. Deeply embedded, yet peculating into the present, anxiety manifests itself in a daily experience of pressure – of limited time in which to get vital tasks completed; living as if each day might be my last; a compulsion to be ready for death. My flat must be spick and span – no muddles. My personal papers must be in perfect order. Fear hovers. Fear of getting caught out, fear of money running out, fear in the present, fear of death itself. Above all, in spite of all the knowledge I have about myself and my history, fear that nothing will change – I shall be in this space for ever. This feeling is unmitigated and has the power to obscure totally the sun. In this space thoughts of suicide are never far away.

It still amazes me just how absolute this experience was, over a period of time, in the present. The power it had to completely block my view of my whole self and also block the view of a positive outcome with Sarah. I don't think that this aspect is understood by many people. The fact that if you are deeply split you can experience being fully in *one* part of yourself and totally lost to the remainder. It can feel, **in the here and now,** that this is all of you – nothing will change – you will be there for ever. Even among people who have studied these things extensively I have met very few who know, first hand, what I am talking about – just one or two.

Around this time, maybe to reassure myself, I unearthed a collection of my uniquely personal Sandplay figures that I have gathered over a period of many years: they are too precious to give to the Hidden Treasures collection because they denote strategic staging posts on my journey. I set them out in a place of honour in my lounge – a reassuring outward sign of a continuum of experience. It interested me that a nativity scene was in the collection, depicting the one and only perfect baby who was born on Christmas Day. Did this event encourage a secret hope of being re-born pure and unblemished? It gave me great pleasure to add the little cluster of figures from my latest Sandplay – the special ones who were still accompanying me to sessions. An additional figure appeared – a bowed figure – set in stone – surrounded by a convoluted chain.

One day, a stranger from the Sandplay appeared on the scene in the therapy room. He confronted Sarah in quite a cheeky and aggressive manner and then lost himself for several weeks. I searched high and low but couldn't find him. I think he represents a part of me who **insists upon having** *something* **even if it is only the crumbs from under the table.** There is a belligerent ruthlessness about this character which is understandable in view of my history. He shouts and swears loudly at motorists who dawdle or cut across my path. He can make life difficult because he is a very disconnected individual and, when I am in that particular slot, it feels, in the present, that I have no freedom of choice. If thwarted he goes into 'don't care mode', which is equally dangerous. He puts me in a position that obscures my truth – and makes me feel that I have no options in the here and now; no freedom to choose.

This little group of figures played a prominent part in the unfolding of my drama right up to the end of my sessions with Sarah. They symbolised and embodied the parts that they portrayed. At any given moment they placed themselves where they needed to be. They appeared and disappeared. They were always ahead of my thinking function and helped Sarah to identify the disparate characters that I was presenting.

Chapter Twenty-four

LIGHT BEGINS TO DAWN

– but will it fade again? It always does

During the following weeks these characters revealed more of themselves by sitting in different chairs in the therapy room. A child in the green chair was angry with the jolly one in the turquoise blue chair. She described her as wilful, naïve, too trusting, seductive. She could and did 'get us into trouble'. She saw her as 'possessed by the Devil'. This is how it looked from her point of view – from the position she had been forced to adopt – the Catch 22 crucifixion place; life or death – heaven or hell. She wanted to kill her because she was an actual danger. She was also a persistent tormenter – brandishing temptations.

Another violent response occurred when I was sitting in the turquoise chair holding the dolls. Acting upon my suggestion, Sarah was asking me some questions. I experienced a strange dulling of my brain. It felt as if my mind was being subjected to overload; like an elastic band being stretched beyond its inherent capacity to give. Then, similar to what occurred in my GP's surgery, an impulse came from some area out of reach of my conscious mind and I threw the dolls with great force on to the floor. Later, a voice said, *"I don't want to see them (the dolls) ever again."* This was repeated many times with the rider, *"I don't know who this is speaking – whether it is me or my mother, but someone in my head does not want to see those dolls ever again."*

All that week the dolls were banished. Rage was very near the surface. No windows. No glimpses of light. Dreariness under-laced by rage.

The following week Sarah happened to be ill and couldn't see me. You've guessed it – I went berserk with anger. The fury boiled over – rage, murderous rage at whoever Sarah represented. "Go to hell – that's where you belong – in hell." It was a quality of unadulterated ferocity which wanted to tear raw flesh and draw blood. It was turned both outwards and inwards: most of all it was directed against myself. I really wanted to tear my own flesh to shreds and see the blood flow freely. I wanted to smash all the pieces of my Sandplay to smithereens…to stamp upon the special dolls and crush them to pieces.

As time passed, the familiar pattern unfolded; the rage turned into 'don't care' mode. Nothing mattered any more. Nothing was of any value. I could drink myself into unconsciousness. Kill myself…nothing had any meaning or relevance. For a while I was totally indifferent to the dolls and their subtle significance.

Alongside, there was a deep fear and concern in the present; fear that I might not be able 'in the now' to get back to the place where I was feeling able to open up to Sarah from that very deep, vulnerable child place – the place where I was held by a gossamer thread. This fear had sadly been realised with Peter. Although I had continued to work with him for some years after his crash I was never able to get back to the space I was in before the accident occurred. There was genuine fear (based upon valid experience) that the same could happen now in the process that was unfolding with Sarah. The thread was so delicately translucent. I had no access to choice in this area – what happened, happened…or didn't happen; that child trusts or she doesn't trust; she opens up or she doesn't open up.

This was the lowest point in my journey with Sarah. It was extremely tough for her too. Just before seeing her again I wrote, "I am writing this just before the session. I have been too detached to write before. I am completely disconnected from the whole process. I don't want to face the day. I don't want to go on living. There is no meaning anywhere – going to see Sarah has no significance whatsoever." However, and this was a crucial decision, I decided to take with me to my next session the symbols that had come to represent the various parts of me – a shred of faith was still present!

We weathered the storm. Retrospectively I see the next few weeks as a 'black chair' experience; a familiar space after I left Philip and also after Peter's accident. I was spinning on the end of a gossamer thread in utter confusion – falling to pieces...breaking up... disintegrating. Once during the night I wrote, "I am in pain...in my innermost self I live in a black hole of hell!" I was aware of being in a place of death...nothingness...a total absence of life.

In a strange way fragments from different areas would merge during the hours of the night. At one point I felt completely enclosed, shut away, couldn't get out. A small voice said, *"I can't lift the lid."* This would be the lid of a large wooden box where smoked hams were kept. I have often had panics around hiding in this box and not being strong enough to lift the lid from inside.

At other times I seemed to be trying to push somebody away but it was impossible. I tried with all my strength but he was too strong. Often these flashbacks were accompanied by the familiar feelings of breathlessness, choking, helplessness. Strangely enough, it was around this time that the male Sandplay figure who had materialized many weeks ago and confronted Sarah suddenly reappeared! There was some hesitation from the assembled company but finally he was allowed to sit on the fringe of the scene!

This period holds a touch of mystery. Very positive voices were heard to speak. For example there is a voice in my repertoire which often chats about things she likes or things that attract her attention. She operates from outside my body, which is full of pain and loss, and makes pertinent comments. It was Christmas and this voice said,

A baby comes at Christmas – a very special clean one. I had a clean one once – I wonder if I could have a new one. They make a lot of fuss about this baby…sparkly things and jolly music.

Another time, when I was experiencing tasks to be unbearably heavy she chipped in with quicksilver energy in her voice,

I can do things very easily. I can soon get them done – I know a lot of things.

I was quite anxious at this time about a forthcoming holiday that had been booked a year in advance. Holidays have always been very special events to all my selves – a treat – an escape. Going on a gleefully anticipated holiday feeling deeply depressed felt like a severe deprivation – a punishment. A small voice kept saying, *"I want my holiday…I want my holiday."* Another child's voice piped up with, "Don't let it go…it's yours…your special thing…don't let 'them' take it away." This little person was angry and very upset.

Then something important happened during a session. It was another of those pivotal moments when a spontaneous gesture is released from the depths of consciousness. A very small child's voice was carefully explaining to Sarah from the green chair that, *"Somefing very bad had happened."* She didn't seem to know exactly what it was but she knew that *'somefing'* had happened. She was intensely upset and agitated about it. **But,** in exactly the same split second, another child was at my side giggling because the window cleaner had chosen this crucial moment to clean the outside of the windows in Sarah's room! Looking back, it is clear that being aware of both child selves **at the same time** was vitally significant and resulted in more access to the disparate selves during the holiday.

I was about to set out upon a long anticipated tour of South Africa. It was to be a re-run of the trip that I had organised many moons ago but I felt that the profound depression cast a spell of doom over the whole enterprise. I felt overwhelming dread about travelling with a group of strangers from the deadly depressed space in which I had been living for so many weeks. I think I would have cancelled the trip if it had not been for the voice of the angry child who blurted out, "Don't let it go…it's yours…your special thing…don't let 'them' take it away."

In the event, and to my great relief, right from the beginning of the tour I charmed everybody and was the acknowledged queen of the group! We had an hilarious time, enjoyed magnificent scenery, mountains and seascapes, viewed memorable historical sights, vying with each other all along the way for the best photographic and camcorder shots. My sense of humour was very sharp: in public I was right on the ball, a lively part of the group: another self was in despair when alone in my room. Bizarre.

In private some of the horrendous depths of the deadly depressed state of being emerged into consciousness. One night I had a sense of my whole self being in excruciating pain. I will copy out what I wrote at the time:

> "My body is wracked with pain. I am pinned down. Can't move. My breasts are being ravished. My whole body is being ravished. Some kind of bestial attack. I am being used for somebody's pleasure…being crushed…choking …being battered…my head bursting…no breath… helpless…just longing for death."

My only wish was to die. This was a totally different experience from wanting to return to my mother's womb in order to be born again all clean and sparkling. This was wanting death because life had nothing for me but a bottomless pit of agony and dereliction. She, my sparkly self had gone…she wasn't available to me…I was alone…utterly alone…filled with pain and anguish. Abandoned. ALL I WANTED WAS DEATH.

Then followed an appeal to the universe,

"Please give me death...just death...I don't want anything but death...nothing but death can get me out of here. I'm crushed...completely crushed...all the **me** has been crushed out of me...'she' has gone...'she' is safe but I am here **for ever and ever.** Life is just full of excruciating pain. I am being crushed, twisted...something/somebody has me at their mercy...I am utterly helpless, unable to do anything to help myself. I could be in my mother's birth canal...completely stuck against hard bone. Or...a man could be ravishing me for his own pleasure...or both. I have trouble with breathing...choking...wanting to vomit. I don't have to know exactly where I am and what is happening...all I know is that 'she' has gone and I want what is happening to stop. All I know is that 'she' has gone and I want death. *DEATH IS THE ONLY THING I WANT...NOTHING ELSE...JUST DEATH...PLEASE TAKE ME OUT OF WHERE I AM.*

It was wacky. During the day we were travelling and seeing exciting places. I was in my 'belle of the ball' space where everybody loved and admired me. All and sundry were so gracious – giving me practical help on all sides. Yet, alone in my room I travailed with this longing to die.

I wrote a lot during those days...pages and pages. These reflections explained a great deal about how I have experienced myself in everyday life. Forever poised on the edge of life and death. Always on red alert. Caught in the fight or flight reflex. Poised on the perimeter of an abyss, always expecting to be caught out, always expecting to fall over the rim. From the beginning of time I have judged myself to be bad – a fundamental, rock-bottom badness; a foundation badness to which everything carrying the same label has automatically been added. No escape. A lifelong scenario of trying to sort out something that is by its very nature 'unsortable'.

Clearly I have lived my life in a state of war with an underground resistance movement actively in situ. Two different scenarios running alongside with their separate communication systems, their spies, panics: their deeply intricate manoeuvres, closely guarded territories, set up for good reasons and fully justified in the circumstances. All necessary for survival.

The holiday gave me space for quiet reflection. I found myself pondering upon some of the favourite precepts of certain therapists, particularly in regard to 'acting out', personal discipline, and freedom of choice: useful tools for some people but infuriating to clients suffering from dissociative disorders because they do not take into consideration the pivotal ground base of the problem. Such precepts are gobbledygook if you are a family of selves because you may well be both the war and the resistance. I also found that 'reflecting back' could take me right off a useful track which I was endeavouring to put into words. If the therapist, in an attempt to elucidate the situation, reflected back *in his/her words,* the effect of this intervention was the reverse of clarification – it left me tied up in knots puzzling over the new definition of what I had tried to explain. Here I have to apologise for the number of times I have fallen into this trap myself.

I reflected upon my lifelong problem regarding words. As a child I was taught with absolute authority that every word in the Bible was true and yet in my secret heart I could never reconcile the contradictions this presented – the inconsistencies that were constantly acted out before my very eyes. I think that normal communication has always been a complicated trap for me. My attention gets caught up between the actual meaning of the words being used and the expression on the faces and body language of those concerned in the interaction.

I remember a horrendously entangled communication dilemma I once had with professional colleagues. I was accused of being secretive. This was the truth but now I can understand why the whole issue opened up caverns of profound terror and pain.

It is also very easy to understand why life in the Community at Lee Abbey, where openness was the accepted rule of life, was so threatening for me. The thought of just speaking the simple truth must have exposed a quagmire of unidentified, impending chaos and doom.

Reared in an alternative environment, I think I might have been quite a talkative child. Had this been the case, knowing that I had to be careful about every word uttered, having to guard my mouth constantly, feeling impelled to keep silent in case any secrets slipped out must have been a perpetual nightmare. Being told 'to keep my own counsel' when I went out to tea must have filled me with anxiety. This is another aspect of what it must have been like living on an edge of impending disaster.

A further sense of reassurance slowly dawned upon me during this time. I was no longer wracked by doubts regarding sexual abuse. I was able to recognize that I had been brutally abused as a small child and that this did not have to be just one incident. There was no longer an agonising urge to know exactly what had happened – to know all the details – time, place and who was involved. **I didn't have to know.** It was that simple.

I was aware that some of the utterances of my child selves that I had recorded did not add up. There were inconsistencies which readers might question. There would also be voices and flashbacks that I did not remember, remarks that I didn't record. But it wasn't important. It all hung together in its own way – **truth recognised truth**. I knew what I needed to know and could at long last be at peace.

I was also able to come to terms with the grief-stricken suffering of my body – the ugly, bad, hated, tormented, tortured shell that had no hope whatever of becoming, once again, the fairylike dancing figure that had once been the delight of the little girl who skipped through a field of buttercups.

When I was sunk into the depths of longing for death I often found myself thinking of the evangelist Jonah. I visualised him as a creepy, repulsive, unattractive man who would perfectly fit the bill of being a pervert. I had always hated him staying in the house and, as an ageing adult woman, my body still instinctively cringes and moves away at the thought of him coming close and touching me. When I read in the press cases of sadistic child abuse I picture a man like Jonah. He *could* so easily have been devious, twisted, cruel, violent. He was soaked in religious jargon and this thought gives depth to my sense of having been invaded and polluted by religion. But I do not need to know whether he abused me or not – the issue is laid to rest.

During this time I also thought of all the things I had jotted down about my father. I pondered deeply. Any association with him would have been part of my secret life and would, of itself, have carried a load of guilt. My feelings of deep love for him would have felt shameful: my longing for his attention, my sense of his isolation and loneliness, my desire to make up to him for what was missing in his life. Any close interaction with him would have been fraught with inner conflict; any pictures of playing with him charged with a mixture of joy, fear and excitement – a cocktail of ingredients that might have got out of hand. But somehow I don't feel tarnished as I close this paragraph.

Chapter Twenty-five

AT LAST!

– the pieces fit together

During the week after my holiday I felt drained of energy. I found it really hard to function. It would have been easier to stay in bed all day. It is difficult to describe the intensity of the depression – the all-pervading dreary gloom – the total lifelessness of it. I looked into my eyes and saw dead eyes. I said, "You are dead. You might as well be in your grave. Yet, if you were in your grave the rest of you might be alive." And a little voice said, *"It's all gone…gone…all gone…not there any more."* There was no resting place…no outside skin…no comfort anywhere…blocked off…wholly detached… beyond reach…completely shut down…dropped out of life…beyond reach…nothing in my consciousness except this experience of deadness.

But, in the next few sessions several remarkable things occurred. For the very first time I was able to register, with clarity, an aspect of my dilemma that was crucially significant. **The complete darkness of the depressed place would always be exactly as it was – a place of utter darkness and despair. It would not change. It was fixed in time. If I was in that position this is what I would experience. The nature and character of the space was set in stone at the point in the trauma at which the clock had stopped.**

On one occasion I was sitting in the turquoise chair facing Sarah and there was a lot of energy in my hands. Both hands formed a fist. The right fist was full of dynamic energy – rather like the powerful male energy which had entered the room and challenged Sarah. The left was a tiny fist – light hearted, jokey, a bit teasing – playfully pretending to fight with the big fist; rather like David daring to face up to Goliath. However, when they locked together they suddenly seemed to be on the very edge of a God almighty explosion. Weirdly dramatic.

I had just purchased a new digital TV and a modern combi-recorder. They arrived with two giant remotes, each tightly packed with rows of tiny buttons. The well-informed expert who installed the equipment explained the system. I was expected to be capable of controlling all four electronic wonders at the same time – to bring to the screen at will or to record on video or DVD any programme of my choice.

I took the remotes to my session with Sarah. I held them in my hands. Then I looked, as it were, across at the TV and the recorder. My reaction was electric. An overwhelming sense of unutterable bewilderment and befuddlement. An immediate connection to a mind-boggling confusion in my brain regarding communication. It was another of those unforgettable moments that I shall never forget. My feelings demonstrated the utter impossibility of understanding the intricacy of these electronic wonders that I was holding in my hands – of cooperating with the minutely interlocked connections in these gismos and discovering how to make them obey my commands. This pinpointed and reflected back a very familiar, frozen in time, state of affairs in my head.

There was a connection between these two enactments. What happened with my fists seemed to be demonstrating a crucial fusing of two separate elements in my body. It was followed by the chaos in my brain caused by the image of linking the two remotes to the TV and the combi-recorder. Something was going on. Some system was being demonstrated that was on automatic – a device that kept components apart, that prevented different parts of me communicating in a direct way.

This intrigued me and captured my interest. I found myself experimenting – as if moving to a crisis point from two different directions – speaking and writing. One voice which I called 'She' seemed to be saying **that it was too dangerous, in the here and now,** to detect the nature of this device. It was extremely odd because, in reality, in the present, I also had great difficulty in actually speaking the words: there was an automatic resistance to the sounds passing my voice box. The words became stuck in my throat. The choking breathlessness experienced in so many flashbacks returned. I felt in real danger of falling into an abyss – I was on red alert with life and death implications. **I felt compelled to move into another part of my brain and try to write the words instead of speaking them.** In actual fact I noted the time on my pad – 1.14p.m. Yet, strange as it may sound, I couldn't hold this position either. The strength drained from my hand and I had to return to the effort of speaking.

Clearly I was dealing with two elements which my personal history decreed had to be kept apart at all costs. This accounted for the degree of compulsion and the extreme emotional and physical discomfort involved. The nature of the disaster which had to be avoided felt of gi-normous proportions.

I have been looking at the notes written at the time and listening to the voice on the small Dictaphone that I used. There are frequent breaks in continuity with exact times noted down. Part of this dialogue occurred during the night and at one point a very concerned, very small voice said,

> *"I would really like to stop for a bit and see whether I want to go to sleep. I'm not tired but I do like to look after this poor old body as much as I can and would like to see whether it needs to go to sleep. I really do try to look after this poor old body even though it cannot be like the sparkly, agile little body I once had...but I still want to look after it. I know 'she' hates it but to me it's a bit like having an old grandmother."*

While all this was happening there was an interested observer who was watching all the moves, interpreting them with apt fascination. I was aware that I was actually approaching the second at which the clock had first stopped. I was keenly aware that I have lived my life around the site of this trauma. What was happening made complete sense of the story I have written in these pages.

During the days when this was happening I was waking up in the morning in a strange space of unreality. I wasn't sure who I was – whether I was truly present or not. It took a while to adjust to this but I felt that it must be part of what was unfolding and found it helpful just to accept it and continue to write down or speak whatever happened. **I was actually living what I had previously known about in theory.** One night I was sitting on the edge of my bed with my hard-backed A4 writing pad on my knees. I was aware of a strong desire to stop thinking and recording – I just wanted to lie on the bed and go to sleep. I was tired. I started to write in capital letters so that I was sure that my writing could be understood. I quote:

> "Part of me…in reality…in 'now' time…really wants to avoid being in both sides of myself simultaneously. In the now…it is difficult to stay in both places…as if some force…out of reach of one part, is in 'now' time endeavouring to keep me from meeting up…in 'now' time with the other part. This force is on auto pilot. My observer self was watching the process unfold. I was aware that, way back in time, my inner clock knew when and why it had stopped. The ultimate crisis point had been reached. I had to cut out – split – there was no other choice."

The written account continues,

> "In order to process what I have just commented upon, it is necessary not to have a voice…to actually stay

with…not avoid…being present at the exact 'Catch 22' point…the actual second when I cut out. There is a strong urge to get out…break the chain…break the continuity. At this very moment I want to put my pen down, stop writing this with my aching hand and lie down on my bed. It is such a strong compulsion…an urge in the now…affecting my breath…it is really hard to get access to breath at this moment of time in my body."

Someone within me was deliberately wanting to avoid what was happening yet was managing to stay with it and also to record the process in writing which could be used as evidence afterwards.

"I am deciding – at this very second – to stay with my aching hand which is in the process of creating this evidence…such a pull here to get out…a strong force trying to stop me. A compulsive intricate piece of machinery – with almost digital precision – similar to when a PC crashes and throws up a box saying what has happened. There is a slight easing of the compulsive 'on automatic' releasing of breath, in my body, at that second. A voice in my head says, 'Get out and allow your body to lie on your bed,' but my aching hand is using every bit of concentration to continue – not to split off.

"Physically it is almost impossible to hold on to the process of getting these words written. Being in my body, in 'now' time and allowing this verbal route to be constructed across this gap in my brain. Each additional word I manage to get hold of becomes, in itself, the path which joins…this sentence wasn't completed. There was such a pull to break the connection and lie on the bed. My brain seems to be grappling for 'good enough' words to convey meaning while my body is struggling to remain in league with my brain.

I note that my writing pad is about to run out and I am crucially aware that I must not break the contact physically by going to fetch another one. Any movement of my body at this crucial second would *break this fragile, gossamer thread.*

"My back and my hand are aching more and more but some wise part of me knows that I can complete this task – I can manage not to press the 'red alert' button. It is imperative that this second is recorded in words that can be read – before the page runs out. This wise part of me knows – it is an 'all seeing, all knowing, wise, informed part'. It knows more than I know and this has been difficult for me to deal with. It has been hard for me to trust. But it also recognises just *how* difficult it has been for me – difficult while living from the black hole. The black hole which also turns out to be the **black whole** and there is just time to get this written *before I run out of road.*"

The words 'run out of road' are written at the end of the bottom line of the inside cover of the notebook! At this point I search for a blank page further back in the notebook and write, "A voice at 2.26 a.m. says with relief, "Oh my God," breathes a sigh of relief and allows her body to lie down on the bed. A small person giggles as she reflects upon this piece of my journey because it is so extraordinary!"

Is this the same character who giggled when the window cleaner arrived at a moment of crisis in Sarah's room?

Chapter Twenty-six

SARAH'S STORY

– professionals don't usually reveal their side of the story

I was intrigued by Betty's written history, which I read before our first meeting, but slightly concerned. For some reason her account and the language it used suggested to me that she might feel more at home with a psychodynamic approach to therapy. Although I use psychodynamic ideas in my work, I in no way felt qualified to undertake therapy using this as a main focus. The referring psychiatrist was requesting Cognitive Behavioural Therapy but I was not happy with this either! I don't like to decide which approach is best before meeting the person concerned.

I have most often used a broadly cognitive approach together with narrative ideas; that is, working with a person's story to understand how their sense of self has developed and where things have gone wrong. A distorted sense of self, or of the world, most commonly leads to depression (self is bad, worthless, inadequate) or anxiety (world is dangerous and unpredictable). Following this I use whatever works with a particular individual to encourage alternative, more adaptive, rules to live by.

I was also concerned that the referring letter from her GP made no mention of possible trauma but instead just highlighted long-term depression.

It is strange but I don't actually remember my first meeting with

Betty in detail, but instead have a sense of the 'flavour' of those first meetings. My impression was of an articulate and vibrant but confused person, veering between hope that another opportunity to make sense of the incomprehensible had been offered, but perhaps not daring to hope that anything else could really make a difference. The longed for peace and sense of completeness might always be just out of reach.

One thing I was certain of from the first two or three sessions. I felt strongly that what was in front of me was not a classic depression, where the person feels inadequate and worthless. Betty, in her 'light' place knew only too well about her considerable personal qualities. In fact in some way she was **always** aware of these, but, when in the dark place she could not reach them, could not feel them, was completely cut off from them. In fact, it was this sense of disconnection that I felt was the most important 'symptom' and one that I was familiar with in the clinical work I had done in the area of trauma. I also felt instinctively that Betty would not react well to intrusiveness on my part and that she needed space to communicate in her **own way**.

Another crucial factor that arose from the assessment was Betty's descriptions of the separate 'selves' that operated in her experience of life. Whilst not completely dissociated in as much as Betty was always aware of the disparate 'selves', it was clear that Betty's sense of self and how she operated in the world was extremely split, again a common consequence of trauma. For this reason I felt that what might arise in therapy was quite unpredictable and therefore an open, exploratory approach would be best. Part of this decision was based on the fact that Betty, despite everything, has a very strong sense of self and ego. On some level she can continue with normal life whilst working through the most primitive and painful material. A more disordered person would not have been able to cope with jumping into the dark places with someone else **just being there**, not making suggestions. In a strange way, I feel that for Betty, the nondirectiveness of the therapy was actually one of the factors that made it containing for her.

Something else arose from the assessment sessions that was very important for the work ahead. Betty was quite preoccupied with the reality or otherwise of possible memories of sexual abuse. Would she ever know for sure and how could she tell if the memories were real? I felt an important starting point was to acknowledge that I certainly could not verify or otherwise whether particular events had or had not taken place, and perhaps Betty could not either. **But this was not important.** What I focused on was the reality of her emotional reactions, the feelings in her body and the profound sense of shock, pain and splitting. This is what was crying out to be heard and what we needed to work with.

The goal for Betty seemed to be to find 'the switch' that could link everything together. Years of therapy and personal growth work had explored and unravelled the various facets of her life experience and their consequences. However, something was missing, the essential ? which linked them all. Without this, the gap between the alive, joyful part and the dead, hopeless part was infinite and unbridgeable.

Betty reacted with surprise when I offered her twenty sessions of therapy to begin with. She though ten might be enough! I think this was possibly because she felt so close to the elusive 'switch'. But the gap between the light and the dark, the knowing and not knowing, which seemed so small, proved to be a split second of enormous magnitude which would take an epic journey to cross. Luckily we both had the necessary courage, fascination, sense of adventure and humour to undertake this remarkable journey. It changed both of us in the process and is an experience I will never forget.

When thinking about how the therapeutic work with Betty progressed, I find it hard to conceptualise it in a 'linear' way, with a beginning, middle and end. What stands out for me are the central issues of the relationship between us, how we communicated and how this changed over time.

When we began working together Betty tried to convey, over some weeks, the complexity of the 'map' that she had developed over the years; how all the complex strands of her life and experience fitted together and had brought her to where she was now. In this way she was attempting to bring me 'up to speed' so that I could have some idea where she was starting from; what she did understand about herself and what remained hidden. Betty at this point was very much talking **about** different parts of herself rather than talking **from** these parts. At this stage I felt like an observer but in an active way. The mental effort needed to assimilate and make some sense of all the information was considerable.

This process also tested my ability to keep quiet, as I was making so many links and associations as Betty talked but was acutely aware that I had to hold on to them. I knew that Betty would ask when she wanted my views but the process of holding all the material in my head felt overpowering at times. However, I felt it was important that I made these links in my own thinking space; in a way I was weaving a map of my own that ran alongside Betty's map.

I am a very verbal person. I conceptualise the world in words not pictures and the art of reducing a mass of verbal material into themes comes naturally to me. At the beginning, I had little idea of Betty's difficulty with words, especially as she was so articulate. However, I was aware that she was a visual and artistic person. From the beginning Betty brought in pictures, collages, and photographs to illustrate her 'map' of herself. I found these incredibly helpful, even if I did immediately 'translate' them into verbal concepts. The immediacy of a visual image cannot be overestimated. One can try to describe, as Betty did, the experience of feeling as if an explosion had gone off in her head, but seeing a drawing of a huge phallic object exploding into the outline of a head, taking up most of the space inside the head and surrounded by chaotic black lines, tells the story in a completely different way. It hits you in the stomach, it has **sensation**, a very physical presence. Trauma is often encoded in a sensory way and so it seems logical that the best medium to express it incorporates a sense of the physical. This interplay between the verbal and the visual seemed very important throughout our work together. In particular, my natural inclination to translate images into words mirrored the need for Betty to name and give a narrative to the isolated traumatic experiences that had never been encoded. Words confer a sense of time; a past, present and future.

Over time, Betty moved away from the position of just describing her split self and actually began to express from these various selves. At these times, her whole presentation would seem to change; her voice, her posture, and her reactions to me, but she was always aware of what was going on and could comment when she 'returned'. Her use of different chairs to express the different selves was especially powerful. Those chairs took on such significance that if anyone had come in and sat on one of them I would truly have felt as if they were sitting on an actual living person.

At times, Betty felt that she was hanging on by a 'gossamer' thread to herself, with a terrible fear that she would disappear into the dark place and never get out again. Getting closer to that original experience of 'falling through the gap' and being nowhere intensified this fear. Despair and fear were close at these times. I too felt this fear and it was at these times that my faith was really tested, as I questioned the integrity and safety of what we were undertaking. Living through these times was so crucial, for both of us. This was not just a question of resilience and getting past these painful points. Being able to **stay with** the uncertainty and the fear and not push them away, accepting these feelings that were coming from the darkest of places, helped to give them a place to be.

The stone figure surrounded by chains seemed to be at the centre of everything. Eventually, all the other figures faded, the chains came off and this one came alone, its head in its hands, unable to change, 'set in stone'. Just being with this part, accepting it, holding it, not trying to sublimate or change it, seemed to be so important. It was this part which had 'fallen through the gap' and lived in perpetual isolation and darkness. Where I was mistaken early on was to believe that I had to help bring this part out of the gap, out of the darkness. What in fact was needed was to accept fully and be with the darkness itself.

The last few sessions, where things seemed to remarkably come together, are most clearly described by Betty. In a strange way this part of the therapy is the part I find hardest to describe, to get a handle on. Perhaps because Betty was experiencing herself *as* herself, as a whole for the first time, my function as an intense 'holding place' receded somewhat. However, two things stand out for me:

- Firstly, the realization of what the clock standing still meant for Betty was fundamental – that 'split second' moment when light turned into darkness would always be 'for ever'. It could not move on in any way. It could not move on in the way that ordinary experiences do – it could not become ameliorated and softened by the effects of time passing. This is the essence of the nature of time in trauma and understanding this proved a revelation to Betty.

- Secondly, the moment when she looked at me and didn't recognise me I felt strongly she was seeing either a new or previously unrecognised part of herself, perhaps the 'someone' she had previously described as being behind her eyes, looking out.

The process of Betty 'bridging the gap' across the split second by truly experiencing and expressing in writing the feeling of putting together the two halves of the brain (as it felt to her) was a truly amazing and intense experience for her. The urge to just 'get out' whilst she was doing it was very powerful.

The process of Betty and I reviewing our work together provided a final synthesis, a 'making sense' that in itself seemed to serve a function of even greater integration. As we reached the end of this process, Betty surprised me by asking what I 'made of the incident with the gypsy'. I immediately took this to mean did I think it was real, had it really happened? I responded that I had always taken it to be a traumatic memory. What had been triggered in Betty was a deeply painful feeling of not being believed, that parts of herself could not risk believing it, they had to reject it in order to carry on, to survive.

The following day Betty sat opposite me and said she could finally say 'it happened to *me*', and associated with this was a sense of a 'good' grieving. This grief extends to her body. She no longer wants to rip it to shreds but accepts it as a 'warrior' – a body that has lived and endured. She sees it as a young child sees their grandmother's body and knows it cannot be the 'sparkly little body' she once had. There is a sense of being in her body now and Betty felt strongly that when she had looked at me and not recognised me, she was seeing herself 'embodied' for the first time.

Going way back in the therapeutic process, the agonising sense of 'not having a place to put myself' was perhaps resolved. So, I wanted to know what was different for Betty. We professionals have to prove that something has changed *'in the real world'* not only the internal world! Betty described how she no longer felt an endless pressure of 'things to do' and a nagging sense of having to get everything 'sorted' all the time. This struck me as very important and shows how the outer world mirrors the inner. Betty had always felt that nothing was completely 'sorted' in her head and everything was endlessly repeated on a loop with no finishing line. This is how she experienced everyday life as well. Nothing could ever be finally sorted and the sense of having to go back to things again and again felt like an interminable and dragging torture. Now she can be fully 'in the moment' and do what needs to be done without feeling there is a finite 'space' in which everything has to be achieved.

And what did I learn about myself as a therapist, as a human being? Betty told me that what was most helpful to her was to have a space where she could 'be' from one part, move on and let me 'hold' that part, keep it on the table so to speak, so that it was not lost. But the most important contribution that our sessions made for Betty was that everything she showed was accepted without question. This reinforced something that I hope I already know and practise. It is so simple really. People need to tell their story in the way that seems most natural to them, and be accepted for who they are at each stage of the process. When people come for help they are often constricted by lifelong feelings of inadequacy. To be accepted, honoured and liked *as they are* is a prerequisite for change.

What makes Betty's story remarkable and so important is that in her quest for wholeness, she has attempted to write an account that captures all the facets of what trauma means. Yes, the experiential side is important, but so is the science, what we know about the brain in trauma. Not only was this knowledge crucial for Betty's own process of integration, the knowledge we have as therapists and clients also needs to be integrated. In a strange way the development of knowledge about trauma has been as fragmented as the experience of suffering from trauma. Betty's account attempts to integrate the different perspectives, to give a sense of wholeness and a message that the darkest of experiences can be understood, the light can be shone on it and the truth revealed.

CHAPTER TWENTY-SEVEN

WE COMPARE NOTES

— two sides of the same coin

Sitting face to face with Sarah and comparing our stories was a deeply moving experience. I immediately picked up on what she wrote about the process of 'testing her ability to keep quiet'. This was so critically significant. When I was confiding in her from one particular part of myself, responding to any verbal intervention would have involved moving out of that self into another: continuity would have been broken at that point. This was pivotal. I was aware that listening, recording and holding on to all the miscellaneous fragments that I was throwing at her must have taxed her powers of concentration to the limit.

Yet, at some profound level, knowing that Sarah was enfolding all the disparate parts of me in her consciousness made it safe enough to explore the component parts separately. My awareness of the fact that she was viewing the scene and making her own map from a different access point gave me deep confidence.

I am aware that we are actually living in an era of unpremeditated research into the long-term effects of trauma. Horrific cases of abuse are currently being unearthed after lying hidden for many years. In addition, hundreds of service personal returning home are finding, quite unexpectedly, that they are still suffering from nightmares and flashbacks from the unutterable horrors of experienced on the battle field.

This pinpoints something of immense importance which I suggest even the most highly qualified professionals and practitioners in any branch of counselling, therapy, or any alternative models of personal growth need to be aware of. If deep trauma is included in any case history then it is crucial to tread extremely warily and it is vitally important to create an atmosphere in which the client feels safe and comfortably supported. He or she needs to feel secure in the knowledge that whatever material may be revealed, in whatever form it may be presented, it will be accepted without question. Flexibility, being prepared to learn from the client and allowing him/her to dictate the pace are invaluable attributes.

It may even be necessary to call in specially trained, highly skilled help. If there is no recognition by the practitioner of the presence of dissociated 'selves' within the client then an added element of intense suffering and frustration that can be experienced by the patient concerned and, sad to say, much time and much money can be wasted.

In my own case, it moves me profoundly and still brings tears to my eyes when I write, "**At long last, I felt that my scrambled brain had an ally – somebody who knew and understood that I was dealing with a mechanism which had been overloaded and crashed.**" As simple as that. In Frank Lake's language, a piece of 'elastic' had been stretched beyond its capacity to give and had snapped. Living with that degree of splitting had been a nightmare: especially throughout the long years during which I knew the theory but did not fully comprehend the implications of such early traumatic experiences. The phrase 'did not fully comprehend' is the crucial factor in this context. In my experience it is possible to continue exploring one's personal history – in depth – for decades without coming to grips with the crux of the problem.

While writing these last few chapters I had an extremely vivid dream of being back on the counter as a travel consultant and being asked to make a simple booking for a family and car to travel by ferry from Holyhead to Dun Laoughaire. My head was in a whirl.

I knew where the places were but couldn't find them on the map. My boss was standing at my side breathing heavy sighs of frustration as I made muddle after muddle. It was a simple booking and I knew where to find all the information but I couldn't put my finger on it – I couldn't collate the pieces, I couldn't work out the prices. I got the names of the passengers, the ports and the ferries mixed up and at the end of the dream felt that I had been put through an old-fashioned clothes mangle. I pondered upon this dream and for some strange reason it was this trail of thought that led me to ask Sarah, "Do you think that the account of my encounter with the gypsy is authentic?" The question surprised her because she had quite simply accepted everything that I presented to her as being an essential part of the whole. What happened when and with whom was not relevant – it was not encoded.

I found that a small child wanted to move to the blue chair and ask, "Do *you* believe me, Sarah? '*She doesn't.*" '*She*' being the part of me that had blocked out the secret. There was so much pain and grief in this question – as if down through the decades, since this scene with the gypsy first burst forth into consciousness, with such dramatic consequences in my life in the present, this little person has been left struggling. "*Do they believe me or don't they?*" And 'they' have often been the trained professionals who unintentionally, unknowingly or unconsciously have backed up the child *who needed to keep the truth blocked out.*

This interchange underlined the agony of a child whose perception of truth is questioned – an anguish that can continue throughout extended years of therapy. At long last I was able to say with simplicity, in a firm voice, "It happened to **me** – this drama of sexual abuse **and**, in addition, the further jumble of traumatic experiences, influences and conditionings which have been coordinated during my journey with Sarah – this all happened to **me**. All of this makes sense of the way in which I have experienced myself in the world throughout the length of my long life."

There was something very affirming about this declaration. I have grieved my losses many times but at this moment, sitting opposite Sarah, there was a purity of grief – grief directly connected to the root cause and I found this deeply healing. I reiterate what I said in Chapter Twenty-four, it all hangs together in its own way – truth has recognised truth. I know what I need to know and can at long last be at peace.

This line of thought led me to picture that child after the horrifying experience with the gypsy going on to school as if nothing had happened. Everything had been blanked out but life went on. She had to sit at her desk as if nothing out of the ordinary had occurred. It is not surprising that I have found learning such a problem. Even as I write I can feel the way in which my brain would go into a kind of fuzz – as if the simple task of sorting information was beyond what could be coped with. This is where Sarah's input about the way in which the brain deals with trauma was so enlightening.

The knowledge that I was very split had dawned upon me quite early on in therapy. I had become aware that deep feelings could be triggered by some simple stimulus in the present. When this occurred the surge of emotion was totally out of proportion to the trigger point in the present. I had lived with this phenomena and understood the theory – but the drive to repeat makes sense when the way in which the brain deals with trauma is understood. Sarah explained this in very simple language and was impressed that I could regurgitate the information as follows:

> "As you go through life you filter information via the splitting – good and bad are kept separately, there is a gulf between. Because the traumatic experience exists in a constant present the healing aspect of time cannot operate on it. Feelings cannot fade when they exist in a constant present. In normal life emotions never stay the same. They never stay at the same pitch – they shift, they vary; one mood changes to another mood. Being frozen in a split

82 Chaos, excitement, distortion, creativity, mayhem, pandemonium – pure, colourful energy twisted and entwined with death – innocence betrayed – confusion beyond the ingenuity of 'the thinking man' to disentangle.

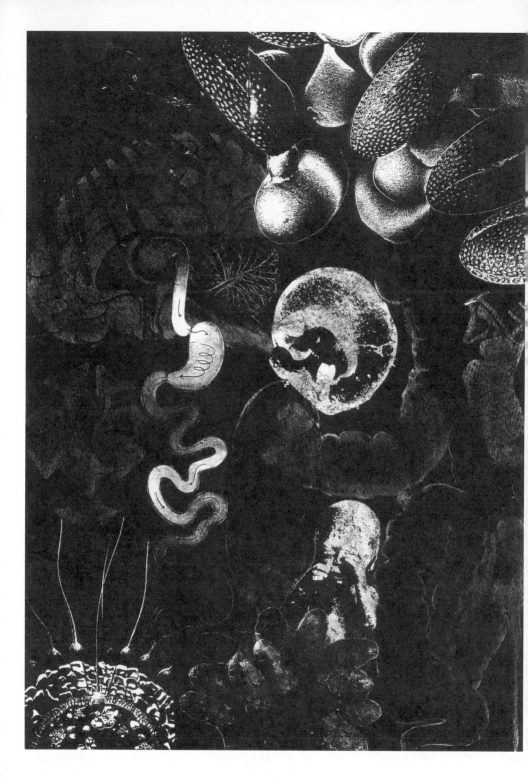

83 & 84 Nightmares.

85   I celebrate my eighty-fifth birthday.

86 *Abuse and betrayal.*

It's
POWER
IS STILL
ACTIVE
IN THE
NOW

DEAD

GONE — FOR THERE

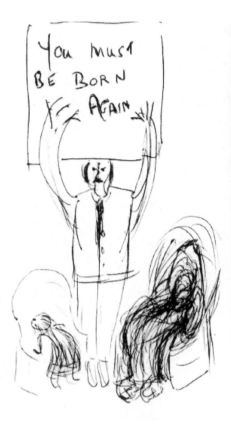

You MUST
BE BORN
AGAIN

*87, 88 & 89 Spontaneous sketches drawn
during the night while working with Sarah.*

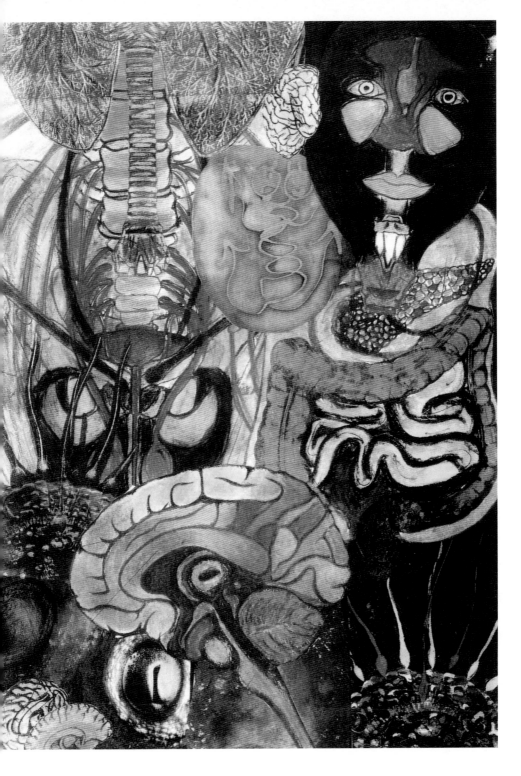

90 I love this picture. I think in some way it is symbolic of feeling good about my body, my mind, my energy, my origins – beautiful colours coordinate and draw everything together.

91 My past is contained, placed in the centre of this beautiful sunflower. Symbolic of nature's drive to heal, make good, reclaim, renew, recycle, give birth? Make of it what you will. I like it.

second of time creates a different situation which is never ameliorated – it exists – it is 'now' – it cannot be reversed. All senses flip back to this split second. Emotional responses, when triggered by trauma, create a situation in which an alarm is set too sensitively – the original extreme emotional reaction is triggered by a very low level of stimuli – it takes very little to set it off. Until processing of the trauma occurs – i.e. is integrated on a cognitive level – verbally on the time line – the unprocessed, unintegrated material will emerge repeatedly."

Sarah also explained that the age of a child at the time of the abuse was a factor to be taken into consideration because it involves the different stages at which a child's brain develops and encodes information. For me this accounted for the fact that the abuse by the gypsy was in the form of a coherent story whereas the earlier abuse appears in fragmentary format.

I found this information extremely helpful. It made it possible for me to tolerate more uncertainty. It lessened the drive 'to know', which had grown in line with doubts about my own perception. During sessions with Sarah and during the sleepless hours of the nights that often followed our times together, flashbacks, dialogues and important insights would frequently occur. I found that this information regarding the way in which the brain operated in regard to trauma helped me to accept each fragment in its own right. It was not necessary for it to be set in time and space. This was such a relief. The element of 'not knowing' versus 'the need to know' had been such a dominant and persistent on-going struggle.

It was a great help to me that Sarah allowed herself to be informed by the Sandplay figures which I brought to sessions: in particular the sequence in which each one was acknowledged, took his or her place, was seen, heard and recognised. Until finally, the bowed figure set in stone appeared on its own surrounded by a length of entangled chain. This is where our faith was most tested.

Sitting in the red observer's chair opposite to Sarah I expressed my doubts and fears and looked across to see whether these were reflected in her eyes. But, somehow, we were able to hang in there and I was quite amazed later when I looked at the chain to discover that it was not a straight piece of chain but rather a series of loops made up of individual links. The intricate way in which simple objects can convey hidden meaning never ceases to surprise me.

Towards the end of our sessions a number of things happened in incredibly quick succession and it was useful to sum them up them clearly:

- The first was the enlightening recognition that the place of isolation and darkness would not change. If I was in that place that is what I would feel.
- The second was that I now have a resting place in regard to sexual abuse. I have brought out into consciousness all the essential elements. I do not need to have an exact time, person or location – the scattered, disparate evidences speak their own truth. **I know enough.**
- I became intrigued by what seemed to be a new part of myself – a part which hadn't been fully recognised before. Sarah and I talked about this and exchanged impressions. Since way back in the early days of therapy I have been aware of the wisdom and clarity of a small self perched up on the ceiling commenting upon life and its vagaries. This new self seemed to have these qualities but we both shared a sense that this self now appeared to be embodied. There was something very solid and grounding about this realisation.
- We both feel astonished at the sequence, written at dead of night, describing bridging the gap. There is something so entirely authentic about it. I experienced it as a scientific enactment of linking past and present

- of processing a word link which the brain was able to grasp.

In my very last session with Sarah a tiny object accompanied me – on its own, none of the other familiar figures were present. It was a minute 'Jack-in the-Box' pulsating with energy. I took it to the turquoise chair. It was lying on my hand. Sarah and I looked at it in silence. Then I wondered what it would feel like to place it on the palm of her hand. I did this very tentatively. After a pause I felt comfortable about it being there and gently placed my hands *under* her hand creating what looked like a water lily.

We said goodbye.

Chapter Twenty-eight

THE END OR THE BEGINNING?

– or is it a complete circle?

That night I had an intensely powerful experience. I was holding the miniature 'Jack-in-the-Box' in my hand – the very same tiny symbol of pulsating energy that I had placed on Sarah's hand when I said goodbye to her. Quite suddenly and without any warning I felt terrified and completely defenceless.

Throughout my long journey, I have re-connected to many strategic crisis points in my personal history, encountering profound experiences of fundamental intensity and diversity: experiences that have severely affected me emotionally, physically, mentally and spiritually but, at this moment I am having great difficulty finding words to unveil the feeling of utter defencelessness that I describe as 'my life being suspended on the end of a gossamer thread'.

The closing stages of my journey with Sarah had been arranged months in advance and we were both confident that the timing was right. I was ready to continue my journey wherever it was going to take me. So when I experienced this terror I felt strong enough to 'hold myself' in these feelings of fear – **fear that was accompanied by a compelling, powerful desire to put the manuscript of my book away for ever.**

I pondered. My mind drifted gently through the pages of my story and links in the convoluted chain appeared which I hadn't observed so precisely before. I recalled an occasion way back in one of Frank Lake's workshops in Nottingham when a small voice had said with great glee, *"I hid myself where my mummy would never find me – in my clitoris!"* I brought to mind the torture of the teenager who had to sleep, night after night, month after month, physically close to her mother – spoon to spoon. I remembered the intense fear I had experienced when, lying close beside her body I had to tell her that my periods had started – the fatal evidence that proved beyond all doubt that I was becoming a sexual woman. For my mother it would have been a final seal of impurity.

When we were exploring in this area, Sarah gained the impression that I was sleeping with a woman who was in severe conflict concerning her own sexuality. So, throughout puberty I would have been in intimate contact with her anxieties, her unconscious desires, her dreams and her nightmares.

I recalled the agony of observing my breasts develop; the unbearable embarrassment of those soft balls of flesh pushing their way into life. *I finally became one of those unfortunate women who has ponderous boobs – loops of floppy flesh that tend to spill out of any bra or swimming costume. I have always hated them. They have housed my deepest shame.*

I considered the Sandplay scene that I have already mentioned. I pictured the teenage child who, with such anguish, had asked each member of the Small Group whether it was all right to 'tell my mummy'. She did not reveal the exact nature of the secret she was grappling with and I was a bit puzzled by this at the time. I assumed it was probably connected to the abuse. But now the answer suddenly dawned upon me. She was asking whether it would be safe to tell her mother that she was 'there' – actually present – in hiding – in a secret place – in her body. I felt as if the clock had stopped again at that point and, for the first time I was feeling the terror encapsulated in that moment – the terror of revealing my presence within my own body. Of acknowledging to all my selves that I was a sexual woman. This had been jolted into the present by the thought of my book coming out. **I shall be seen.**

This terror lay just under the surface for some days and three small figures found themselves constantly at my side – the black baby who had been hidden in a cage in the Sandplay, the miniature 'Jack-in-the-Box' and a new object – a miniscule, hooded scrap of a person, crouched in the bottom of a tiny corked bottle. In fact, some weeks passed before I realised that it wasn't a new object at all – it had been in my Sandplay scene from a year ago – standing right up in the corner next to my mother and her Lord. This is the fascination of Sandplay. When you are split into different selves, secret symbols are cunningly picked up by knowledgeable members of your cast of players and are strategically placed in the sandtray: they go unnoticed until you, *whoever you are at that moment, are ready to see them!*

The three small figures remained in focus. At one point I decided to remove the cork from the bottle but when I did this the little wisp of a person seemed to crouch even more deeply into her corner. The realisation dawned upon me that she was not only petrified of coming out – she was also terrified of being touched. This opened a parcel of feelings that reverberated throughout my whole body.

Fortunately I was about to attend the annual BPF Conference and I found myself in a Small Group with facilitators whom I knew and trusted. I felt confident that I would be able to explore this terror. I had taken my Sandplay equipment for members to use during the event and observing people absorbed in creating their scenes in such a meaningful way was a great delight. This also gave me access to materials with which to set out my own scene around the black baby, the 'Jack-in-the-Box' and the hooded figure in a cage and I was able to provide a visual context to what I needed to share.

At this stage of my journey I was very aware of the degree of resolution that I had achieved with my clinical psychologist in relation to Post Traumatic Stress Disorder and Dissociation: this natural, built-in coping mechanism which a child resorts to when faced with trauma and a degree of inner conflict that is overwhelming. I reminded my group that when a child has used this survival device and the split off elements have been eased into consciousness, these child selves do not suddenly grow up. In fact, you find them exactly where they were left – stranded within the confines of their own particular restricted space. What a bizarre paradox!

The instinct to stay alive is so supreme that the clock stops, time stands still for each little escapee who falls by the wayside, yet, at the same time life continues to unfold. A deeply conditioned persona develops, grows up and becomes an adult, in all probability a character hampered, restricted and debilitated, only functioning with part of their full personality and essence. Possibly even, a person whose life revolves in continual loops of repetitive patterns of behaviour. Meanwhile, in the background, child selves mutter, whinge, argue and hang on hopelessly to hope!

For myself, discovering and owning these stranded child selves has presented me with an open-ended adventure. It is like opening up my very own individual Aladdin's Cave.

But, to return to the group. First of all, when I took my turn, an aggressive character took the stage and some rage and frustration emerged around the use of words as a substitute for loving care and protection but the crucial enactment was around touch. I requested the male facilitator to sit beside me. I invited the whisper of a touch – his finger laid very gently upon my finger. The quiet perception of my need for the softest, gentlest touch combined with eye contact, opened the door to an agony of response – the bleak pain of total isolation, deprivation of essential needs for survival, yawning despair and acute anxiety poured out. All I needed to do was to just be there – that was enough.

After a while I wondered whether I dare ask the female facilitator to join us – it was risky because she tended to use a lot of words! However, I plucked up courage and a small child thoroughly enjoyed instructing her, *'how to do it properly!'* It was a deeply moving, very primitive experience.

This was followed, in another group, by a deep fear of being touched by the whole group. I had worked in multifarious groups for many years and on one level this was no new challenge but on this particular occasion it felt as if 'the self at the end of the gossamer thread' was daring to reach out and trust the 'family' environment for the first time. I was able to sit in the centre and have each person gather round, touching me gently in a way which felt comfortable for them and for me. Then I have a clear recollection of gazing around the circle and tentatively looking into everybody's eyes. There was a mutual exchange of love and acceptance. We were separate yet together.

Recalling these two experiences reminds me of when Peter had his accident and of other times when I have described myself as being suspended from a gossamer thread, on the edge of an abyss, poised between life and death but never having been picked up and made to feel safe and contained. Yes, that's what its about...the feeling extends beyond being threatened or attacked, it is more akin to an absence of any kind of foundational affirmation of being alive: a sense of being totally exposed, floating in nothingness yet without the containment of an outside skin. A complete lack of essential support, both physical and emotional – the foundational holding necessary for survival – the kind of containment that tells you that you are present, eyes that reflect your eyes, that inestimable 'something' that tells you are special to one special person.

My experiences around touch at this vital stage of my journey lit up the stark simplicity about this powerful drive to attach – it cannot be underestimated especially when a baby has had a traumatic delivery through the birth canal. Infants need to be held and supported unconditionally. I had never been supported – never been held free of rigid conditions. My mother had told me that right from the time she knew she was pregnant that she had offered her new infant to her Lord. She had brought me up within this framework.

At one point during one of the group sessions a remark had been addressed to the little black girl – she was told that she was 'comely'. I hadn't really noted the fact that she was standing so proudly – stark naked with her hair tied in neat little bunches. She responded joyfully to being told that she was 'comely' and it suddenly dawned upon me why, for so many years, I had always felt so free to be totally myself in Africa – it was a country where the native children were black!

One person in the organisation whom I respect deeply happened to remark at breakfast one day that he saw me as 'St Peter at the Pearly Gates'. I really liked this idea but it wasn't until I woke up in the early hours of the next morning that a small voice said out of the blue, *"If I am St Peter at the Pearly Gates then I can let my daddy in!"* Another voice immediately chipped in, *"Will you let yourself in?"* It was the last day of the conference and I decided to go to Holy Communion in the Chapel. As I went forward to receive the bread and wine the three little figures who had taken centre stage were tucked snugly under the open hand with which I received the sacred symbols. The God I know must have clapped his hands with joy to see them.

Chapter Twenty-nine

THE GRAND FINALE

– *surprises right to the end*

Two interesting developments followed. The first was another group holiday: a fascinating tour of Sicily; ancient sites, incredibly beautiful mosaics, rugged countryside. For me it was like the world lighting up, seeing everything in clear focus, having direct access, not being one degree removed from a direct experience.

There was one church in particular where I was moved beyond belief at the sheer beauty of everything around me. An added dimension was that all the biblical stories of my childhood were revealed in colourful accuracy around the high ceiling: Noah and his ark, the feeding of the five thousand and all the characters who had been the heroes and heroines of the biblical fairy tales as listened to by a very puzzled child – a scrap of a person who tried to make sense of it all, yet managed to retain her own perception of the truth.

I was surprised to see where my mother featured in all this religious drama. I often spied her in pictures of the saintly Virgin Mary, or Mary Magdalene sitting adoringly at the feet of Jesus but I gradually became aware of a spunky side to her nature which till now had eluded me. I suddenly recognised *in myself* the repressed side of my mother venturing out into the sunlight and she seemed to give me an unexpected gift: her delight at seeing me freed from some of the complex entanglements of my early years. *It has since dawned upon me that* **she** *probably suffered from dissociation, and*

recalling her mother, my grandmother. I cannot imagine her being
nurtured at a cosy breast.

Bill Swartley, in my Primal Integration Training had always maintained that all the psychological tests he tried gave me an incorrect reading: he was quite sure that I was an extrovert whereas all the readings suggested introversion. Sometimes he said, "Who filled that form in, you or your mother?" But, amazingly and confusingly, on this coach tour it was the extrovert who held the floor. I quickly became known as 'The Baroness' and, whenever the coach stopped, willing hands reached out to help me descend safely! I talked openly about writing my life story and two different people suggested that a film should be made and that the lead should be played by Dame Judi Dench.

I was astounded by the amount of fun we had. I have always managed to put on a good show but throughout my life I have found social situations boring beyond belief. But not this time. Every person on that coach was so intensely interesting: all were over sixty and every one had a fascinating story to tell. And each and every one was interested in *me*. I was the focus of much attention and welcomed it: I cannot remember any ten days of my life when I have laughed with such genuine delight.

In addition, a drama unfolded which added an interesting dimension to the trip: 'God' was on the coach – the 'God' of my childhood who had merged with time into a type of male authority figure who, throughout my life, I have wanted to topple from his perch. There he was, perfect for the part, in the form of the Tour Manager – an arrogant, opinionated masculine figure who always thought he was right. He was dismissive, patronising, was unable to listen and couldn't admit to mistakes. To give him his due, he knew his subject, was an interesting guide and gave clear leadership but he didn't know when to stop talking. He was mesmerised by the microphone: his commentary was attention-grabbing when focussed, but it went on interminably and he seemed quite unaware that everybody had nodded off.

At the beginning I made the mistake of having fun and being quite cheeky towards him but I found that you mock gods at your peril; at root level they are extremely vulnerable and unsure of themselves and quickly spring into attack mode. *They* have to make the jokes; they certainly can't be laughed at, mocked. Early on we had two cryptic interchanges. He knew that I had been in the travel business and on one occasion when I had made a simple suggestion he said, "You are used to giving orders, not taking them, aren't you?" to which I responded, "Yes, I am." Another time when I had irritated him in some way he said, "I can bite," to which I responded, "So can I."

I have been a tour leader and have had some really difficult clients in my time who have worn my patience to shreds. On this tour I recognised that it was an added hassle for the Tour Manager having a disabled passenger on board but looking after everybody impartially is what he was paid for: the essential talent for the job is to listen and then come up with a solution. We crossed swords because he flatly refused to listen and I began to find that this was triggering and challenging me on an extremely deep level. A crisis arose when I started to make a simple request regarding my room at the next hotel and he deliberately shut me up. Very politely I insisted upon being heard and said, "May I finish what I want to say, please?" He answered briskly, "No." I walked out and went up to my room.

I have included this incident because of its impact upon *me*. This was immediate. I lay on my bed more shocked than angry. I couldn't believe what my ears had told me. I felt traumatised. One flick of a man's tongue had tipped my world upside down. Flipped me back into square one. The holiday was finished. I couldn't stay with the tour. Nothing could make it come right again. Something monumental had occurred that could not be put right. My spirit felt totally crushed.

What a re-run of early childhood experience! No wonder the minute scrap of a person had been forced to retreat into the corked glass jar. She had been crushed by big feet. The very essence of her, her exuberance, her joy, her sense of fun, her natural spontaneity had been squashed out of existence.

Fortunately, on this occasion I was able to maintain a deep sense of awareness. In spite of the surge of overwhelming feelings I held on to reality in both time zones: in the present **at the same time** as in the past. My world turned back the right way up and the holiday wasn't ruined. In fact, it proved to be a brilliant, unique experience involving all my selves in unison. I dealt with the inexcusable behaviour of the Tour Manager by letter after I returned home.

The second thing that followed was of a quite different genre. It concerned my deep loathing of my body. My work with Sarah had reminded me of the horrendous body painting session in Bill's group. How could I have put myself through that? Why was I unable to sit comfortably on one side watching the others and enjoying the fun? The experience of forcing myself to participate did me no good at all, in fact it deeply reinforced my sense of shame. Retrospectively it makes me feel angry at Bill's insensitivity and sad that nobody in the group had the perception and compassion to say, "Betty, don't do this to yourself."

The recall of this incident, linked to the illuminating connection to the agonies of the teenager trapped in her mother's bed, alerted me afresh to these symbols of my deepest shame, my ponderous boobs. For the very first time I was ready and open to possible solutions. I recognised that my shoulders and damaged spine were carrying a considerable, unnecessary weight and I decided to investigate the possibility of breast reduction. I carefully considered the psychological implications. I looked up all the relevant information on the internet: it would be an extensive, invasive operation but my body had already been invaded by shame and I felt it would welcome release from the sheer weight of these horrendous appendages.

It was one of the best decisions I have made. The feeling of lightness was exquisite and after suffering all through so many decades you cannot imagine the pure delight of being able, at long last, to wear a flimsy lace bra.

One complication was that after surgery I developed a urinary tract infection, had a fall in my flat and fractured my right shoulder. We are complex creatures and from a psychological viewpoint it is interesting to speculate upon whether there was any deep connection between this sequence of events. I shall never know but what transpired reflects both the best and the worst of our NHS. The UIT was diagnosed in Accident and Emergency but was not treated for about ten days and, as is well documented in such cases, I had a bizarre experience of several weeks of mental confusion and paranoia. At one stage I understand that sectioning me was considered!

Retrospectively, there are certain elements during the course of my illness which seem to carry undertones of regression: craziness, floating out of time, paranoia, shouting into the ether, utter confusion. There was also a general sense of existing in a vacuum: having a vague sense of people being around and certain interactions, yet not being connected or attached. Weird, uncanny.

The most wonderful part of the experience was the way in which I was supported. My niece flew in from Cyprus, my nephew drove up from Devon, and all my relatives and friends formed a cordon of loving care around me that I shall never forget. I understand that they took it in turns to listen to my ramblings on the phone! I am also very grateful to all the staff at the Rehabilitation Centre who were kindness itself.

When I had fully recovered I decided that it was high time to complete my manuscript and get it published but this decision brought with it a final wave of fears and apprehensions. I would be an open book. Some of my innermost secrets would be revealed. What would people make of my wanderings among my fragmented selves? I shall find out.

I am aware, encouraged and excited to know that extensive research is being carried out every day in the field of Post Traumatic

Stress Disorder, Dissociative Disorders and Attachment Theory. This is being undertaken and carefully recorded by extremely erudite, experienced professionals and survivors. I believe that in the future many people will be assisted in finding a quicker route to healing than the one I and many others have had to take. If this account of my own journey adds to this increasing area of knowledge then telling my story will have been worth while.

There will be aspects of the journey that I am unable to explain. For example, a colleague referred to the drama of making contact with such a crucial experience of touching into the exact moment when the clock stood still. I often ponder over this myself and when I open my A4 notebook and read the final page I still smile to myself. The experience is alive in my memory. I was so aware of being in the two separate parts of myself, each using their particular method of communication. I recall the intense 'life and death' pull of resistance and the need to make a clear decision to allow the two parts to come together.

Whatever anybody makes of this staging post, all I can say is that it now much easier to live with my collection of selves with their unique personalities, ages and voices than it used to be. Functioning in this format is interesting, stimulating and often amusing. The characters are so diverse. Each person is a distinct individual. One revels in chaos and untidiness while another is obsessive about neatness and organisation: an extremely hard, merciless monster, who can be abruptly triggered into ruthless rage, is contrasted by a genial, charismatic character; a recluse contends with a person who is spontaneously sociable. Certain triggers or interactions can topple one or another 'self' into re-activation of feelings around pressure, fragmentation, conflict, exposure, being kept waiting, etc. etc. If circumstances permit, he or she is allowed to let rip but, in the main, the inner family has developed tolerance and has negotiated a truce. We all understand how we hang together and in a strange way the panics are more peripheral, life flows and decisions appear out of the network.

I used to live every day as if it was my last but the crucial need to be constantly poised on red alert, permanently equipped for the unknown, eternally prepared for an unidentified, life and death threat lurking round the corner has now ceased. It has been my experience that living frozen in fight/flight mode deadens life and casts an unending vista of meaninglessness into the future. Living with the long-lasting effects of early trauma is still a mystery. Sometimes I find myself expecting the cloud to loom again, occasionally it hovers. Maybe it will descend again. It could happen, but today, as I write this sentence, my past has caught up with my present. I am living in the now and I relish it.

There are advantages in living in a family group. Life is not dull – it is full of interest. Small children live very close to the earth. Their attention is captured by the minutiae of microscopic detail – colour, shape, texture, sound…they are absorbed in the wonderment of the moment and find something new every day. They love watching people, especially small children. I often go down to the beach because the sea fascinates me: it is never the same, its moods change, it lives its own life; a life controlled by hidden laws that are beyond my understanding. I have to keep an eye on the character who likes to sit poised right on the danger line when the tide is coming in, arrogantly confident that he can move back just in time and avoid getting his feet wet.

This character is a strong protector and would leap into action if I was attacked. He has very quick reactions and when I am driving this is a great advantage. But I still have to watch him. He can be very competitive and doesn't run out of swear words when other drivers cross his path or, worse still, when they dither! My computer has escaped being bashed to smithereens when I have been unable to read its mind and, in spite of gargantuan efforts over more than two decades I am aware that errors in this manuscript will creep through the net. I have discovered how to use the new high tech TV and recording equipment and the two remotes have become my friends.

The countryside still draws me with its magic and although I am not as mobile as I used to be I have my favourite places. Holidays are not as exotic but those treasured memories are alive in my consciousness as well as photographically. When I go on holiday my suitcases are always bulging because I never know in advance what anybody may choose to wear.

I am fascinated by human behaviour in all its forms. Like everybody else, reports of human tragedy from all over the world, which hit the headlines day after day, give me an immeasurable sense of being overwhelmed. When it comes to individual cases of brutality and abuse I find that I am forced to consider the plight of both perpetrator and victim. Crime cannot be condoned but many perpetrators of crime have themselves been abused.

I have been abused and throughout my life I have been at the mercy of powerful, controlling drives and compulsions, but these, in the main, have been dysfunctional forces which only have harmed myself. But what if being violently abused, especially by someone who was a trusted, loved companion, left a person with drives and compulsions to abuse others? What if that person was you? I find these thoughts agonising. I have listened to personal stories of people caught up in this horrendous predicament and my heart still bleeds for them.

Some may wonder where I now stand in relation to religious matters. My child selves seem to be freed from overpowering 'Catch 22' pressures about good or bad, acceptable or unacceptable, life or death, heaven or hell – all those compelling no-win situations backed by Almighty God which have come to the surface so continuously throughout my story. I now feel free and sufficiently integrated to exercise choice and, in the right company even take pleasure in an argument. On occasions I even enjoy voicing an opinion during our local Sunday morning religious programme.

I still find labels restricting and this applies to many areas of life – religious, political, moral, educational, therapeutic…if God is God then he must be beyond our ability to know him, to read his mind or fully understand him. I deeply respect people's beliefs but I, myself am unable to say that '**I know**'. Many will think it simplistic to believe that truth is to be found in life itself: that life is the journey, but I often think that when all is finally revealed we will stand back in wonder and amazement because it will be so much simpler than we had ever imagined.

In the meantime, my past has caught up with my present. I have found my pot of gold and it is a wondrous gift to be able to live in the now – my life abundantly enhanced by my journey. I must be one of the richest eighty-nine-year-olds in the world. The primal scream needed to be uttered but it has made way for the delight and enchantment of the primal laugh.

APPENDIX

This book covers wide areas that cause many of us deep concern. Reading it may have raised curiosity, anxiety, interest or a desire to explore further.

This appendix includes details relating to organisations mentioned in the text and additional resources where further information can be obtained.

BODYWORKS
with Tim Brown

Tim is a body psychotherapist and workshop leader.

Individual sessions

Tim offers one-to-one Deep Bodywork, Body Psychotherapy and Postural Integration sessions in Brighton and Hove. Deep Bodywork can contact the deeply held feelings, emotions and beliefs which are held in the body. It can help release old patterns that hold us back, and liberate energy for new movement and growth.

Groupwork

Tim runs groups using movement and bodywork, including trainings tailored to specific group needs. Tim worked with Betty Hughes in creating the Hidden Treasures workshops – mixing creative expression, sandplay, movement and bodywork – and continues to offer this approach to personal growth work.

He has developed Dance of Awareness, which draws on bodywork, bioenergetics, 5 Rhythms dance, and investigation into consciousness. It uses an energetic cycle of sensing, grounding, expressing, releasing, connecting and completing. Tim also runs regular groups in Authentic Movement – a gentle, mindful, body-centred approach to self-awareness. It blends dance therapy with Jungian psychology, movement with meditation, personal growth with group process, in a way that is hard to describe, but extraordinary to experience.

Contact details:
Tel: 01273 271408
Email: timclare@dialstart.net
Website: www.bodyworks.org.uk

THE BOWLBY CENTRE
Psychotherapy at the Bowlby Centre

1 The Bowlby Centre believes that mental distress has its origin in failed or inadequate attachment relationships in early life and is best treated in the context of a long-term human relationship.

2 Attachment relationships are shaped in the real world and impacted on by poverty, discrimination and social inequality. The impact of the social world is a necessary part of the therapy.

3 Psychotherapy should be available to all, and from the attachment perspective, especially those discriminated against or described as 'unsuitable' for therapy.

4 Psychotherapy needs to be provided with respect, warmth, openness, a readiness to interact and relate, and free from discrimination of any kind.

5 Those who have been silenced about their experiences and survival strategies need to have their reality acknowledged and not pathologised.

6 The Bowlby Centre values inclusiveness, access, authenticity and excellence.

Contact details:
Website: www.thebowlbycentre.org.uk

BRIDGE PASTORAL FOUNDATION

(formerly the Clinical Theology Association)

The Home of Clinical Theology

The Clinical Theology Association was established in 1962 by Dr Frank Lake to further the training in pastoral care in general and especially of those whose concern is with persons suffering from spiritual and emotional distress.

People seeking to help others are often aware that they need more resources in order to be effective. Frequently these individuals are also seeking personal development for professional reasons concerned with their work as pastoral caregivers, health care workers, social workers, teachers, clergy, counsellors, therapists or as members of befriending organisations.

Now known as the Bridge Pastoral Foundation, training is offered in pastoral care and self-awareness using experiential learning techniques at three levels. The introductory course of eighteen hours can be followed by the seminar programme, and further training over three to four years leads to accreditation in counselling and psychotherapy. Participants are introduced to various personality types and shown through increasing self-awareness how they can be more effective pastoral carers.

Frank Lake believed that many aspects of personality develop around the time of birth and the foundation offers primal work in small groups to enable individuals to revisit these early times and experience healing. The Bridge Pastoral Foundation has a long history of facilitating groups that enable personal and professional insight and growth. The Foundation works with people of all faiths. and none.

Contact details:

Bridge Pastoral Foundation, 8 Kingsmead Road North, Prenton, Birkenhead, CH43 6TB

Tel: +44(0)151 652 0429

Email: admin @bridgepastoral.org.uk

Website: www.bridgepastoral.org.uk

CLINIC FOR DISSOCIATIVE STUDIES

The Clinic was established in 1998 as a small specialist outpatient mental health service for people suffering from the range of dissociative disorders. Treatment is provided for children, adults, couples and families from all ethnic backgrounds and religions. We work with all levels of learning disability and physical disability.

Centred in north London, the Clinic is an independent provider to the NHS. This means that the Clinic works with NHS patients, subject to the approval of each patient's local Primary Care Trust.

We are a multi-disciplinary group of professionals, including child and adult psychotherapists, psychiatrists, psychologists, art and music therapists. The majority have particular expertise in psychoanalytic psychotherapy.

All assessment and treatment through the Clinic aims at increasing personal and/or family resourcefulness in dealing with the difficult feelings and personal problems caused by dissociative disorders.

Dissociation can be caused by traumatic and frightening experiences. In its milder forms, it can involve feeling disconnected from one's body or surroundings. At the extreme end, it can take the form of Dissociative Identity Disorder (DID).

Clinic Director: Valerie Sinason
Clinic Manager: Nancy Dunlop

Contact details:
Clinic for Dissociative Studies
10 Harley Street
London W1G 9PF
Tel: 020 7794 1655

FIRST PERSON PLURAL

A small registered charity led by abuse survivors with first-hand experience of complex dissociative distress, including dissociative identities / multiple personalities.

It is a membership association open to dissociative survivors, their friends, family, and health, social care and other professionals and workers with an interest in trauma and dissociation. It works to facilitate mutual support and information exchange among its members. It encourages increased social and professional recognition and understanding of complex dissociative distress and the diverse needs of those who experience it.

Its activities include producing a regular newsletter; producing and disseminating other written information resources, including the booklet 'Understanding Dissociative Disorders' published by Mind; and delivering and/or organising training and awareness-raising sessions, including its acclaimed introductory level Understanding Dissociation one-day training course.

Contact details:
First Person Plural, PO Box 2537, Wolverhampton, WV4 4ZL
email: fpp@firstpersonplural.org.uk
Website: www.firstpersonplural.org.uk

THE HOFFMAN PROCESS
'When you're serious about change'

The Hoffman Process is an eight-day intensive residential course of personal discovery and development. Held in a secluded countryside retreat in the UK and in fourteen countries worldwide, it allows you to examine and better understand your life and reveals why you behave the way you do.

Since 1967, more than 70,000 people worldwide have used the tried and tested Hoffman techniques to improve their quality of life and restore relationships with friends and family.

Published scientific research has also demonstrated the long-term positive effects that the Process has had on relieving depression and anxiety.

Some of the reported benefits include a release of pent-up stress, a better work-life balance, increased self-esteem, a clearer personal vision and tools for ongoing change.

To help you find out more we hold free monthly information evenings and phone-ins. Our website also includes articles from those who have done the Process.

This is a once in a lifetime experience, so we're happy to advise you in confidence on the number below, to get the timing right.

Contact details:
Tel: +44 (0)1903 88 99 90
Website: www.hoffmaninstitute.co.uk

LEE ABBEY

Lee Abbey conference, retreat and holiday centre in Devon is:

1 An international Christian Community
   ninety people from fifteen nations, of all ages and many
   denominations, bringing a rich variety of traditions, worship
   styles and experiences
2 A place to be renewed and inspired by God
   with amazing stories week after week of God at work in people's
   lives through the teaching, worship, prayer ministry and space
3 Enjoy God's amazing creation
   set in 280 acres of dramatic coastal estate in Exmoor National
   Park, Lee Abbey's location is truly breathtaking.

Our vision is to renew and serve the Church, to build community
and to be God's welcome. We do this through a varied all-inclusive
programme of weekend, midweek and holiday programmes that
include a blend of worship, teaching, workshops and entertainment
in a great community atmosphere.

Contact details:
Tel: 01598 752621
Email: relax@leeabbey.org.uk
Website: www.leeabbey.org.uk

The 'Lee Abbey Fellowship' is a registered Company (4428890)
and Charity (1094097).

THE OPEN CENTRE

Founded in 1977, the Open Centre is one of the longest established centres for self-development and personal growth in the UK and offers group and individual work in Bioenergetics, Deep Bodywork, Feldenkrais Method, Primal Integration, Psychodrama, and Pulsing.

We offer people an opportunity, both in group work and individual sessions to increase their awareness of themselves – an opportunity, in a supportive environment, to look deeply and realistically at all aspects of themselves – body, mind, feelings, spirit – relationships with others – assumptions and decisions about life and work, etc. This requires responsibility and commitment on the part of the people who work with us, and we encourage them to translate what they learn at the Open Centre into everyday life to make their own loves more fulfilling and to help enhance the world we live in.

Contact details:
The Open Centre
188-192 Old Street
London EC1V 9FR
Tel: (020) 7251 1504
Email: ocinfo@opencentre.com
Website: www.opencentre.com

THE PLAY TEAM

The Play Team continues the work of Dr Rachel Pinney, Virginia Axline and others, who were greatly influenced by Margaret Lowenfeld, one of the early pioneers of Play Therapy. The approach is both Person Centred (Carl Rogers) and Self Directed and follows the core conditions of empathy, congruence and being non-judgemental. We hold the belief that everybody has the ability to achieve positive development and change, given the right environment.

Our training teaches practitioners how to interact with children in a time that is designated as special and individual.

During this time the child can play and explore an array of material:

➢ Sandtrays	➢ Paints
➢ Craft materials	➢ Dolls
➢ Miniatures	➢ Puppets
➢ Marbles, etc. etc.	

Why is play important?

- ➢ Play is vital to every child's emotional and social development.
- ➢ The child has an opportunity to explore his/her hopes, fears and difficulties without judgement.
- ➢ The playroom becomes a growing ground for the child.
- ➢ Children can work through many of their problems when given the space and time to do so.

Contact details:
Anna Clarke
The Old Rectory, East Marden, Nr Chichester, PO18 9JE
Tel: 01243 535208
email: annabclarke@lineone.net
website: www.ukplayteam.org

THE SURVIVORS TRUST

The Survivors Trust is the UK umbrella agency for specialist voluntary agencies working with victims/survivors of rape, sexual violence and/or childhood sexual abuse. We have 130 member agencies based throughout the UK, including rape crisis and sexual abuse support services.

Our core belief is that sexual abuse and/or rape of girls, boys, women and men is preventable and we challenge society to acknowledge both its reality and our individual and collective responsibility for it.

The Survivors Trust supports working in ways that:

1 Recognise human rights and dignity;
2 Appreciate the variety of human experience and culture;
3 Demonstrate a commitment to showing justice in dealing with all others;
4 Encourages the continual development and improvement of professional knowledge of its members group

Survivors Trust member agencies provide an extensive range of specialist services for victims/survivors including rape and sexual abuse crisis support, helplines, counselling and therapy, Independent Sexual Violence Advisors, information, support groups, support and therapy for people with learning disabilities, residential workshops, art therapy and web forums.

Contact details:
Website: www.thesurvivorstrust.org

TAG

TAG is a group studying and supporting work concerning trauma, abuse, and dissociation

How TAG came about

The group exists to provide information, support, training, encouragement and networking for counsellors, therapists, professional workers, carers and indeed anyone who is concerned or interested and any that are working with individuals who have suffered trauma and abuse. As a group we acknowledge the contribution of survivors to increased understanding in this area and respect the great value of their insights.

Dissociative Identity Disorder is neither a psychosis nor a personality disorder but rather a sophisticated survival mechanism for coping with overwhelming, often enduring, childhood trauma.

Trauma in this context is any globally overwhelming experience – it therefore includes neglect, abuse, abandonment, and medical intervention.

Successful Treatment is more dependent upon the client/counsellor relationship than on which model of therapy is adopted. Seeing the client as a person rather than as a 'condition' and listening to and learning from the client are vitally important.

Contact details:
TAG, P O Box 3295, Swindon SN2 9ED
Website: www.tag-uk.net

WILLOWS COUNSELLING SERVICE

Willows Counselling Service, Swindon, is a charitable trust, providing:

- ➤ Confidential counselling for self-referring adults or couples, of any faith or none, regardless of gender, sexual orientation, ethnic or cultural background
- ➤ Training in counselling from Level 2 Introduction to Pastoral Counselling, through Level 3 Certificate in Integrative Counselling, up to level 4 Diploma in Therapeutic Counselling
- ➤ Supervision, Support Groups and Continuing Professional Development for Counsellors, Supervisors and Staff
- ➤ Advice, support and bespoke training for churches and other voluntary and statutory organisations seeking to work with survivors.

Willow's particular area of interest is in supporting adult survivors of childhood neglect, trauma and abuse as they seek to work through the long-lasting, multi-faceted sequelae.

As all our counsellors and supervisors work on a voluntary basis we are able to offer low cost counselling, adaptable to people's circumstances, and without a fixed time limit.

Contact details:
Willows Counselling Service
11 Prospect Place, Old Town, Swindon, SN1 3LQ
Tel: 01793 426650
Email: willows@willowscounselling.org.uk
Website: www.willowscounselling.org.uk